Fighting
for the
Faith

Fighting
for the
Faith

The Many Fronts of Medieval
Crusade and Jihad
1000–1500AD

David Nicolle

Pen & Sword
MILITARY

First published in Great Britain in 2007 by
Pen & Sword Military
an imprint of
Pen & Sword Books Ltd
47 Church Street
Barnsley
South Yorkshire
S70 2AS

ISBN 978 1 84415 614 6

Typeset in Plantin by Phoenix Typesetting, Auldgirth, Dumfriesshire

Printed in the U.S.A.

Pen & Sword Books Ltd incorporates the Imprints of Pen & Sword Aviation,
Pen & Sword Maritime, Pen & Sword Military, Wharncliffe Local History,
Pen & Sword Select, Pen & Sword Military Classics and Leo Cooper.

Book Club Edition

Contents

List of Plates

Maps

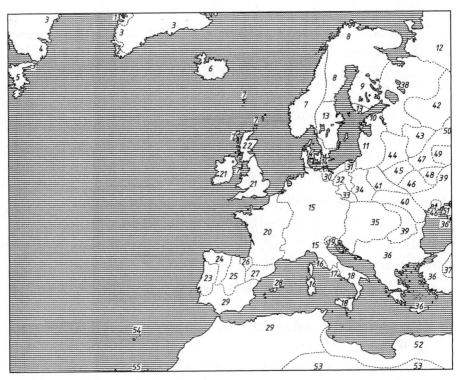

1. Europe, circa 1180

1	Norse Western Settlement	19	Venice	36	Byzantine Empire
2	Norse Eastern Settlement	20	France (inc. estates of Angevin King of England)	37	Saljuqs of Rum
3	Inuit-Eskimos			38	Novgorod
4	Markland?	21	English kingdom of suzerainty	39	Kipchaqs
5	Helluland?			40	Galich
6	Iceland	22	Scotland	41	Volhynia
7	Norway	23	Portugal	42	Vladimir-Suzdal
8	Saami-Lapps	24	Leon	43	Smolensk
9	Finns	25	Castile	44	Polotsk
10	Estonians	26	Navarre	45	Turov-Pinsk
11	Baltic peoples	27	Aragon	46	Kiev
12	Finno-Ugrians	28	Murabitin	47	Chernigov
13	Sweden	29	Muwahidin	48	Pereyaslavl
14	Denmark	30	Pomerania	49	Novgorod-Seversk
15	The Empire	31	Pomerelia	50	Murom-Ryazan
16	Pisa	32	Great Poland	51	Khazaria
17	Papal States	33	Silesia	52	Ayyubids
18	Kingdom of Sicily	34	Little Poland	53	Arab tribes
		35	Hungary	54	(uninhabited)
				55	Guanches

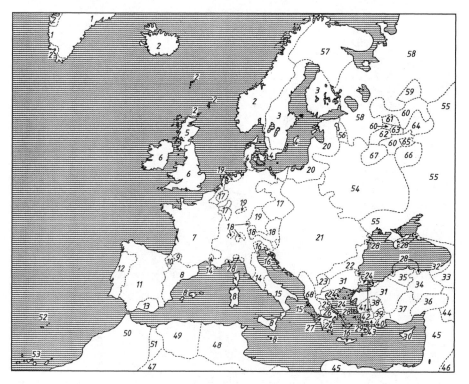

2. Europe, circa 1382

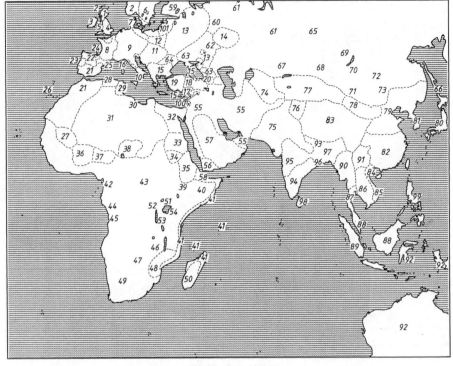

3. Europe, Africa and Asia, circa 1100

1	Scotland	37	Hausa	71	Keraits
2	Norway	38	Kanem-Bornu	72	Mongols
3	Irish kingdoms	39	Galla	73	Tatars
4	England and Normandy	40	Somalis	74	Qarakhanids
5	Welsh principalities	41	Arab coastal and island	75	Ghaznawids
6	Sweden		settlements	76	Kashmir-Ladakh
7	Denmark	42	Fang	77	Qara-Khitai
8	France	43	Azande	78	Tanguts
9	Germany	44	Loango	79	Empire of China,
10	Italo-Normans	45	Bakongo		Jurchen
11	Hungary	46	Baluba	80	Japan
12	Poland	47	Balunda	81	Koryo
13	Russian principalities	48	Kingdom of	82	Empire of China,
14	Volga Bulgars		Monomatapa		southern Sung
15	Byzantine Empire	49	Khoisan peoples	83	Tibet
16	Pisa	50	Meri'na	84	Annam
17	Cilician Armenia	51	Kitara	85	Champa
18	Danishmandids	52	Nkole	86	Khmer
19	Saljuqs of Rum	53	Rwanda	87	Dvaravati
20	Georgia	54	Ganda kingdoms	88	Dvipantara
21	Murabitin	55	Great Saljuqs	89	Sri-Vijaya
22	Leon-Castile	56	Local Yemeni states	90	Pagan
23	Portugal	57	Qarmatians	91	Nan-Chao
24	Navarre	58	Adal	92	Aboriginal peoples
25	Aragon	59	Western Finns	93	Nepal
26	Guanches	60	Eastern Finns	94	Cholas
27	Ghana	61	Ugrians	95	Chalukyas
28	Hammadids	62	Kipchaqs	96	Kalinga
29	Zayrids	63	Alans	97	PaLas
30	Arab tribes	64	Pechenegs	98	Lanka
31	Berber and Tuareg tribes	65	Samoyeds	99	Maid
32	Fatimid Caliphate	66	Ainu	100	Crusader enclaves
33	Makuria	67	Kimaks		
34	Alwa	68	Kirghiz		
35	Ethiopia	69	Oirats		
36	Mossi kingdoms	70	Merkits		

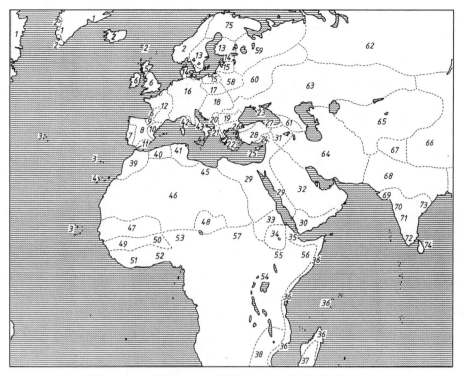

3. Europe, Africa and Western Asia, circa 1300

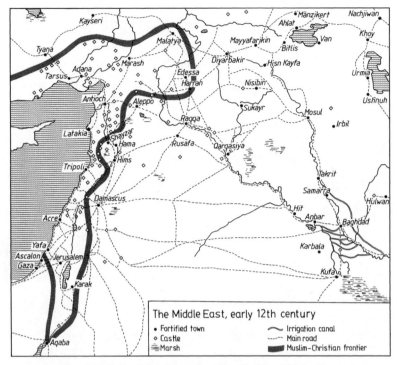

5. The Middle East in the Early Twelfth Century

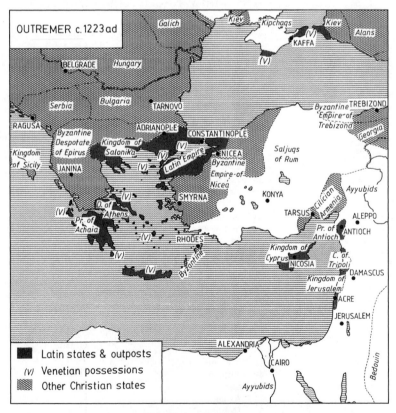

6. Outremer, circa 1223

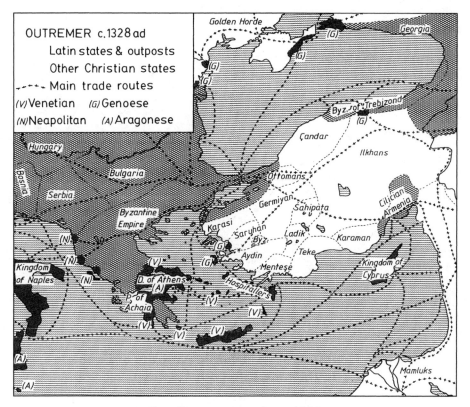

Golden Horde

Georgia

(G)

(G)

(G)

(G)

Byz.or Trebizond

(G)

Hungary

Çandar

Ilkhans

Bosnia

Bulgaria

Serbia

Ottomans

Byzantine
Empire

Germiyan

Sahipata

Cilician
Armenia

Karasi

Byz.

Ladik

Karaman

Saruhan

(N)

(G)

(N)

Aydin

Teke

Kingdom of
Cyprus

(V)

(G)

Mentese

Kingdom
of Naples

(N)

D. of Athens

Hospitallers

(A)

P. of
Achaia

(V)

(A)

(V)

(V)

(V)

(A)

(V)

(V)

Mamluks

(A)

7. Outremer, circa 1328

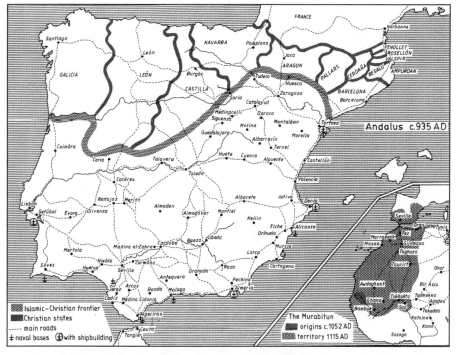

FRANCE

Santiago

Narbonne

León

NAVARRA

Pamplona

FENOLLET
ROSELLÓN
VALSPIR

GALICIA

LEÓN

Burgos

Jaca

ARAGON

PALLARS

CERDAÑA

BESALÚ

AMPURDAN

CASTILLA

Tudela

Huesca

BARCELONA

Barcelona

Soria

Catalayud

Zaragoza

Medinaceli
Siguenza

Daroca

Molina

Montalban

Andalus c.935 AD

Coimbra

Guadalajara

Albarracín

Morella

Tortosa

Coria

Huete

Cuenca

Alpuente

Castellón

Talavera

Teruel

Cacéres

Toledo

Valencia

Lisbon

Badajoz

Mérida

Albacete

Jativa

Setúbal

Olivenza

Almadén

Almodóvar

Montiel

Denia

Evora

Hellin

Elche

Alicante

Mértola

Córdoba

Madina al-Zahrás

Baeza

Úbeda

Lorca

Murcia

Seville

Orihuela

Silves

Niebla

Carmona

Baza

Cartagena

Ordea

Tunis

Fez

Huelva

Seville

Granada

Pechina

Marrakesh

Jerez

Antequera

Almería

Massa

Sijilmasa

Arcos

Ronda

Malaga

Taghaza

Cadiz

Medina Sidonia

Taurirt

Ghat

Algeciras

Awdaghost

Timbuktu

Todmekka

Agades

Bir Aslu

Katsina

Ceuta

Ghana

Tangier

Bambuk

Salaga

Kano

Tekedda

**8. Al-Andalus and the Further Maghrib from the Tenth
to the Early Twelfth Century**

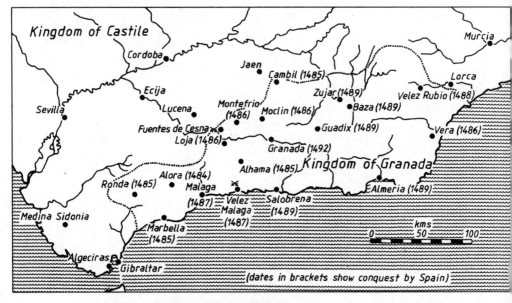

**9. The Conquest of the Islamic Amirate of Granada
in the Late Fifteenth Century**

Introduction

The early medieval period saw the foundations of two major new civilisations being laid, those of medieval Christian Europe and of the Islamic World. They emerged as much as partners as they did as rivals, and the current popular concept of a supposedly inevitable 'clash of civilisations' has no foundation in historical fact. Nevertheless, the worlds of medieval Christendom and medieval Islam often found themselves at war, while also being partners in trade and cultural exchange. Furthermore, both had other rivals, not merely each other. Hence many of those campaigns which were, justly or unjustly, graced with the titles of Crusade or Jihad, were fought against pagans, Hindus, Buddhists, Manichaeans or other 'third parties'. All too often their targets were fellow believers such as Orthodox rather than Latin-Catholic Christians, or Shia rather than Sunni Muslims.

Although western Christendom had regained some of its economic and military strength by the eighth century AD, the first aggressive thrusts into a wider world occurred three centuries later, beginning with the Spanish (or more correctly Iberian) *Reconquista*, the German *Zug nach dem Osten* (or expansion eastwards) into previously pagan Slav lands, and the Norman conquest of Islamic-ruled Sicily. These thrusts would soon be followed by Crusades, initially against the Islamic peoples of the Middle East but then against pagan Baltic and Finnic peoples in the Baltic region. These were in turn followed by Crusades against Orthodox fellow Christians in the Byzantine Empire, the Balkans and Russia, as well as against perceived heretics within Latin-Catholic Christian Western Europe.

The Laws of War
Medieval people were just as concerned about the morality and legal basis of warfare as were those of later centuries. This was particularly true of medieval religious leaders and lawyers who put considerable effort into establishing a satisfactory framework for this least desirable of human activities. In the early fifth century, Saint Augustine of Hippo maintained

that only rulers and officials acting in the line of duty could kill without giving way to hatred. He also accepted the concept that, for a just ruler, the punishment of wrongdoers or enemies was an 'act of love' in a sinful world where perfect peace was impossible. This 'radical pessimism' dominated attitudes to warfare throughout the Middle Ages and it was also widely accepted that the sin of waging unjust war fell upon leaders rather than their followers.

The Byzantine Empire also inherited the Roman concept of victory in battle as a judgement from God and this element of 'trial by combat' persisted at least until the tenth century. Byzantine armies also tried to maintain a Roman tradition of limiting the destructiveness of war, and in this respect the Byzantines were remarkably similar to their Islamic neighbours. However, despite Byzantine influence upon many aspects of warfare in the Orthodox Christian states of Eastern Europe, restraint was clearly not characteristic of warfare in medieval Russia. Here instead the members of a prince's *druzhina* or armed retinue were motivated by honour for themselves and glory for their leader, just like the knights of Western Europe.

The medieval Western European Christian Church had few moral problems with warfare and frequently took part itself, but until the late eleventh century spiritual punishments were often imposed upon soldiers, for example insisting that they undertake a fast or other form of penance. In other respects Christian concepts of 'Just War' and 'Holy War' came to be seen as punitive responses to perceived injuries inflicted upon Christ or upon the Christian community. During the twelfth century, the lawyer Gratian of Bologna was the first to make a clear distinction between 'Just War' and 'Holy War', the former being to protect the state, the latter to protect the Church. Such canon or religious law provided a moral framework for aggressive campaigns like the Crusades and 'Holy War' was eventually regarded as an attempt to further 'God's Intentions' in this world. In such cases one side stood totally in the right – namely the Christians – while the other was totally in the wrong.

Medieval soldiers had their own accepted ways of waging war and it was widely regarded as 'dishonourable' to stray outside such rules. Those most closely involved in war, especially the Western European aristocracy, had their own concept of 'Good War' and 'Bad War'; the former being characterised by restraint and honourable behaviour, the latter by cruelty and dishonesty. Each class of society had its own code of conduct, that of the military aristocracy evolving into the concept of chivalry. In several respects chivalry had its origins in the Church's efforts to promote the idea of the Christian *miles* or knight back in the tenth century. He, it was hoped, would be a warrior who served the interests of the Church and lived, as far as possible, according to Christian principles. In return, the Church now offered such a fighting man a recognised role within Christian society.

A tendency for Just War and Holy War to fuse into one struggle called Crusade was first seen along western Christendom's frontier with Islam, most notably in the Iberian peninsula. In fact many legal thinkers during the centuries of Crusade and *Reconquista* were clearly influenced by Islamic ideas where the legal framework of warfare was concerned. In the thirteenth century, for example, the three preconditions laid down by Saint Thomas Aquinas for Just War had clear parallels within Islamic Law; these being due authority, just cause and good intentions.

The Papacy, having given the *miles* or knightly class a new role in Christian society, soon tried to divert the *miles'* warlike energies against the Islamic peoples whom the Catholic Church described as the 'most blameworthy nation'. Only the Church could proclaim a Holy War or Crusade and the religious lawyers of the late eleventh to thirteenth centuries developed a legal framework for such Crusading warfare, promising participants the status of heroes in this world and salvation in the next. Before long, however, some thinkers were suggesting that the repeated failure of such Crusades showed that they were at best misguided and might actually be immoral aggression. To counter such views some canon lawyers maintained that God permitted Islam to exist merely to enable Christians to gain merit by fighting against it.

The legal framework in which war took place was more defined in the Islamic world than in Christendom. Some historians disagree on just when the legal and religious framework of Islamic society came into being, denying that it can be traced back to the time of the Prophet Muhammad himself. It certainly existed from an early date and Islamic 'laws of war' were firmly based upon Koranic Law. It is also clear that Islamic concepts of Just War, as distinct from Holy War, drew heavily upon the tribal traditions of pre-Islamic Arabia, being characterised by a wish to dominate politically rather than convert religiously. In other words, conquest was a means to an end rather than an end in itself.

The Koranic basis meant that the 'physical' or secondary *jihad*, as distinct from the superior 'spiritual' *jihad*, was the only strictly legitimate form of warfare. The *Hadith* or 'Sayings' of the Prophet provided more detailed guidelines; for example stating that even sinful Muslim rulers should lead the *jihad* and that the help offered by a non-combatant towards the equipping of a *mujahid*, or soldier in *jihad*, was itself a form of *jihad*. Furthermore, all defensive wars were to some degree a *jihad* because Islamic civilisation was theoretically theocratic. So injury to the state was an injury to Islam and thus to God.

The waging of *jihad* soon became an important way for Muslim rulers to demonstrate their own political legitimacy, but by the eleventh century it was little more than a political tool in the hands of the ruling élite. The European Crusades then led to a revival of interest in the laws of *jihad*, the most famous legal scholar of this period being Ibn Rushd. His treatise, written in 1167, remained a standard work for centuries, maintaining that *jihad* was essentially defensive and that the enemy could be any polytheist (believer in more than one God which, in Muslim eyes, included the Christian concept of the Holy Trinity). However, the enemy could not be attacked before being offered a chance to accept Islamic rule and to pay the *jizyah* tax demanded of all non-Muslim subjects.

The *siyar*, or regulations governing a soldier's behaviour, had been codified in the mid-eighth century. These prohibited the killing of women, children, the old or sick, the destruction of various economic targets or private property. Furthermore, soldiers should not mutilate the enemy nor break promises or offers of safe conduct.

Despite this legal framework underpinning the conduct of war in Islamic civilisation there remained a considerable contrast between theory and reality. A survival of tribal traditions in frontier areas could meanwhile lead to un-Islamic barbarism. For example the Saharan Berber Murabitin may have introduced head-hunting to the Iberian peninsula, a practice then occasionally adopted by their Christian foes, though both sides apparently returned the decapitated bodies for burial.

The ferocity characteristic of pre-Islamic Central Asian warfare had different origins, stemming from the difficulty of survival in a singularly harsh environment. In fact the Mongols are said to have regarded their own lives as the property of their rulers, and that they slaughtered their opponents because the latter were an enemy ruler's property. In fact the perceived non-acceptance of established 'rules of war' by such Central Asian armies led to widespread terror and confusion amongst their medieval Christian and Islamic foes.

The basic Central Asian legal 'code' was the *yasa* or tribal law. Even after a Turkish or Mongol tribe became Muslim, it generally took several generations before their old *yasa* gave way to Islamic law. This was particularly apparent in the conduct of warfare, with a mixed tribal and Islamic code sometimes called a *siyasat* often characterising the intervening period. For example, the Mamluk Sultanate of Egypt and Syria, despite being the champion of Islam against Mongol aggression, remained sufficiently close to their Eurasian steppe origins to regard the *Great Yasa* of Genghiz Khan as a suitable legal model.

In medieval India the code of the warrior and the laws of war were based upon Hindu scripture. The duties of the high status *kshatriya* warrior caste had, for example, traditionally been laid down in the ancient Vedic 'Laws of Manu'. As in pre-Islamic Sassanian Iran, victory in battle decided which side was right and which wrong. Might was right and military success was essential to maintain a ruler's legitimacy. A soldier captured in battle became the servant or slave of his captor, though only for as long as it took to pay off his ransom. The captive could then hope to be freed and 'born again' as a member of the *kshatriya* caste.

Chapter 1

The Rise of the Crusade

During the tenth century, the political fragmentation of the unified Abbasid Caliphate with its capital at Baghdad in Iraq had been accompanied by some degree of cultural and even religious fragmentation within the Islamic world. Consequently the confrontation between Islam and Christendom in the Middle East, Mediterranean and Iberian peninsula became a struggle between many armies using increasingly different military systems and tactics. The Arabs had already declined in military importance to be replaced or supplemented by Iranians, Turks and Berbers. In addition to the Byzantine Empire and Iberian Christian states which had long been the primary protagonists, other peoples were similarly drawn into this struggle on the Christian side, ranging from Nubians and Ethiopians in Africa, Armenians and Georgians in the Caucasus, to Italians in Europe.

In some places the border between Christendom and Islam was remarkably blurred. In eastern Anatolia, for example, half-Armenian half-Arab dynasties arose, claimed by neither side and an enemy to all. Various minor religions or heresies had also found a refuge in this area, including Paulicians, who were largely Manichaean in belief and had much in common with the later Bogomils of the Balkans and the Albigensians of southern France.

The Muslim Arabs had been the first conquerors of Central Asia to come from the west since Alexander the Great, but once their first wave of expansion ended in the eighth century the only large-scale spread of Islam resulted from the peaceful activities of merchants or missionaries in Central Asia, Africa and the Indian Ocean. Meanwhile, the Islamic world, like Christian Europe, was wracked by internal conflicts as the central authority of the Abbasid Caliphate crumbled, most of the regional successor dynasties being built upon military power.

In the steppe lands of Central Asia some Turkish peoples had already adopted Buddhism, the Nestorian sect of Christianity or had converted to Islam, though those further to the north and east largely remained shamanist-pagan. One powerful group, the Khazars, had adopted Judaism while far to the west in Morocco most, though not all, of the Jewish Berber tribes had converted to Islam. Nevertheless the heretical Judaeo-Islamic Barghawata of the Atlantic coast remained a powerful force well into the tenth century.

The Struggle for the Mediterranean

The strongest naval powers in the Mediterranean before the rise of Italian naval power in the late tenth and eleventh centuries were the Byzantine Empire, the Fatimid Caliphate and the Umayyad Caliphate in the Iberian peninsula. Islamic forces had conquered the island of Sicily in a combined operation which involved shipping substantial forces from Tunisia. Naval warfare and communications were, in fact, notably more advanced in the Mediterranean and the Indian Ocean than in the northern seas, with correspondingly more ambitious attempts at such combined operations. Nevertheless this should not be overstated. Political changes in Islamic North Africa left the virtually autonomous Islamic state in Apulia on the heel of Italy cut off from support, resulting in its defeat and absorbtion in the early tenth century.

In naval warfare there was a clear distinction between piracy and official warfare against enemy vessels or coasts. Sea battles were usually a matter of grappling and boarding rather than ramming, while the artillery aboard ships was primarily for use against stationary coastal targets rather than other vessels. In strategic terms several geographical factors gave a clear and persistent advantage to the naval powers of the northern shores of the Mediterranean. Here there were more island 'stepping stones' and good harbours while the winds were generally more suitable for coastal navigation in the north.

Nevertheless, medieval requirements were different from those seen in later centuries and as a result Malta was not much used as a naval base in the Middle Ages because it lacked timber. The northern shores' abundant sources of timber with which to build ships may have been even more important. Egypt's shortage of timber was so acute that, by the tenth century, wood was being imported from Italy, Dalmatia and Crete. Later it was even being imported from India. Raiding the enemy's shores and burning his stores of timber and sails, as happened, clearly played an important part in naval strategy.

The change from hull-first to more economical frame-first construction had started during the early Islamic period and the Muslims' lack of timber may subsequently have stimulated a revival in the construction of very large and powerful ships which were more economical in terms of resources and were better able to defend themselves. The widespread use of the lateen sail could similarly be attributed to the Arabs as a result of Indian Ocean influence.

Byzantine and Islamic Mediterranean warships were the same, with considerable exchange of both technology and terminology. Some war-galleys had a single bank of oars, some two; some a single mast, others up to three. By the tenth century the ship-breaking ram had been replaced by the oar-breaking and boarding beak, probably a result of a shortage of timber increasing the value of ships and making it more desirable to capture them intact. The normal Byzantine galley had 100 to 200 oarsmen, with a maximum of 150 marines concentrated in the forecastle, while both the Islamic *shini* and *shalandi* galleys had two banks of oars.

Some transport ships were similar to barges in being propelled primarily by oars rather than sails; these including the *qarib*, *ghurab* and *tarida* specialized horse-transport. Standard late tenth-century North African *tarida* horse-transporting galleys could carry forty animals, whereas the Italian or Byzantine ships used by the Normans in their invasion of Sicily in 1061 still only carried about twenty. Possession of a fleet capable of transporting troops enabled the later Fatimids to hold on to a string of harbours on the Palestinian and Syrian coasts long after the interior had fallen to invading Crusaders.

The Muslims' general shortage of trained naval troops meant that the *ghazi* volunteers were trained to fight on both land and sea. Both sides relied mainly on archery and javelins, plus special long-hafted anti-rigging axes and long spears to attack opposing oarsmen. There were also references to mysterious 'snakes' which were probably a form of incendiary weapon. Whereas Byzantine marines made considerable use of *solenarion* arrow-guides to shoot short darts, an élite unit of eleventh and early twelfth-century Egyptian Fatimid marines used hand-held crossbows in addition to ordinary composite bows.

From an early date, the most powerful Byzantine *dromond* galleys had been armed with three 'Greek fire' projectors. This is said to have been propelled through a bronze tube and the Abbasid fleet was clearly using comparable *naft* by the mid-ninth century. A century later the Fatimids of Egypt were considered to be superior to their Byzantine foes in pyrotechnics, Egypt being in commercial contact with China where fire-weapons were even more advanced.

Although a major shift in naval strategy became apparent by the tenth century, when Islamic navies pioneered a change from coastal raiding to attacking enemy ships in the open sea, coastal attacks remained more important through the medieval period. Several states had, in fact, developed sophisticated coastal defence systems, the Muslims having observation points along the Syrian coast which, with intelligence reports, could warn of the approach of an enemy fleet. During the summer when the 'seas were open', infantry and cavalry garrisons were encamped on the coast itself, whereas in winter when the 'seas were closed', a few soldiers manned the watchtowers while the garrisons withdrew inland. Some ports were more strongly protected, often with floating chains across the entrance and with stone-throwing engines on their sea walls. The Byzantines had, in fact, been on the receiving end of naval raiding throughout the early medieval period, from Slavs and Scandinavian Russians as well as Muslim Arabs. Things became particularly serious in the later eleventh century, after the Byzantine Empire's collapse in Anatolia and the appearance of a Turco-Islamic fleet based at Smyrna (Izmir) on the Aegean.

The Byzantine Empire

A constant feature of Byzantine military history was the Empire's shortage of military manpower, particularly on the eastern frontier, which resulted in frequent transfers of population into Anatolia. Recruitment from outside the Empire was another solution but despite the fact that hiring mercenaries was a cheap way of acquiring an experienced army, the proportion of foreigners and external allies was always higher when Byzantium was on the offensive rather than the defensive.

By the ninth and tenth centuries the bulk of the Byzantine army probably consisted of men obliged to give service in return for land or other privilege from the state. These formed the famous *theme* or provincial armies which first appeared in the threatened eastern regions. *Theme* soldiers would not have farmed their own land but might have lived off its rents, and *theme* armies normally included four times as many infantry as cavalry. Some of the former probably formed an armoured élite, as they did in the regular units based around the capital, while poorly equipped provincial javelin troops and infantry archers were not regarded as regular soldiers.

Some of the non-Greeks recruited into the Byzantine army were not actually foreigners, with Armenians playing a prominent role in all ranks including senior commanders. The majority appear to have been infantry and were highly regarded in siege warfare. On the other hand Armenians were suspect as heretics or, worse still, members of the essentially non-Christian Paulician sect. In fact the brutality with which the Byzantines crushed the Paulicians in eastern Armenia had led large numbers to migrate to more tolerant Islamic rule where they were still recorded in Middle Eastern Islamic armies as late as the twelfth century.

Other warriors crossed the frontier in the opposite direction, including substantial numbers of Arabs, some Kurds and a few Persians who converted from Islam to Christianity. Central Asian Turks in the tenth-century Byzantine army came from pagan, Buddhist and Zoroastrian regions beyond the existing Islamic frontier, though by the mid-eleventh century the Byzantines were also enlisting many Pecheneg Turkish prisoners-of-war from the Balkans.

Slavs as yet played a minor role in Byzantine armies, though many Bulgarians were recruited after Byzantium's reconquest of the southern Balkans and by the eleventh century Slavs were second only to Armenians amongst the non-Greek troops of the Byzantine army. Similarly the *Rhos* or Russians would have included men of Scandinavian origin who had played a significant role in the foundation of the first Russian state. Other non-Greek recruits from the west included Albanian mountaineers, Romanian-speaking Vlach nomads from Thessaly in Greece and, in the mid-eleventh century, Norman heavily-armoured cavalry who arrived via southern Italy. Meanwhile the Byzantine Emperor Constantine IX disbanded some 50,000 local Armenian troops, many of whom subsequently entered the service of the Islamic Fatimid Caliphs of Egypt.

The Byzantine Empire had been divided into smaller military zones as a result of civil wars and by the tenth century the state had become highly militarized. Metropolitan forces around the capital of Constantinople such as the *Tagmata* regiments and guard units served as a strategic reserve. Here it was easy to keep en eye on the kit and competence of military units, but to check provincial units the Byzantine government held occasional *adnoumia*, local musters or reviews. If a man was considered too poor to maintain himself as a properly equipped member of a field army he might be transfered to the irregulars or sent to garrison a fort.

The structure of the Byzantine army remained quite complex throughout the early medieval period, with the *Domestic* as the most senior officer, assisted by various senior officials and officer grades. The bulk of the army was also theoretically divided into *turma* (brigades), each of three to five *droungoi* (battalions) in turn consisting of five *banda* (companies), the smallest tactical units traditionally consisting of around thirty cavalrymen. The normal operational formation was a *parataxis* theoretically of three hundred men, and by the tenth century a typical Byzantine operational infantry formation supposedly consisted of five hundred armoured *oplitai* regular troops, two hundred javelin-armed and three hundred archer auxiliaries.

The structure and organization of Byzantine provincial and frontier *theme* armies differed from that of metropolitan forces. In the war-ravaged east the whole *theme* structure had been renovated in the ninth century and was then extended to the western or European coastal provinces. Subsequently, the fragmentation of Islamic frontier territories in the Middle East led to Byzantine frontier defences themselves being subdived into smaller units to face smaller but more numerous enemy centres. Military commands known as *kleisourai* or mountain passes now appeared, each with their own relatively small forces, backed up by the *theme* armies in case the Muslims launched a more substantial invasion. From the late ninth century the military initiative passed to the Byzantines and the frontier was again reorganized, with new offensive forces under the command of *Dux* or *Turmach* officers being added to the existing military structure while the *kleisourai* seem to have been re-absorbed within the overall *theme* system.

Anatolia had been a major recruiting ground for the Byzantine army, despite the fact that large areas had been dominated by local magnates who were almost beyond imperial control. The eastern frontier was, in fact, the setting for the heroic *akrites*, frontier warriors whose exploits filled the pages of medieval Greek tales. Elsewhere the perhaps less epic but equally important provincial military gentry came to be known as *stradiotti*. As the Armenians declined in military importance, their place was to some extent filled by Norman, Varangian and other Western mercenaries in the mid-eleventh century. However, Norman heavy cavalry knights and Varangian heavy infantry did not form fixed garrisons, being intended to act as a field force operating out of the main Byzantine strongholds. *Theme* forces developed later in the western part of the Byzantine Empire, and in many cases supported provincial navies rather than land armies. However, the *theme* armies of Byzantine southern Italy were disbanded around 1040 AD, to be replaced by local militias backed up by units sent from Constantinople.

The tenth century saw the Byzantine Empire go on the offensive against neighbouring fortified Islamic cities. Here the Byzantines had several strategic advantages because the geography of northern Syria enabled them to approach their targets indirectly, rather than being confined to a small number of mountain passes. Whereas the Byzantine 'target' population was rural and dispersed, that of Syria was concentrated in cities surrounded by intensively cultivated, and thus vulnerable, areas. As a result Byzantine offensives were carefully planned to conquer one city or cultivated zone at a time, necessitating self-sufficient, highly mobile and adaptable armies.

Georgia and Armenia

Virtually nothing seems to be known about the military organization of the Christian kingdom of Georgia in the Caucasus mountains. Meanwhile Christian Armenia had regained its ancient independence and wealth under the suzereinty of the Islamic Caliphate in the mid-ninth century. The countryside was dominated by a military aristocracy of *nachararks*, most of whom had their own *azatk'* forces maintained by an agricultural class of non-military serfs. In fact, medieval Armenia had a large and notably well-equipped army which was capable of fending off both Byzantine and Islamic interference until the Byzantines took control of eastern Anatolia in the mid-eleventh century.

More is known of the simple strategy adopted by the small Christian states of northern Iberia. Until the eleventh century, Christian Spanish warfare was largely modelled upon that of Islamic Andalusia, with raiding by light cavalry being the main form of offensive operation. In tenth and eleventh-entury León and Castile, a *fonsado* or major expedition would, however, involve infantry if an enemy town was to be attacked or battle with a large enemy army was expected. It is also worth noting that the high plains of La Mancha and Extramadura in Spain were not the cereal growing regions seen today but were characterized by sheep ranching, raiding and rustling. Meanwhile both Christians and Muslims attempted to control the passes through the sequence of *Sierras*, east-west mountain ranges which straddle the Iberian peninsula.

The Islamic World

Following the fragmentation of Abbasid authority in the Islamic Middle East, power often fell into the hands of soldiers of slave-recruited Turkish *mamluk* origin who formed a military élite separate from the Arab and Persian religious and commercial élites. This *mamluk* or *ghulam* class perpetuated itself by purchasing further military slaves to be trained and freed. It was also characterised by a system of *sinf* or loyalty in which *mamluks* were remarkably devoted to those who had purchased, trained, freed and paid them. Of course Turks or other *mamluks* were not the only troops in the Islamic Middle East and similar loyalty was found amongst other military groups, often being based on ethnic origin or regimental identity.

Meanwhile the smaller successor states had to recruit from a more limited area and their armies thus varied. Many rulers also believed that recruiting from several different sources promoted competition, inhibited military coups and provided a balance of forces. The Samanids, for example, had used Turkish *mamluks* to balance the indigenous Iranian *dihqan* minor aristocracy while also enlisting Tajiq eastern Iranians and freeborn Turkish nomads, Arab and Kurdish cavalry, Daylami infantry from south of the Caspian Sea and Hindu Indian infantry. The assorted *muttawiya* religiously inspired volunteers were still mentioned as a separate entity in the eleventh century, generally being orthodox Sunni Muslims who included *ghazis* or men who dedicated their lives to defending Islam's frontiers, plus retired old soldiers, runaway peasants and *azadaya* short-term volunteers. Fiercely fundamentalist *khawarijis* were similarly operating in the eastern provinces of the Islamic world, though they were more prominent in the Middle East and Arabia.

In northern Iran, Daylamis and troops from neighbouring Tabaristan were used to balance the ubiquitous Turks. In fact backward, poor and mountainous Daylam became a major exporter of highly regarded infantry. Further west, in the Fertile Crescent and mountains close to the Byzantine frontier, Arab tribal forces had been downgraded but never disappeared. Now they re-emerged to establish a number of small but potent successor states such as the Banu Kilab of northern Syria and the Banu 'Uqayl of northern Mesopotamia. In contrast the the Kurdish Marwanid dynasty in Armenia was founded by the leader of the local religious volunteers. The tenth and eleventh centuries produced, in fact, some of the most varied armies in Islamic military history. The army of the Arab Mirdasid dynasty in northern Syria was at one time commanded by a Christian *wazir* while the walls of the great city of Aleppo was defended by its Christian and Jewish as well as Muslim inhabitants.

The armies of the Islamic successor states in Egypt and North Africa largely drew upon different recruits. Slave troops of black African origin played a major military role, particularly in Egypt and Tunisia, most Islamic armies in North Africa still largely consisted of local Berbers commanded by an Arab officer class.

The military structures of most post-Abbasid successor states attempted to imitate the great days of Caliphal power and in many areas raising money to pay the army, either by direct taxation or a system of *iqta'* fiefs, became the primary function of the state apparatus. Retaining the loyalty of *mamluks* once their original purchaser and patron had died was more difficult, though there were examples of regiments lasting for up to three generations through new recruitment. All too often, however, such soldiers transferred their loyalty to their own senior officer and sometimes became little more than wandering bands of mercenaries.

Elsewhere things evolved differently and the way in which the Islamic frontier regions attempted to defend themselves was illustrated in remarkably detailed information dealing with the major fortified city of Tarsus in Cilicia. Here counter-raids against the Byzantines were normally summoned during the main Friday religious service. Much of the city's population was, in fact, still dedicated to *jihad* with the *ghazis* or 'fighters for Islam' including permanently-resident as well as temporary volunteers.

In Syria, *ahdath* urban militas also reached their peak of effectiveness by the early eleventh century, their members often being paid a regular annual salary and sometimes acting like a regular army, raiding Byzantine and subsequently Crusader territory or fighting in open battle against invaders. In Egypt the Arab Bedouin remained something of a state within a state, playing a small but locally important military role.

In Iran there had been a revival of many aspects of pre-Islamic Persian civilization under an Islamic veneer. Annual military reviews, for example, were sometimes carried out on the festival of *Nawruz* which was the old Persian 'New Year'. A great deal is, in fact, known about the military organization of the Samanid dynasty which ruled Transoxania and eastern Iran before the arrival of the Saljuq Turks. This Sunni Islamic state was administered through a *diwan al-jaysh* or 'war ministry', a *diwin al-barid* 'communications service' and a *diwin al-mushrif* 'intelligence gathering service'. The forces of the rival Shia Islamic Buyid dynasty of western Iran and Iraq was a organized in a manner halfway between the old mixed armies of the Abbasids and the new *mamluk* forces. It was also characterized by a system of public oath-taking ceremonies and chains of such oaths to cement loyalty between the ruler, his officers and their men, though not with great success.

Far away on the easternmost frontier of the Muslim world the little-known Karakhanid state ruled the steppe frontier of Central Asia and straddled the Tien Shan mountains into what is today Chinese Turkestan. Though the settled Iranian minor aristocracy of *dihqans* saw a brief military revival under the early Karakhanids, this state was essentially Turkish and clung to Turkish nomadic military traditions, being divided into tribal fiefs whose loyalty to the *khan* or ruler depended almost solely on his character and military success.

As with military organization, so with strategic concepts, the successor states of the Abbasid Caliphate attempted to continue existing and highly respected traditions. Raiding into Byzantine territory continued, though now usually as reprisals for Byzantine offensives and as the Muslims were now largely on the defensive it was now their armies which attempted to trap Byzantine raiders either south of the mountains or in the passes as they returned home.

Lance-armed heavy cavalry had revived in Byzantine armies as the Empire took the offensive in the tenth century and there may have been a revival of horse-archery under the influence of the Turkish *mamluks* of neighbouring Islamic armies. Nevertheless, such heavily-armoured cavalry remained a feature of metropolitan rather than frontier forces and the bulk of Byzantine archers remained infantry rather than horsemen. Generally speaking, Byzantine armies found it easier to cope with the bull-headed tactics of their Western European rivals than with the sophisticated tactics of Central Asian Turks and Middle Eastern Muslims. Yet the sophistication of Byzantine tactics enabled them to vary their formations to meet different challenges. The *Tactika* attributed to Nicephorus was primarily concerned with large-scale offensive operations, mainly against Islamic territory, indicating that purely cavalry as well as mixed cavalry and infantry forces could be sent into the plains of the Arab Fertile Crescent. In the latter case, cavalry ideally operated from a defensive square of men on foot; normally with four infantrymen to each horseman. Square or rectangular Byzantine infantry formations left gaps through which their cavalry could launch counter charges, these usually being followed by lighter cavalry skirmishers while the infantry remained on the defensive.

Byzantine armoured cavalry on armoured horses were first mentioned in 965 but, being so slow and tiring so quickly, they were used for a final decisive charge. They also advanced at a measured pace, not a gallop, with the ordinary cavalry close behind. This was the same shock cavalry tactics which would characterize the subsequent 'knightly' armies of Western Europe but, unlike Western armies, the Byzantines also made use of as many horse-archers as were available. Although Western Europe clearly did not invent this form of shock cavalry warfare, it is doubtful whether the Byzantines did either, since the same tactics were being used by the Abbasids in the ninth century if not earlier. A blunted wedge-shaped cavalry formation was, however, said to have been 'invented' by Nicephorus Phocas. This had archers on armoured horses at the centre surrounded by men with swords, maces and axes, with lancers in the front rank and on the flanks.

Military training in the professional armies of the Middle East and eastern Asia involved structured programmes and exercises, many of which had evolved over centuries. For example, Byzantine archery tended to emphasise accuracy and power rather than speed of shooting. In the late-eleventh century, infantry archers were trained to shoot in disciplined ranks, sometimes at a diagonal angle in order to get around the opposition's shields, and there is no reason to believe that this was a wholly new idea.

Infantry often had higher status in tenth- and eleventh-century Islamic armies than in the Byzantine Empire. Armoured Daylami foot soldiers, for example, had younger warriors as shield bearers in battle, suggesting that such shields were large enough to be called mantlets, while the importance given to infantry by the east Iranian Ghaznavids clearly showed that the prestige of foot soldiers had risen since pre-Islamic Sassanian times. The Ghaznavids also used larger numbers of elephants, each with four spearmen or archers on their back and towards the mid-eleventh century the Buyids brought a few of these animals to the Middle East, probably for parade purposes. On the other hand the Arab armies of Syria included relatively few infantrymen, the most important being archers.

Several Arabic military manuals survive from the early medieval period but have yet to be studied to the same extent as comparable Byzantine military treatises. At least one late ninth-century example included a chapter on 'Shadowing Warfare', decades before the more famous

Byzantine work on the same subject. Meanwhile most other evidence indicates that, on the march, the armies of post-Abbasid successor states still used the classic *khamis* array first recorded in pre-Islamic southern Arabia. In Abbasid times the centre would have consisted of heavy cavalry with heavy infantry and infantry archers behind; the right and left flanks, van and rear largely consisting of light cavalry. The baggage, hospital and any siege train would follow, with flocks of animals as a food supply. Each division ideally marched in a rectangular formation where each man supposedly kept strictly in position while reconnaissance parties rode a day's march or more ahead.

In open battle it was still normal for Islamic armies to await an enemy attack before they themselves moved, as would remain the case throughout the medieval period. Even *naft* fire-grenade throwers could be used against static lines of enemy shield-bearers, though not always with success. Arab Islamic cavalry traditionally advanced in lines rather than the Byzantines' wedge formation, launching measured and repeated charges.

In open battle most Islamic forces still preferred to adopt a defensive array and await the enemy's first move, infantry normally hoping to exhaust an enemy by absorbing his attacks before themselves advancing in solid phalanxes. According to one eleventh-century book of military theory, a different *shi'ar* or battlecry was assigned to each unit, while commanders might take position on available raised ground, or use a camel as a command post to gain the best possible view over the battlefield. Additional details show that Islamic armies were by now also effective in night fighting, as their pre-Islamic southern Arabian ancestors had been, and that *haraqat* fire ships were used in river warfare at least in Iraq.

The Arab-Islamic conquerors of the Middle East had inherited not only training grounds but also their predecessors' professional attitudes towards military training. As a result theoretical and practical military manuals survive from a remarkably early date, though the Abbasid Caliphate of the ninth and tenth centuries saw the golden age of such *furusiyah* literature. Large reviews also gave a senior commander a chance to practice the movement of large bodies of men as well as testing battlefield communications, discipline and responsiveness. As a result medieval Islamic cavalry took part in various exercises including polo, which the Arabs had learned from the Sassanian Iranians.

Practice to improve individual skills also featured prominently, and from the late ninth century cavalrymen were tilting with spears against metal rings mounted on top of columns to improve their dexterity. The Abbasid Caliph Harun al-Rashid is credited with introducing archery as part of established military exercises while Turkish influence lay behind the later adoption of the *qighaj* or *qiqaj* exercise in which a horseman shot at a ground-level target at very close range while on the move. This had more military application than the *qabaq*, a target mounted high on a pole which was used to improve a horse-archer's dexterity. Infantry skills were still in demand and could involve unusual training devices such as a tenth-century Syrian archery target in the form of a stuffed animal mounted on a four-wheeled cart which was rolled downhill.

Military recruitment in the eastern Islamic territories continued to reflect earlier traditions until the coming of the Mongols in the thirteenth century. For example, the later Ghaznawids, whose state was centred upon Lahore in what is now Pakistan, recruited a multi-ethnic army which included local Indian converts to Islam, while the Ghurids, who overthrew the Ghaznawids in the later twelfth century, continued to rely heavily upon soldiers of slave *mamluk* origin.

The Coming of the Saljuq Turks

By the time the Saljuq Turks swept across the eastern provinces of the Islamic world and dominated most of the Middle East, they were already under strong Islamic military influence. However, they would, in military terms, teach as much as they learned, having come from a part of the world which already had its own highly effective military traditions. The fragmentation of the early medieval Great Turk Empire and its most civilized successor, the Uighur Khanate in what is now Chinese Turkestan, had resulted in a period of great instability in the steppes. This caused another wave of migrations which had their impact upon southern Russia, eastern Europe and the Byzantine Empire. However, it would be wrong to think that the peoples of Central Asia were any more warlike than, for example, the peoples of medieval Europe.

Nor did the Turkish, Mongol and other peoples of Central or Inner and northern Asia only inhabit the steppes. Many tribes lived in the Siberian forests rather than open grasslands or semi-desert areas. The Mongol Kitai, for example, inhabited the forests of northeast Mongolia and southern Manchuria while the Turkish Qarluks included both settled and nomadic elements, many of whom became Nestorian Christians. In contrast, the Semirechye region south of Lake Balkash was largely settled and agricultural. Here Islam spread rapidly after being introduced to Central Asia. Having been displaced by the Uighurs in the mid-eighth century, it was the Qipcaq Turks who eventually re-established relative stability in the steppes from the borders of Transoxania to the Hungarian frontier, at least until the rise of Genghis Khan.

The armies of the *khans* of the steppes appear to have been largely recruited from within the dominant tribe or tribal confederation. Only on the southern and western fringes did the existence of other, sometimes non-Turkish peoples, encourage more varied recruitment. Hence the urbanised Semirechye region had become a semi-independent part of the Islamic Karakhanid state by the eleventh century, with a local army recruited from Muslims, Christians, Buddhists and others.

Those Bulgars who had migrated to the Balkans in the early Middle Ages had been absorbed by their Slav subjects, whereas those who migrated north and created the Volga Bulgar state in what is now eastern European Russia became Muslim in the early tenth century. The latter soon fielded a powerful army which dominated, as well as recruiting from, the neighbouring Slav and Finnic tribes. Their neighbours, the Bashkir or Bashjirt, also converted to Islam and dominated the local eastern Magyar tribes. Many other Bashkirs entered western Magyar or Hungarian service in twelfth-century central Europe.

The Khazars, who expelled the Bulgars from the western steppes and established a particularly long-lasting state in southern Russia, had at first been a typical Turkish tribal force, but their aristocracy converted to Judaism in the eighth century. Their successors in the western steppes were the Turkish Pechenegs who, defeated by another wave of westward migrating nomads in 1116 AD, were driven northward into Russian or southward into Byzantine territory along with their rivals, the Torks and Uzes who, like the Saljuq Turks, were a branch of the Oghuz people.

The Qipcaq Turks who expelled these Pechenegs now established a sophisticated and militarily effective state divided into semi-independent eastern and western 'wings' or 'flanks', while the many trading towns under their control were inhabited by Persians, Jews, Armenians and others, some of whom provided military support. Nevertheless, the role of non-Turco-Mongol peoples in the armies and empires of the steppes tended to be localized. The Finn and related Ugrian tribes were widely regarded as fearsome fighters, but only rarely emerged from the forests north of the steppes, while Iranian-speaking Alan tribal nomads played a prominent role in the valleys and foothills of the north Caucasus mountains and neighbouring plains. In the coastal mountains of the Crimean peninsula, on the northern side of the Black Sea, a Germanic Goth community survived the nomadic invasions which dominated the steppes, perhaps being reinforced by Anglo-Saxon recruits to the Byzantine Varangian Guard in the late-eleventh and twelfth centuries. After the Mongol conquest, however, this isolated Germanic community disappeared.

Unlike the Arab Bedouin nomads of the Middle East, nomadic Turco-Mongol steppe societies were basically self-sufficient. Although there were plenty of small towns in and around the grasslands, most peoples also being involved in agriculture, mining or metallurgy, the social organisation of Central Asian nomadic tribes was on basis of 'heads' rather than land or property. As a result such tribes were already structured rather like armies. The main problem for these tribes was to maintain the enormous horse-herds upon which their power depended, particularly when they conquered intensively cultivated or semi-desert lands.

Islamic dynasties had dominated Transoxania until the rise of the partially Mongol and Buddhist Qarakhitai in the twelfth century. These Qarakhitai were unlike previous Central Asian nomad states because their culture and military organisation were strongly based upon those of China, the army being divided into small, almost regular units which appear to have been paid by the ruler rather than maintained by military or tribal fiefs. In many respects the Qarakhitai state was similar to that of the subsequent Mongols and the non-Islamic Qarakhitai may have been one of the realities behind stories of a great eastern ruler named Prester John who, Western European Crusaders piously hoped, would join them in a great war to crush Islam.

The life of steppe nomadic tribes normally meant a wide dispersal of people and military manpower. It thus took considerable time to assemble an army, while the horses were usually considered 'ready for war' by autumn, which thus became the main campaigning season. Turco-Mongol nomad armies also tended to follow uplands or watersheds, avoiding the main rivers which were not only significant obstacles but whose banks tended to be settled by non-nomadic populations. Mountain ranges rarely formed a barrier against Turks or Mongols because both use Bactrian camels for transport; such animals being capable of enduring high altitude as well as rough terrain and extreme cold.

Even within the open steppes, a cavalry army which found its archery outclassed would attempt to close with the enemy in a massive charge. Judging by Chinese descriptions of Great Turk armies in eastern Turkestan, such horsemen would advance in a wedge or arrow formation, making repeated attacks and withdrawals. How far such tactics were an indigenous development, or showed either Chinese or Iranian influence is unknown. How far the later Byzantine wedge-shaped cavalry formation owed to the Turks also remains unknown.

Arabic evidence confirms that Central Asian Turkish cavalry were normally lighter and swifter than their Islamic counterparts. An account of the 'battle plan of the Khaqan' in a thirteenth-century Indo-Islamic military treatise was probably based upon the tactics used by the twelfth-century Qarakhitai. Its similarity with tactics adopted by medieval Chinese forces when facing Central Asian nomad foes is remarkable, the *Khaqan*'s army being arrayed in nine separate groups rather than ranks forming a three-by-three formation.

Large ships had sailed the Caspian sea since at least early medieval times, even including a 'Viking' fleet which raided northern Iran after sailing down the river Volga. The importance of water-borne communications was emphasised by the man-made, sometimes silted and as often cleared, Uzboy channel which linked the Caspian Sea and Amu Darya river as a sort of 'Suez Canal' in the heart of the world's largest land-mass.

The Saljuq Turks were of Islamic Turkish tribal origin, first rising to power along the lower Syr Darya river in Transoxania, but as they spread their authority over the larger part of eastern Islam and the Middle East they again turned to traditional Islamic methods of military recruitment. In fact, many of the so-called Turks who first broke through the Byzantine defences into Anatolia around 1025 were not Saljuqs, nor even other Turks, but Persians, Daylamis and Kurds.

Non-Saljuqs certainly played an important role in the armies of various minor Saljuq leaders in eleventh-century Syria, including other Turkish nomads – better referred to as Turcomans since the Saljuqs themselves were no longer really nomadic. Armenians offered military support to the Saljuq governor of Antioch at the end of the eleventh century while the highly experienced warlike urban militias of northern Syria and the Jazirah (northern Mesopotamia) defended their walls both for and against the Turks during a period of near anarchy. By the end of the eleventh century some of the existing Christian military aristocracies of these areas had been 'Turkified' through intermarriage and it seems inevitable that some Western European, ex-Byzantine, mercenaries found themselves serving Saljuq rulers in the years immediately before the arrival of the First Crusade.

Crusader Armies and Tactics

The Islamic and Byzantine world both faced assaults from Western European Christendom during the twelfth to fourteenth centuries and there was also migration into the Balkans by waves of Turkic nomadic peoples from the steppes. This period was, in fact, characterised by militarily significant migrations, the most obvious being the Turkish conquest and settlement of the eastern half of the Byzantine Empire. At the same time the Muslim Kurds took over large areas which had previously been Christian Armenian, Muslim Arabs began to dominate North Africa at the expense of Muslim Berbers, Muslim Arab tribes pressed southwards into the Christian Nilotic Sudan while the Turkification of previously Iranian Transoxania continued.

The forces which marched east as the First Crusade were unlike normal Western European armies in their composition but not in their organisation, with participants grouping themselves around the most senior lords. Crusading was expensive and some poorer knights pooled their resources. Similarly the bulk of foot soldiers in the early Crusades appear to have been prosperous peasants, townsmen or professional *sergeants*. Women sometimes accompanied their husbands on Crusade and proved to be a morally stabilizing influence as well as working in camp and even mounting guard when necessary. In the early-thirteenth century the Pope also permitted monks to go on Crusade, but by the early fourteenth century monks were again confined to their monasteries.

However, military recruitment within the Crusader States in the Middle East differed from that of Crusading expeditions which originated in Europe. Large-scale migration to the Crusader States virtually stopped after the disaster at the Battle of Hattin in 1187, though individual families continued to make their way east, often as a consequence of political exile at home. Most of the nobility of these new states were from relatively modest knightly origins, the knights of the Middle East being known as *chevaliers de la terre* by friends, and *poulains* or 'runts' by unsympathetic sources. Members of this class could be involved in warfare as early as fifteen years old and were still liable for active service until sixty. The lack of agricultural land in the Crusader States also meant that the bulk of the thirteenth-century, and perhaps even twelfth-century, military aristocracy lived in towns and came to form a bourgeois knightly class similar to that of Italy.

Non-knightly troops included professional infantry and cavalry 'sergeants' paid by the towns and the Church, most having been recruited from local commoners and visiting pilgrims. In an emergency a general levy or *arriere ban* produced larger numbers of infantry sergeants and barely-trained militias, including men from the Arabic-speaking indigenous Christian communities. The merchant class of the coastal ports similarly formed *confraternities* or 'brotherhoods' to defend their own walls, while during the thirteenth century the various separate Italian *communes* within these cities provided highly effective infantry militias.

Mercenaries were essential to the Crusader States in Syria and Palestine, a steady stream of these being much preferred to sudden hordes of uncontrollable Crusaders. These were distinct from knights who were paid stipends via 'money fiefs' because the latter were theoretically still part of a feudal system of military obligation. From the mid-thirteenth century to the fall of Acre, other outside troops arrived in the Kingdom of Jerusalem; for example, the force of southern Italian cavalry brought by Filangieri, Emperor Frederick's *bailli*, or governor, during his brief rule over the Crusader States, and the French regiment brought east by King Louis of France. This was maintained by the French crown until the fall of Acre in 1291.

Armenian mercenaries were particularly numerous in Edessa (Urfa) and Antioch where their military engineers built and operated many of the Crusader States siege machines. The Principality of Antioch received less support from the West than did the Kingdom of Jerusalem and so relied to a greater extent on local recruitment, including a large Greek community and the better known Armenians. Syrian and Maronite infantry archers from Lebanon were more characteristic of Tripoli and Jerusalem.

The Crusaders would not apparently accept defeated Muslim troops into their service but there were significant numbers of ex-Muslim soldiers in the armies of the Crusader States. These were the *Turcopoles*, a word of Greek origin which initially referred to captured Muslims who had converted to Christianity and continued to fight as light cavalry. Subsequently the term *Turcopole* applied to troops fighting in Islamic style though not necessarily being converted Muslim prisoners, many apparently being eastern Christians and a few the descendants of Latin settlers. They were also seen in Crusader Cyprus where some may have been of purchased slave origin.

By far the most important non-feudal military forces in the Crusader States of the Middle East were the Military Orders. The two biggest Orders, those of the Templars and the Hospitallers, attracted men from all over Western Europe, though the majority came from France. At first recruits only had to be free but later those becoming 'brother knights' had to be of knightly origin. Sergeants in these Military Orders again had to be free, usually of artisan or peasant background but not serfs. In fact the Military Orders came to be seen as a good career for the younger sons of knightly families, particularly as they did not involve the same degree of 'renunciation of the world' as did the regular monastic orders. Visiting pilgrim knights could similarly attach themselves temporarily to one of the Orders while in the Holy Land.

Much of the military élite fled to Cyprus before and during the collapse of the Crusader States on the Middle Eastern mainland. Even so mercenaries and foreign allies played an increasingly important role because the number of Cypriot-Crusader knights was always small. From the later thirteenth century onwards the Italian, Catalan and Provençal merchant communities in Cypriot towns became increasingly important, as did the Military Orders, contributing to the defence of the island. Armenian and Syrian Christian refugee communities also had a military role, though many *turcopoles* appear to have been Greek.

The military organization of the Crusader States was essentially that of Western European armies, with a few local variations. As elsewhere the king could create additional knights when needed, the knightly class distinguishing itself from the bulk of the population by wearing brightly coloured clothes and highly-decorated military equipment.

Most Crusading expeditions continued to be organized around the most senior lords taking part, lower ranking Crusaders attaching themselves to the retinue of one such leader while some infantry fought in 'national' groups reflecting their place of origin. Ordinary pilgrims and Crusaders not involved in major expeditions tended to travel eastward individually or in groups known as *socii* under the leadership of a knight or lord, the size of such groups aboard one particularly well-documented sea voyage ranging from three to twenty persons.

Within the Crusader States the feudal élite declined in wealth and power during the late twelfth and thirteenth centuries, and the knightly class was soon almost entirely confined to the towns where their superior status in comparison to the merchant class was maintained by law rather than wealth. Meanwhile there appears to have been a steadily increasing proportion of non-noble sergeants, most of whom were raised and paid by the Church. Religiously-based *confraternities* similarly flourished in the thirteenth-century Crusader States, often forming the basis for urban militias and sometimes associated with a particular 'national' or ethnic group.

The king of Jerusalem commanded the army, usually in consultation with leading barons and the commanders of the Military Orders. Consequently the military organisation of the Crusader States remained rather temporary and almost amateur. In practice, the *Connétable* led the army, sorted out the *batailles* (military formations) and took command when the king was not present. His second in command, the *Maréchal*, recruited troops, controlled and checked their kit and organised supplies, while the *restor* system of replacing knights' horses enabled the *Maréchal* to ensure the army was properly mounted. Immediately beneath the *Maréchal*, the *Grand Turcoplier* commanded *turcopole* light cavalry and was permitted to command knights on reconnaissance but not in battle. The king's *Seneschal* was in charge of all castles and their *baillies* or commanders, except those who were members of the Royal Household.

The military organization of the County of Tripoli and Principility of Antioch were almost identical to that of Jersualem, though on a smaller scale. The feudal structure of the short-lived County of Edessa appears to have been more rigid and even more specifically military than those of Western Europe. There were also references to a rank of *rais* in charge of local security in groups of two or three villages, these men probably being recruited from the indigenous population.

The Military Orders each formed a highly disciplined and immediately available regiment. These Orders were usually given castles in the most exposed and dangerous frontiers but only a small proportion of the overall membership of the Templar, Hospitaller and Teutonic Orders were stationed in the Crusader States, these being supported by much larger structures in Western Europe. Within the Kingdom of Jerusalem the local Templar Commander was supported by a *Drapier, Sous*

Marechal and *Gonfanonnier*. Hospitaller organization was similar, though by the early fourteenth century the Hospitaller Grand Commander of Cyprus was supported by seven senior officers; Marshal, *Hospitaller*, Drapier, Treasurer, Admiral, *Turcopolier* and Conventual Prior, while the Master Crossbowman and Master Sergeant were not members of the Order and may have been mercenaries. While on a *caravan* raid a Templar force was organised by the Marshal then put under command of the *Gonfanonier* who organised squires when they were foraging away from camp. Otherwise the squires and grooms appear to have been under the authority of the Master Esquire of each 'convent' or barracks.

Whereas the political organization of the Crusader Kingdom of Cyprus was a mixture of Western and Byzantine systems, its military structure was almost entirely European and virtually the same as that of the Kingdom of Jerusalem. The king took the lead in war, retained control of the main towns and castles and, in the Byzantine manner, the main roads. Late in the fourteenth century the island was restructured into twelve *chevetaine* or military districts, each under a captain, because of the threat of war with Mamluk Egypt.

Throughout most of the twelfth century the Crusader invaders and settlers were trapped within a traditional view of their own military superiority. During the later twelfth and thirteenth centuries the Crusader States finally accepted the need for caution, a general avoidance of offensive operations, and that their greatest strategic asset remained divisions amongst their Islamic neighbours. Crusades launched from Europe never lost their grander strategic ambitions, their main strategic hope being to conquer Egypt. In practice, however, most major Crusades were launched in response to Islamic successes. Most offensive operations launched by the Crusader States themselves were similarly retaliatory, the most effective being rapid *chevauchée* raids by fast-moving and relatively lightly-armoured forces known as *caravans*.

More attention seems to have been given to maintaining cohesion on the march than any other aspect of warfare in the Crusader States because relatively slow-moving Western-style forces remained vulnerable to their more rapid and manoeuvrable Eastern foes. As a general rule, a rectangular formation was adopted in open country, a column with strong flank guards in the hills. According to *The Rule of the Templars* no one was allowed to leave their allotted place while on the march, with squires riding ahead of the knights and baggage bringing up the rear.

The precise function of Crusader castles remains a matter of debate. They could not realistically 'plug' invasion routes and their role as places of refuge in case of defeat must have been limited. In the twelfth century they were probably intended as garrison bases for offensive operations, evolving into defensive garrison bases during the thirteenth century. The successful defence of the Kingdom of Jerusalem against Salah al-Din in 1183 focussed on retaining control of water sources, then remaining on the defensive until the thirsty Islamic army was obliged to retreat after failing to lure the Christians into battle. In contrast, it was the Crusaders' failure to avoid major battles that led to their most serious strategic defeats.

The tactics soon adopted by the Crusaders in the Middle East mirrored those of Byzantium and may have been a common response to a common foe rather than direct learning from the Byzantines. Perhaps the most immediate response was the use of smaller cavalry units than in Western Europe, this giving a commander more flexibility, and even in the early twelfth century they were usually sent against the enemy in sequence rather than all together. On the other hand, smaller cavalry formations were more vulnerable if the enemy counter-attacked, particularly as the majority of Islamic cavalry tended to be faster and more responsive, though more lightly-armoured. Nevertheless the cavalry charge remained virtually the only offensive tactic available to Crusader armies when facing Islamic foes in the field.

The Rule of the Templars sheds interesting light on how knightly cavalry charges actually worked. Apparently brother knights would attack in a single line of *eschielles* (squadrons), with a more densely-packed formation of mounted sergeants in support plus a guard of ten men to protect the *gonfanon* (banner). The function of the sergeants was to keep the enemy at a distance while the knights reformed. The squires seem to have come behind the sergeants with spare horses while the *turcopoles*, though normally operating as a separate unit, could, like the sergeants, be distributed in support of the knights.

Meanwhile, crossbowmen and other infantry kept enemies at bay until an opportunity came to use the knightly charge, or to protect the knights if their charge failed. As a result the Crusaders' single most important military capability was to endure prolonged harassment and attack, rather than themselves attacking the enemy. These passive tactics led to close cooperation between horse and foot. Even in the twelfth century the most common Crusader battle formation appears to have been cavalry placed behind a defensive array of spear and bow-armed infantry – exactly as their Fatimid (rather than Turkish) opponents did. Clearly King Richard's use of a line of infantry and dismounted knights, those with spears kneeling with the butts of their weapons thrust into the ground while crossbowmen and their loaders stood behind them, was not as new as Richard's sycophantic chronicler suggested, this idea having long been used by both Islamic and Crusader armies.

The success of defensive tactics was not disproved by the great disaster at Hattin in 1187. Nevertheless, late thirteenth-century European observers were aware of the limitations imposed by such traditional tactics, some of them urging Crusaders to adopt the highly disciplined formations of the Mamluk army, though not saying quite how this was to be done. A few decades earlier some military commentators were suggesting that the most effective troops against both Islamic and Mongol light cavalry were mounted crossbowmen, but it seems that such soldiers remained rare in the Crusader States. Instead, infantry crossbowmen remained vital for all the Crusader States, whether in the Middle East or Greece, and the overall proportion of infantry to cavalry seems to have been increasing throughout the twelfth and thirteenth centuries. Though a crossbow's slow rate of shooting compared to the hand-held bow could have been a severe disadvantage for Crusader infantry, the normal Islamic cavalry tactic of separate, rather than continuous, cavalry attacks apparently gave the Christian foot soldiers time to reload.

Although early forms of tournament were held in Crusader Antioch in the mid-twelfth century they do not seem to have been recorded in the Kingdom of Jerusalem until the late thirteenth century. The rules of various Military Orders do, however, shed light on training within the Crusader states. *The Rule of the Templars*, which largely dates from the mid-twelfth century, shows that training was tactical rather than theoretical, while information about the Hospitallers shows that exercises were mostly performed in the afternoon, three times a week, featuring drill and the use of weapons, including the crossbow.

Fatimid Armies and Tactics

While there were significant differences between Crusader and rival Islamic armies, there were also many similarities. These were more apparent in the Fatimid Caliphate of Egypt than elsewhere. The army of the Shia Fatimid Caliphate had a long and varied history, its recruitment and structure changing from the early days in North Africa, through the conquest of Egypt and Syria, to the final period when the Fatimid Caliphate controlled little more than Egypt, where the Caliph was a puppet of his *wazir* and army commander. By then the majority of the Fatimid army was Sunni, despite the fact that the Caliphate itself was Shia.

Generally speaking ethnic or linguistic groups which had played a prominent military role in the early days of Fatimid history were downgraded or disappeared when new sources of recruitment became available. Berbers had, for example, remained important until the mideleventh century, but virtually all Berber units were disbanded by the Armenian *wazir* Badr al-Jamali in 1073 AD. African troops played a major role in Fatimid forces and in the early eleventh century Masmuda Saharan Berbers may have formed the bulk of Fatimid garrison infantry.

Other *Sudani* or 'blacks', as they were called in Arabic sources, included Zanj sword-armed and other mercenary infantry from Eritrea, Ethiopia and beyond, as well as slave-troops purchased via Christian Nubia. Nubians themselves also served in Fatimid armies.

Though fewer in number, Arab troops of Bedouin origin played a highly influential role after the Fatimids moved their capital from North Africa to Cairo. Some served as auxiliary cavalry, others as professional cavalry, infantry and in the fleet. Arab soldiers similarly fought for the Fatimids in Syria and Palestine, enabling the Fatimid port of Asqalan to hold out against the invading Crusaders for several decades. Arabic-speaking but non-Bedouin inhabitants had a limited military role under the Fatimids, normally in urban *ahdath* militias though these were more typical of Syria and Palestine than Egypt. The substantial Jewish population of Jerusalem also fought in defence of the city against the First Crusade.

The Fatimids' first Turkish troops were *mamluks* inherited from the previous Ikhshidid dynasty of Egypt, but these were few in number. Experience of fighting against Turkish *ghulams* in Syria and Palestine then convinced the Fatimid Caliph that he should build a new army on the same pattern as his eastern rivals. Not surprisingly these rivals did not want high quality Turkish *mamluk* recruits to reach the Fatimids, so the latter were never able to obtain as many as they wished.

Daylami infantry from Iran were particularly welcome because, like the Fatimid Caliphate, they were Shia Muslims and may have formed the Fatimid army's *naffatun* corps of 'fire-troops'. Armenians were recruited in larger numbers, especially after the Byzantine Empire largely disbanded the Armenian frontier units of eastern Anatolia. In fact several Fatimid *wazirs*, senior ministers or army commanders, were Armenian in the late eleventh and twelfth centuries. Amongst other nationalities recorded in the Fatimid army were Kurdish archers, Russian prisoners from the Byzantine army, Christian Sicilians, Western European and Greek mercenaries known as *Rumi*, and slave-recruits of supposed Slav origin known as *Saqaliba*.

In North Africa the Fatimid army seems to have been a tribal structure, but once established in Egypt the Fatimids attempted to copy classic Abbasid military organisation. During the tenth and eleventh centuries they maintained a substantial garrison in their new capital of al-Qahira (Cairo) though the bulk of the army was stationed in Syria. Even after the Saljuq Turks conquered most of this area the Fatimids clung to several coastal ports, which was the situation when the First Crusade arrived. The south of Egypt was meanwhile defended by a smaller garrison at Aswan, though there was little threat in this area as the Fatimids tried to maintain friendly relations with the Christians states of Nubia.

The Fatimid army now consisted of divisions and regiments identified either by the ruler who first raised them, by the name of their commanding officer or by their technical function. One distinctive formation was the *Hujariya*, essentially a military training structure arranged in age groups. Regiments were subdivided into smaller units down to groups of ten men, while officer ranks included three grades of *amir*, three grades of lower rated *khassa* (ruler's attendants) and *qa'ids*, much as had been the case in the earlier Abbasid army.

Their loyalty was encouraged by the system of patronage known as *istina'*, but as the Fatimid Caliphate declined during the late-eleventh and twelfth century, so the army's cohesion fragmented and the soldiers' loyalty tended to focus on their own senior officers rather than the Caliph. Nevertheless the slave-recruited palace corps of African origin was a notable exception, remaining fiercely loyalty to the Fatimid ruler.

The Fatimids rarely adopted the system of *iqta'* fiefs. Instead senior soldiers took over the tasks of tax farming, part of these revenues being retained to supplement normal military pay. The soldiers themselves fell into four financial categories depending on whether they were permanently assigned to a castle, stationed in one area but subject to rotation, attached to a mobile field army, or regarded as mercenaries to be paid via their commanding officers. An army secretariat was also responsible for listing their names, where they were stationed, and organizing reviews, most of this military bureaucracy being carried out by Coptic Christians.

The main problems faced by the Fatimids after they conquered Egypt was the smallness of their armies and the unsuitablity of their largely Berber troops, above all their lack of archers when facing Turkish *mamluks* who were the finest horse-archers of the Middle East. Even the use of infantry archers and lance-armed local Arab cavalry equipped in essentially the same style as the Byzantines did not solve this problem. The Fatimids' adoption of horse-armour in the later tenth century was another response to the menace of Turkish archery. Meanwhile, the best Fatimid foot soldiers operated as mounted infantry, riding camels or horses and including many infantry archers.

The Fatimids claimed that their tactical concepts were based on the military actions of the Prophet Muhammad and the Caliph Ali, but in reality they were essentially the same as those of their Abbasid rivals. Additional details which stemmed from Abbasid practice and probably applied to most professional Islamic armies, included parading flags before marching to ensure that every man recognised the banner of his own unit, checking thickets and clumps of trees for ambushes while pursuing a seemingly beaten foe, and adopting a rectangular infantry and cavalry formation known as a *hisn* or 'fortress'. Here both cavalry and infantry were said to form up behind their officers in such close ranks that no one else could squeeze through. In battle the cavalry ranks were straightened by their officers before a charge, while commanders employed aides-de-camp who carried orders to units on the flanks.

The basic battle tactic was an infantry charge supported by cavalry on the flanks. If the enemy counter-charged, Fatimid infantry were trained to kneel behind their shields and thrust the butts of their spears into the ground as pikes, with armoured men in the front rank supported by archers and javelin throwers. Any hesitation on the part of the enemy would result in a limited counter-charge by a minimal number of men. A general advance was only permitted once the foe had clearly been defeated and with the troops maintaining their original formations. If the enemy broke completely he would be pursued by cavalry and light infantry archers in case this was a ruse. An interesting tenth-century Byzantine reference to *Aethiopians* in a Muslim battle array probably referred to African or Nubian troops in Fatimid service. They were described as infantry archers wearing quilted armour and using very large simple bows (as opposed to composite bows), operating ahead of the cavalry and, like other Islamic infantry, often riding pillion behind a cavalryman to give the army greater strategic mobility.

Atabegs, Saladin and the Mamluks

Perhaps the most significant military development in the Middle Eastern heartlands of Islamic civilization during this period was a further professionalisation of most armies, with the skills demanded of a soldier now being so high that the old militias and tribal forces could no longer compete. The twelfth and early thirteenth centuries also saw a brief but limited revival of Abbasid military power in Iraq and western Iran. Here the Sunni Caliph's small army included nomad Turcomans and refugees from the Khwarazmian army defeated by Genghis Khan. Similarly small armies characterized the *Atabeg*, or successor states, of the Fertile Crescent following the fragmentation of the great Saljuq Turkish Sultanate. Typically such rulers could only afford a small *askar* body-guard of slave-recruited *ghulams* or *mamluks*, forming the core of a larger force of *jund* provincial soldiers, most of whom were Turks or Kurds. *Ahdath* urban militias still played a role and in specifically Arab areas, like the Syrian city-state of Shayzar, women not only fought in defence of their homes but donned full armour when the need arose.

One of the best-documented twelfth-century *Atabeg* armies was that of Damascus. This again consisted of slave-recruited and largely Turkish *ghulams* under their own officers, tribal Turcoman volunteers who served on a short-term basis, some Kurdish archers and a small numbers of Arab auxiliaries or support personnel. In 1138 one Damascus army also included Armenians described in the Arabic sources as sun-worshiping *ariwurik*, probably residual members of the Manichaean-Paulician heresy from eastern Anatolia. The city militia was now largely recruited from the urban poor and early twelfth-century Damascus was also home to many refugees from coastal areas that had been conquered by the Crusaders. These included the garrisons of Tyre and Sidon who now fought for Damascus. Finally there were untrained religiously-motivated volunteers, the *mutatawi'ah* who were organised on a semi-permanent basis.

The largest *Atabeg* army was that of the Zangids who ruled northern Iraq and Syria. It was recruited along the same lines but included siege engineers not only from Aleppo but also from eastern Iran, as well as Armenians and professional *naffatun* fire-troops. Salah al-Din was at first merely the Zangid ruler Nur al-Din's deputy in newly-conquered Egypt. Here he and his Ayyubid successors built a powerful military system incorporating both Zangid and Fatimid principles. Though Salah al-Din was himself of Kurdish origin, the role of Kurds in Ayyubid armies has been greatly exaggerated. Most of the Kurds were auxiliaries, as were most tribal Turcomans while the *halqa* élite of Salah al-Din's army were slave-recruited Turkish *mamluks*. Such men remained the backbone of all subsequent Ayyubid forces.

Salah al-Din also inherited the military service of Arab tribes in southern Palestine, the Sinai peninsula and Egypt from his Fatimid predecessors. Their descendants continued to garrison Damietta in the western Nile Delta in the thirteenth century. Other Arabic-speaking troops included Muslim refugees from Crusader territory, and a *jund* or territorial Egyptian militia who seemed to consist of spear-armed infantry.

The ex-Fatimid infantry guard regiments of black African slave origin proved unreliable and were soon disbanded, as were the Armenian ex-Fatimid regiments, though Armenians who had converted to Islam continued to be recruited by minor Ayyubid rulers in thirteenth-century Syria. North Africans or Maghribis were considered the best sailors in the Islamic world and many were recruited for the Ayyubid navy, some coming from as far west as Morocco. Various soldiers of Western European origin also served the Ayyubids, including large numbers of renegades following Salah al-Din's reconquest of most of the Crusader States. Another wave of captured Crusaders converted to Islam in the mid-thirteenth century and were found in the armies of Egypt and Aleppo.

The army of the Mamluk Sultanate which replaced the Ayyubids in Egypt in the mid-thirteenth century was initially the same as that of the preceding dynasty. However, major changes soon appeared in the status and size of units and their recruitment. *Mamluks* of slave origin were now the ruling as well as the military élite. Under the *Bahri* ('River') Mamluk

Sultans of the thirteenth and fourteenth centuries the majority were of Turkish, above all Kipchaq, origin, but in the late fourteenth-century the *Burji* ('Tower') Mamluk Sultans took control. They and their supporters were described as Circassians from the Caucasus mountains, though in reality they included men of Russian, Alan, Greek and even Western European background. Islamic soldiers of slave-origin had always maintained some contact with their homelands, but under the *Burji* Sultans many *mamluks* who achieved high rank invited their original families to take up military or administrative posts in the Mamluk state.

Freeborn troops had a lower status in the Mamluk army than under the Ayyubids. Nevertheless they still formed the *halqa*, which remained the largest part of the army, though no longer an élite, and included the *awlad al-nas*, a unit recruited from the sons of slave-origin *mamluks*. In Egypt, by the later fourteenth century even ordinary civilians could buy the status and privileges of a *halqa* soldier, though in Mamluk Syria the *halqa* continued to consist of freeborn soldiery. Even here, however, the *halqa* soon largely consisted of infantry rather than cavalry.

Other freeborn troops in Mamluk Syria included Turcoman, Kurdish and Arab tribal auxiliaries, a few Anatolian Turkish professional soldiers and large numbers of Oirat Mongol tribesmen who had deserted from the Il-Khan Mongol rulers of Iran and Iraq. In Egypt, meanwhile, the status of Arab auxiliaries declined sharply and Mamluk persecution of Egypt's Bedouin was one reason why so many migrated southward into the Sudan. The Mamluk authorities were more sympathetic towards the infantry archers of the Lebanese mountains and Beqaa valley who defended their own territories as virtually autonomous vassals of the Sultan. A small number of Europeans entered Mamluk service, including some members of the knightly class of the Crusader States who remained under Islamic rule, in some cases converting to Islam and receiving *iqta'* estates from their new rulers.

The Armies of Iran and Eastern Islam

Traditional systems of military organization and recruitment characterised the eastern regions of the Islamic world until the Mongol invasions. For example, in Afghanistan and northern India the Ghaznawid army was still administered by a government department called the *diwin al-ard* based Ghazna or in Lahore where religious volunteers assembled. Similarly the Khwarazmshahs who took over Transoxania and eastern Iran following the decline of the Great Saljuqs employed troops of slave origin, though the garrison which defended Samarkand against Genghiz Khan reportedly included Turks, Ghurids, Khurasanis and others.

The Great Saljuq Sultanate of Iran and much of the Middle East was itself initially divided into twenty-four military zones by the famous *wazir* Nizam al-Mulk. Each was commanded by an officer who was expected to raise, train and equip a specified number of local troops then lead them during a military review each spring. However, this system proved inadequate and the Saljuq Sultan soon had to hire mercenaries, purchase *mamluks* and demand contingents from vassals. Similarly there was a great extension of the *iqta'* system of money-raising fiefs which dominated Saljuq military administration by the start of the twelfth century.

In the late twelfth and thirteenth centuries the Abbasid Caliph also tried to make himself the spiritual leader of existing *futuwa*, religiously-inspired 'brotherhoods', and militias in an attempt to win greater influence throughout the Islamic Middle East. Nevertheless, the success of the Great Saljuqs' successors, the *Atabeg* dynasties, the Ayyubids, Mamluks and subsequently the Ottoman Turks in expelling the Crusaders and then defeating a whole series of additional Crusades was certainly not a result of religious fanaticism or greater numbers. Rather it reflected superior organisation, logistical support, discipline, tactics and to some extent armaments.

The army of twelfth century *Atabeg* Damascus can be taken as an example. It was divided into five sections according to the origins of the soldiers or their specific role. The militia, though primarily intended to defend Damascus, sometimes took part in offensive campaigns against the Crusader States. Like the militia, the *mutatawwi'a* religious volunteers were paid, being more like a permanent part-time force rather than short-term auxiliaries. Regular troops generally lived within the city whereas tribal forces summoned for a single campaign camped in the irrigated area outside. In most small *Atabeg* armies *iqta'* fiefs were allocated to the ruler's *askar* of regular cavalry. These were organised in *tulb* platoons and their weapons were stored in the ruler's *zardkhanah* or arsenal.

However, there was another small but distinctive Muslim military force also operating in the Middle East; the *Isma'ili* or so-called 'Assassins' of mountainous northern Iran and western Syria. They held a few castles and very little territory, but exerted an influence far beyond their numbers. The military and entire organization of these 'Assassin' mini-states was based on Shia religious concepts, the Isma'ili *da'i* preachers or religious leaders also becoming political and military leaders. Next in rank came the *rafiq* comrades, the *fida'i* fighters, and the *lasiq* beginners. By the early thirteenth century some senior Isma'ili officers came under the overall command of a *naqib* supported by a *janah* ('wing') or *nazir* (inspector) while the *da'i* in charge of a castle was now called a *wali*.

Islamic Tactics, Strategy and Naval Warfare in the Eastern Mediterranean

Ayyubid power arose in and continued to be centred upon Egypt, but Egypt was seriously short of pasture to maintain adequate cavalry horses. So Ayyubid sultans relied upon small numbers of exceptionally well-trained and equipped cavalry, with larger mounted forces being stationed in Syria. The élite of the Ayyubid army was the *jandariyah* which largely consisted of slave-recruited *mamluks*. This *jandariyah* formed part of the professional *halqa*, the officers of both groups acting as a military staff on campaign. Another cavalry unit known as *qaraghulams* probably consisted of lower grade *mamluks*. *Rajjala* infantry remained essential for siege warfare but mostly consisted of mercenaries and volunteer auxiliaries.

Ayyubid tactical units appeared to have varied considerably, often overlapping or being created in response to military problems. The term *janib*, for example, simply meant a unit of infantry or cavalry, the *tulb* being a smaller cavalry platoon, the *jarida* perhaps a cavalry unit designated to act independently, the *sariya* being smaller than a *jarida* and used for ambushes, while the *jama'a* seems to have been a group of around three *jaridas*. Ayyubid logistical support organization was especially sophisticated, consisting of an *atlab al-mira* (supply train) in addition to a recognized *suq al-'askar* or mobile military market formed of civilian, though specialized, merchants.

The army of the subsequent Mamluk Sultanate became the reason for the state's very existence. The most important element was the *mustakhdamun* or *mamluks* of the ruling Sultan who included those of previous rulers and those whose commander had died or been dismissed. The *khassakiya* formed a bodyguard within these *mustakhdamun* and were mostly stationed in Cairo's Citadel, being trained for higher officer rank. Lower in status were the *mamlukun* or *mamluks* of senior *amir* officers. The third element was the *halqa* or freeborne cavalry which included those sons of *amirs* and *mamluks* who chose a military career. The status of the *halqa* was, however, in steady decline within Egypt.

The Mamluk army's ranking structure was equally elaborate and until the late thirteenth century the most senior was the *na'ib al-saltana* viceroy of Egypt, though later the *atabak al-'asakir* ('father-leader of soldiers') became senior. Some senior ranks concerned administrative, disciplinary or training functions. Otherwise, ranks were based upon the number of soldiers the officer in question maintained in his own retinue rather than the number he commanded on campaign. For example an *amir* of one hundred maintained a hundred horsemen but theoretically commanded around one thousand.

The *iqta'* system of fiefs was more important under the Mamluks than the previous Ayyubid rulers, some of the biggest estates being in territory recently reconquered from the Crusaders. An officer who held an *iqta'* was called a *muqta'* and was expected to appear at the head of an agreed number of properly equipped and trained soldiers, some of whom had small *iqta'* fiefs of their own. Nevertheless, the Mamluks were extraordinarily reluctant to live on their *iqta'* estates, preferring whenever possible to live in Cairo or at least Damascus, although retired *mamluks*, some of whom had been pensioned off with the honorific Turkish title of *tarkhan* or 'hero', sometimes retired to the countryside.

Despite the overwhelming military and political domination of Cairo, provincial forces remained vital for the Mamluk state, each *qirat* military district theoretically being capable of supplying one thousand soldiers. Syria was by far the most important region outside Egypt. Here the *na'ib al-saltana* or viceroy of Damascus was appointed by the Sultan and probably arrived with his own force of *mamluks*. A separate viceroy called the *na'ib al-qal'a* was, however, in charge of the Citadel in Damascus – perhaps as an insurance against political coups by either senior *na'ib*.

Under the Ayyubids most senior military positions had gone to members of the ruling family rather than to specially trained officers, but the Fatimid *hujariya* training system continued in a modified form through to the Mamluk period. No less than twelve *tibaq* training schools, as they were now known, existed in Cairo's Citadel under the Mamluks, each selecting youngsters of a specific ethnic origin. Those slave recruits who passed through these training barracks were freed on completion of their courses, though they proudly retained the name of *mamluks*, meaning 'property of the ruler'.

Each Islamic city had one or more *maydan*, parade or military training grounds comparable to the old Roman *campus martius*. In times of military emergency troops also trained in the courtyards of their own or their officers' houses and individual weapons training may normally have been carried out in such privacy while the *maydan* was reserved for training in unit or battlefield manoeuvres. Other *maydans* were designed for long-range archery 'flight shooting' with a line of ranging markers.

Although surviving training manuals include quotations from much earlier sources, these sometimes anachronistic insertions generally dealt with tactics and theory rather than training exercises. Nevertheless the Mamluks, had a profound faith in 'square-bashing' as a way of producing good soldiers with a habit of immediate obedience. The skills involved in *furusiyah* exercises were above all use of the lance, plus other weapons, polo, hunting and horse-racing.

Warfare in the Islamic Middle East was particularly constrained by summer heat, winter rains and the availability of water. Even unexpected sandstorms could endanger an army moving through a desert area like the Sinai Peninsula, adding just one more reason why armies avoided real deserts whenever possible. Salah al-Din's strategy was also deeply influenced by the relatively few passes through the mountains of northern Syria, it being vital to secure these if troops operating on the coast were to maintain secure communications with their bases in the main inland cities.

The Muslims had also learned that the only way to overcome the Crusader States was by reducing their castles and fortified cities one by one. Here the main professional army protected siege operations largely carried out by urban volunteers. A major army might also seek to draw the Crusaders' field army into a major battle while auxiliary forces harrassed a less manoeuverable foe, raided enemy territory and diverted attempts to lift a siege. The main difficulty in such campaigns was that seasonal, tribal and volunteer forces tended to drift home if operations went on too long.

The Ayyubid armies had special units or formations for this sort of warfare, most of them organized on a temporary basis to meet an immediate military need. These included a *yazak* advance guard selected from the best cavalry which was expected to carry out reconnaissance and poison the enemy's wells. The *jalish* appears to have been a special vanguard carrying banners at the head of the main force who also served as shock cavalry against enemy encampments or protected their own technicians during siege operations. The *qufl*, or 'fortress', may now have referred to soldiers sent to close main routes; the *harafisha* or 'rabble' were guerrillas or commandos operating inside enemy territory, whereas the *lisus* were light cavalry attacking enemy supply routes.

There was similar variety amongst eastern Islamic troops, ranging from the Ghaznawids' axe-armed heavy cavalry to the heavily-armoured Turkish horse-archers of thirteenth-century northern India. In general, however, the armies of the Islamic Middle East were more lightly equipped than those of the Crusaders but were better disciplined and more responsive to orders, with a greater reliance on horse-archery and tactical mobility. Heavy cavalry remained a minority, particularly those using horse-armour, and leather body armour was at least as common as that of iron.

The arrival of the Saljuq Turks had led to a localised and relatively brief dominance of Central Asian dispersal and harrassment horse-archery tactics, before the region's tradition of concentrated shower-shooting horse-archery revived. This was more suitable for Middle Eastern conditions, requiring fewer horses, being less tiring for the archers, tactically more versatile and permitting the use of heavier armour. Yet it demanded a high degree of professional training, with the best horse-archers supposedly able to loose a sequence of five arrows within two and a half seconds.

Military theoreticians writing in places like Egypt had plenty of traditions to draw upon, including that of the ancient and Hellenistic Greeks; sections of Aelian's archaic *Tactics* being translated in some *furusiyah* training manuals. Most *furusiyah* texts were, however, based upon or were merely repeats of Abbasid *furusiyah* works from the ninth and tenth centuries. Nevertheless they were used selectively and critically. Furthermore the best Islamic Middle Eastern armies relied on tactics which demanded initiative and discipline from junior officers, as well as elaborate systems of signal flags, drums and couriers to pass orders.

Furusiyah literature dealt with every aspect of warfare, including raids and naval conflict. Here the link between reality and theory was clear. For example, when a Turkish fleet from Aydin landed a small expeditionary force on European soil in 1337/8, the *azap* infantry archers moved cautiously ahead of the *ghazi* cavalry, just as suggested in *furusiyah* manuals. A similarly strong connection can be drawn between theory and reality when an army was on the march. For example large Islamic forces could easily cross twelfth-century Crusader-held southern Palestine to maintain the link between Egypt and Syria. Smaller groups needed a strong military escort and a section of one early thirteenth-century Ayyubid military manual was dedicated to this problem.

Ambushes were, in fact, frequently launched when an enemy was ending his line of march, at a moment of vulnerability known as *nuzul*. This is probably what happened at the Battle of Arsuf, which began when Salah al-Din's best archers were sent forward to harras the Crusaders as the head of their column hurried towards that night's camping place. According to the *Nihayat al-Su'l*, one of the oldest Mamluk *furusiyah* manuals, ambush tactics formed a major part of a military leader's knowledge. In one such attack in 1192 a wave of Arab light cavalry burst through a Crusader supply column before luring the enemy's escorting cavalry out of position so that they could be hit by a concealed force of Turkish horsemen.

Large set-piece battles feature more prominently in accounts of medieval warfare than they did in reality and this was as true of the Islamic world as of medieval Europe. Nevertheless when they did occur, certain features remained clear. For example the Turks' use of harrassment archery techniques gave them a huge advantage over Arab forces in eleventh-century Syria but failed against the First Crusade only a few decades later. Thereafter Islamic commanders adopted a more cautious approach, usually relying on evasion and harrassment. Traditional Middle Eastern shower-shooting tactics had sufficiently revived by the late twelfth century for Ayyubid and, subsequently, Mamluk forces to face the Crusaders with greater confidence. The Mamluks then used these tactics with considerable success against Mongol invaders.

The primary aim of all Muslim commanders seems to have been to separate the enemy's cavalry and infantry. Once that had been done the enemy's horses could be shot down at long range though even in close combat an opponent's horse remained a primary target. If the enemy cavalry could be dispersed or driven away, then his infantry was usually helpless.

The actual formations used in such set-piece battles remained traditional, with infantry forming a defensive shield-wall supported by archers while the cavalry were divided into offensive *shuj'an* and defensive *abtal*. A late twelfth-century military manual written for Salah al-Din, but based on Fatimid traditions, described an ideal battle array in traditional terms. Another manual written a few years later agreed in principle but added that a commander should try to face the enemy's best with his own best, their weakest with his weakest. He should seek to launch counter attacks against those enemies who had just attacked his own line, in the hope that they would be tired, disorganised and perhaps weakened by casualties.

The evidence of actual battles shows that Islamic commanders of this period hid their reserves behind hills or other natural features, and that the ability to resupply troops with arrows during the fighting could tip the balance. A reference to thirteenth-century Mamluk cavalry charging the centre of an enemy's line to overthrow his flags and shoot his signal drummers, thus depriving the commander of his means of communication, was in line with long-established practice. Battlefield communications were, in fact, of paramount importance in an army like that of the Mamluks where tactical formations were controlled and reassembled by means of drums and trumpets.

According to Ibn Khaldun, known as 'the father of modern history', early fourteenth-century Mamluk forces habitually divided into three formations drawn up one behind the other. The men then dismounted, emptied their quivers onto the ground then shot from a kneeling or squatting position. Each rank was protected by the one ahead, which suggested that they might have been trained to move forwards or backwards in an alternating sequence of ranks. A somewhat 'desk-bound' Mamluk theoretician writing at the end of the fourteenth century suggested engaging in battle when the sun, wind or dust were in the enemy's eyes and dismounting one's own cavalry if they themselves were suffering from the dust, this being more of a problem for cavalry than for infantry.

The individual skills demanded of troops within this overall military tradition seem to have put as much emphasis on avoiding an enemy's charge as on making a charge themselves. In fact the skill of generally lighter Islamic cavalry and infantry in avoiding the fearsome Western European knightly charge eventually rendered that tactic almost redundant. Once Islamic forces developed the skills to lure and then counter-attack a Crusader charge in the flank or rear, then such a charge became extremely hazardous. One of the main concerns for an Islamic commander was to ensure that the terrain immediately in front of his position was unsuitable for a Crusader cavalry charge. This resulted in the adoption of positions behind steep rocky slopes or patches of soft sand, while the troops themselves were trained to watch for the moment when the enemy 'put their lances in rest' – in other words lowered them for a charge.

Less anecdotal information from the Islamic side of the frontier pointed out that a horse-archer was always vulnerable to a lancer if the latter attacked from the right side, but that a heavily-armoured European knight, though virtually invulnerable when mounted, was almost helpless once unhorsed. On the other hand, the twelfth-century Arab *amir* Usamah Ibn Munqidh recommended that his compatriots adopt the European-style couched lance, though not to the exclusion of other methods. Around the same time a scholar writing for Salah al-Din stated that a horse-archer should aim at an opponent's saddle-bow so that the arrow hit the horse if it flew low or the rider if it flew high. He should have his sword and shield ready in case he hit the horse rather than its rider, and if he was attacked by both a lancer and a swordsman he should try to shoot the lancer first. Otherwise archers were advised to disperse when harrassing a group of enemy soldiers, to reassemble if they came close and where possible to keep the foe on the own shielded left side.

According to a late twelfth-century manual written for Salah al-Din, infantry archers could hold their bows horizontally when shooting from behind a wall, while horse archers should keep three aditional arrows in their left or bow hand while shooting. By the mid-fourteenth century the use of crossbows on horseback had been added to these skills, being described as a suitable weapon for a small or inexperienced man. A special clip had also been invented to hold the bolt or arrow in place if the horse made the crossbow unstable, a feature which would not be known in Western Europe for another century.

Late fourteenth-century Mamluk training manuals summarized cavalry skills as attacking, maintaining such an attack, feigning retreat, wheeling around in battle, evading an enemy and renewing an attack. Infantry skills were more prosaic, being summarized as marching long distances, anticipating enemy attacks, taking cover, checking and chasing cavalry, scattering and frightening horses. Earlier manuals had been more specific and had included chapters dealing with the use of specific weapons against opponents armed in a variety of ways, horseman against horseman, infantry against infantry, and in mixed combats.

Unit manoeuvres were at least as important as individual skills, each such team exercise being called a *bab* or 'gate' and involving individuals doing a sequence of actions in turn or as a group. The Khurasani method of using a cavalry spear was comparable to nineteenth-century cavalry 'tent-pegging', while the *Muwallad* style was suitable for an unarmoured man since it involved lying flat on the horse's neck to reduce one's own target area, and the 'Syrian Attack' was the couched lance by another name. Aiming a spear to the rear was intended to fend off a pursuer.

Naval warfare in the Eastern Mediterranean was essentially the same as it had been in the preceding centuries. A remarkable similarity of ship design sometimes meant that Christian and Islamic vessels were only differentiated by their flags and the fact that Christian sailors tended to be clean-shaven while Muslims were bearded. During the thirteenth century a so-called 'crossbow revolution' in naval warfare meant that armoured crossbowmen formed a specialist élite of marines. Crossbows were also used aboard Islamic ships, though to a lesser degree because composite bows and javelins continued to play a vital role.

During the eleventh and twelfth centuries most European galleys had changed from having oars evenly spaced, usually at two levels, to having oars grouped at a single level. Byzantine and Islamic fleets may have been slower to make this change but all had done so by the late thirteenth century. In contrast Islamic shipwrights were more advanced in building large merchant and transport ships, three masted vessels being known since at least the eleventh century.

The Crusader States largely relied on Italian vessels, particularly for ambitious assaults upon Egypt. Nevertheless the County of Tripoli created its own small fleet after Egyptian warships broke into Tartus harbour in 1180. The Military Order of Hospitallers similarly had their own small fleet from the late twelfth century, including some ships based at Tripoli, Tyre and Marseilles, but the Hospitallers, like the Templars, only assembled a true navy after the fall of Acre.

These Crusader vessels included *chelandre* horse-transports because the ability to carry cavalry mounts and perhaps new breeding animals from Europe remained vitally important. Shallow draught vessels could be brought close inshore to bombard an enemy marching along a coastal road, particularly when that road was forced to the water's edge by coastal mountains. In a naval battle transport-galleys such as the *tarida*, being a sort of landing craft for cavalry, could also serve as a reserve. Deeper draught vessels such as *uissiers* probably stood further off the coast and sent their cargoes ashore in smaller craft. In fact five large vessels were reportedly capable of carrying 7,000 troops during the Fourth Crusade. Other evidence from the thirteenth century indicates that horses were taken into some Crusader transport ships through doors near the stern of the vessel, these then being sealed for the duration of the voyage. Cyprus served as a vital assembly point for several naval Crusades as well as being a basis for Christian piracy. In fact Western European naval domination of the Eastern Mediterranean enabled Crusaders, Italian merchant republics and pirates alike to maintain footholds on mountainous coasts where local Islamic rulers found it difficult to concentrate their forces and thus evict the intruders.

In 1220-9, during preparations for his proposed invasion of Egypt, the Emperor Frederick of Germany and Italy ordered specialised shallow-draught ships capable of operating and making amphibious landings in the confined waters of the Nile Delta. Against Dumyat in 1223 and 1249, Crusader ships had mangonels (stone-throwing engines) with which they bombarded Islamic ships on the Nile; and during the final defence of Acre in 1291 one Crusader ship had a mangonel on board, though this was destroyed in a storm. For their part the Muslims attacked a Crusader fleet with fire-ships outside Dumyat in 1169, and in 1220-1 the Egyptians sank block-ships in the Nile to stop the Crusader fleet penetrating further upriver.

In 1170 Salah al-Din retook the Crusader-held castle of Qa'at Fara'un on a small island in the Gulf of Aqaba after having small prefabricated boats brought across the desert. But why did the Muslims need to carry these vessels overland in the first place? Perhaps the Crusaders who held Aqaba also dominated the waters of the Gulf of Aqaba as well as posing a threat to Islamic control of the Red Sea. River warfare had never been very significant in the Middle East but it now disappeared almost entirely, the only exeption being Arab river pirates of the eastern Nile Delta who caused Salah al-Din some difficulty in the late twelfth century.

Chapter 2
An Arc of Conflict

The Struggle for Byzantium

The Byzantine Empire's loss of most of Anatolia meant the loss of a major pool of military manpower and at the end of the eleventh century foreign troops may, for the first time, have outnumbered domestic recruits. Subsequent attempts by the Comnenid Emperors John and Manual to rebuild a 'national' army still had to be supplemented by hiring large numbers of mercenaries as well as settling prisoners in strategically important regions.

By the late twelfth century the majority of domestic troops spoke Greek. Amongst them *Archontopoulos*, 'sons of *archontes*', and by the late twelfth or early thirteenth century the *Archontes* themselves formed a provincial élite with military authority but no legal recognition. Nor were they specifically linked with the *pronoia* system of fiefs which was itself in an early stage of development. Non-Greek subject or vassal peoples whom the Byzantine Emperor recruited included Bulgars and Serbs. The Vlach population south of the Danube tended to be unreliable, helping Kipchaq Turkish invaders from the steppes and playing a leading role in a revolt which led to the recreation of an independent Bulgarian state at the start of the thirteenth century.

Turks were similarly recruited, including defeated Pechenegs in the Balkans, many of whom settled in what is now eastern Bulgaria. Kipchaqs later settled in the same area and many Muslim Turks transferred their allegiance to Byzantium following the Comnenid reconquest of western Anatolia. The Saljuq Turkish rulers of central Anatolia also supplied allied troops at various times but the number of previously important Armenians declined steeply. Arab troops included prisoners-of-war whereas Western European recruits were mercenaries. The first Anglo-Saxon refugees from Norman-ruled England arrived around 1075, but the majority are said to have been unwilling to serve in the emperor's *Varangian* bodyguard, so were sent north to the Crimea. Larger numbers came down the river Danube or via the great rivers of Russia in the 1080s and '90s. By the end of the twelfth century the Varangian Guard may have been predominantly English. Normans were also prominent in the late eleventh- and twelfth-century Byzantine army as armoured cavalry.

Following the Fourth Crusade's seizure of Constantinople and a large part of the Byzantine Empire's heartland at the start of the thirteenth century, the fragmented Byzantine successor states had to rely on limited sources of recruitment. The Empire of Nicea, for example, initially relied on mercenaries, including Westerners, before regaining enough territory to recruit domestic armies. By the mid-thirteenth century this Nicean army included Spaniards, Catalans and Sicilians. The first domestic troops included infantry archers from Bithynia who had previously defended the Byzantine frontier against Turkish encroachment, Greeks from Thrace, Vlachs, Albanians and Kipchaq Turks. The *Mourtatoi*, however, are more likely to have been converted captured or renegade ex-Muslim Turks.

The Comnenid Byzantine Emperors of the late eleventh and twelfth century effectively had two armies, one in the European and one in the Asian provinces under the overall command of the *Grand Domestic*. The army was further divided, as it had been for centuries, into central and provincial forces. There usually appear to have been twelve senior *patrician* or strategos general-officers, each commanding around two *turmarch* commanding officers, themselves each heading about five *drungarios*, each over five or so *comites*, over five not entirely clear *quintarchs* who in turn led forty troops further subdivided into units of ten men under a *decurion*. How far this theory existed in reality is a matter of debate. A senior officer called a *sebaste* commanded foreign troops, probably those not fully integrated into the Byzantine military structure.

Byzantine provincial forces never fully recovered from the disasters of the late eleventh century. Some *theme* armies had, however, survived in the Balkans and the far southeastern coastal province of the Black Sea. Elsewhere the Comnenids tried to rebuild a *theme* structure in territory they regained from the Saljuq Turks. Much of the Balkan provinces consisted of two *duchies* though much of the Danube frontier was virtually autonomous under local Turkish chieftains. Provincial forces themselves included many *stradiotti* who either served in person, supplied a substitute or commuted their servive for a cash payment. In the late thirteenth century many of these *stradiotti* were, in fact, too poor to equip themselves properly. During the thirteenth century the Byzantine *pronoia* system of money-raising estates became a military institution to maintain cavalry in an almost feudal manner, but differed from a Western European fief because it was not normally inherited by the holder's son. *Pronoias* also varied considerably in size, though most supported one stradiot soldier or a Western European mercenary knight.

Following the Fourth Crusade's seizure of Constantinople the largest of the surviving Byzantine states, the 'Nicean Empire', established a standing force known as the *tagmata* which included household troops, a field army largely of foreign mercenaries and the remaining *theme* units. Guard units were commanded by the *primmikerios* who could also lead the Macedonian garrisons. Otherwise the army was commanded by the emperor or his *grand domestic* with a *protostrator* as his deputy. Other officers included the *megas konostoulos*, ('grand constable') in charge of Western mercenaries, and various *stratopedarchs* who commanded the local cavalry and infantry regiments. By this time the commanders of Byzantine forts and citadels were known as *kastrophylakes* while their garrisons were under a *tzaousios* whose title came from the Turkish term *çaus*.

Traditional Byzantine defensive strategy had failed against the Saljuq Turks and their allies in the eleventh century because these new tribal invaders occupied the hills as well as the central plains of Anatolia. The Byzantines retained control of the coastal strip along the Black Sea which was protected by densely forested mountains, where Turkish raiders could be ambushed and which was also easily reinforced by sea. Once the western part of Anatolia had been regained by the Comnenid Emperors in the early twelfth century it was secured by a broad band of depopulated no-man's-land backed up by a series of impressive fortresses. Everywhere a first line of defence was provided by garrisons and local militias supported by mobile central forces; a system which worked well until the second half of the thirteenth century. By then, however, the Crusader occupation of Constantinople and much of the Byzantine heartland had weakened the ability of central armies to support the often run-down frontier forces.

Although the Byzantine army never regained its strength in horse-archers after the disaster at Manzikert in 1071, such troops were still trained to shoot in disciplined ranks and to fight in close combat from the twelfth to fourteenth centuries. Western European prejudice against the supposed superior strategy and inferior fighting skills of Byzantine armies during this period may, in fact, have been based on reality; certainly the Comnenid Emperors tried to train their own heavy cavalry on Western European knightly principles. In the event this Western-style cavalry failed dismally against the Turks but may have been more effective against Western invaders.

Despite the Byzantine Empire's unrivalled naval heritage and the fact that it clung to many coastal areas long after losing control of the interior to Turkish and other invaders, the Byzantine navy was in almost un-interrupted decline from the late eleventh century onwards. Efforts to rebuild Byzantine naval power in the early twelfth century had to rely on

Venetian help, though friendly relations with Venice did not last. After the Fourth Crusade the Byzantine Empire developed much closer ties with Venice's great rival, Genoa, and by the thirteenth century Byzantine ships' crews included native Greek speakers, Genoese Italians, ex-pirates and Muslims.

Armenia and Georgia

The Armenians probably started to organise their own defences against the Turkish invaders before the final collapse of Byzantine authority in eastern Anatolia. At the same time there was a massive migration by the Armenian military aristocracy into the mountains bordering Cilicia which became the heartland of a new Cilician Armenian state. By the late twelfth century the military organisation of this new Armenian kingdom is said to have incorporated several Western European features copied from the Crusaders, though this is probably an exaggeration. The army still consisted of *azat* elite cavalry, now often called *jiavors* which was a term of Turkish origin, plus an infantry peasant levy. It was headed by a *connetable* to give him his westernized title, or *spasalar* in Armenian, a *bayl* or *bailli*, and a *marachakhd* or *marshal*; while provincial forces were mustered behind the *avak baron* or chief baron. The few towns and cities in Cilician Armenia had their own militias but the great majority of troops were rural and feudally organized, the élite being spear-armed cavalry supported by some horse-archers. By the mid-thirteenth century this Cilician Armenian army was also recruiting Banu Kilab Arab tribesmen from Syria as well as Latins from the neighbouring Crusader States.

Less is known about the twelfth- to fourteenth-century Georgian army, except that it was organised around the local clan or *t'hemi*, from the Byzantine term *theme*, supported by an *eri* which was probably an urban contingent. The rulers' military household was built around armoured cavalry known as *aghlumi*, a term which stemmed from the Arab-Islamic term *ghulam* meaning soldier of slave origin. Georgia recruited some Western mercenaries, at least in the early twelfth century, while Georgian troops were themselves noted as archers. However, the independent Christian states of Cilician Armenia and Georgia were not the only ones to field independent Christian forces during these disturbed centuries. Young men from the Syrian Jacobite or Syriac Christian community were reported defending local monasteries in the area of Urfa and the mountains near Malatya in the mid- and late twelfth century.

The Crusader States of the Aegean

The Crusader States that were carved out of Byzantine territory in the wake of the Fourth Crusade had a mixed fate. Those established in southern Greece were largely conquered by Crusaders from the Champagne and Burgundy regions of France. However, they contained very little suitable land for use as fiefs and as a result many knights had 'money fiefs' or simply remained in a greater lord's service as household knights. The lack of land, the abundance of islands and the overall naval orientation of Crusader Greece meant that many men of knightly rank became little more than pirates. The poverty of the Latin Emperors of Constantinople also meant that they could not pay sufficient mercenaries to defend their ephemeral 'Empire'.

The large Armenian military community which existed in north-western Anatolia at the time of the Fourth Crusade's conquest of Constantinople appears to have lent ready support to these invaders. Many were transfered to Plovdiv but were largely wiped out when the Bulgarians retook the city in 1205. Their survivors may have included many members of the old Paulician-Manichaean sect and have been responsible for the spreading of the Bogomil-Manichaean sect elsewhere in the later-medieval Balkans.

The military circumstances of Crusader Greece differed from those of Crusader Syria because the previous military aristocracy had been conquered and then gradually assimilated rather than wiped out or expelled as had happened in the Middle East. Though the baronies and fiefs of Crusader Greece were very small, military obligations were strongly enforced because the conquerors were almost always at war with one or more of their neighbours. When Crusader Greece fell under the rule of the Angevin kings of southern Italy, however, a *vicarius* and a *bailli* were sent from Naples as civil and military governors while the main castles were also placed firmly under their control.

The Black Sea region was home to various militarily formidable peoples, ranging from the Christian Georgians to a mosaic of Islamic and semi-pagan peoples, many of them descended from passing conquerors whose remnants had found sanctuary along the northern slopes of the Caucasus mountains. Dotted around the Black Sea in the aftermath of the Fourth Crusade were several strongly fortified Italian trading colonies, some of which survived until they fell to the Ottoman Turks in the fifteenth century.

The Sultanate of the Saljuqs of Rum

The Sultanate of the Saljuqs of *Rum*, or 'the Roman lands', was the most successful of the Islamic states established in Anatolia following the collapse of Byzantine authority in the later eleventh century. Here the new Saljuq Sultans of Rum initially modelled their army on that of the Great Saljuq Sultanate in Iran. At first it consisted of Turcoman tribesmen and a small professional élite of slave-recruited *ghulams*. The latter came from many backgrounds including Russian slaves and Greek prisoners-of-war but, from the mid-twelfth century onwards, the bulk of professional soldiers were freeborn Turkish cavalry holding *iqta'* fiefs.

Another characteristic of the army of the Saljuqs of Rum was its incorporation and assimilation of at least part of the pre-existing Byzantine, Armenian and Georgian military élites, though this was more typical of the rival, short-lived Danishmandid Turkish state in eastern Anatolia. The Saljuq Sultanate of Rum also encouraged urban *fityan* and *ikhwan* Islamic 'brotherhoods' as a source of religiously motivated volunteers, a system which was even more important under the subsequent fragmented Turkish *beylik* principalities of Anatolia.

At the height of their prosperity the Saljuqs of Rum recruited settled Turks, nomadic Turcomans, Georgians, Azerbaijanis, Armenians, Persians, Daylamis, Khwarazmians, Kipchaqs from north of the Black Sea, Kurds, Arab nomads and men from the Syrian towns. They similarly enlisted Christian Byzantines, French, German and other Western European knights and infantry and liberated prisoners-of-war from the Crusader States. For a while the latter actually formed one of the sultan's bodyguard units. Within relatively few decades the army of the Saljuqs of Rum was evolving along different lines to that of the Great Saljuqs. It now consisted of an 'Old Army' mainly of Turcoman tribesmen and the ruler's *ghulams* or *mamluks*, the *havashvi* armed retainers of the *iqta'* fief-holders and urban governors, while a 'New Army' of mercenary units was under the ruler's more immediate control.

Following the Mongol conquest the élite *ghulams* gradually disappeared from the rump Saljuq state to be replaced by Turcoman tribal warriors, most of whom were concentrated near the frontiers under the authority of their own tribal *beys* or chiefs. Local militias of mixed origins known as *igdish* were responsible for maintaining security in the towns and rose to greater prominence during the chaos which followed the final collapse of the Saljuq Sultanate of Rum.

The Turks were newcomers to Mediterranean naval warfare and their first temporary fleets operating from Tarsus in Cilicia in 1085 were probably set up in cooperation with the long-established Arab fleet from Tripoli in Lebanon. The Turkish fleet which operated from Smyrna (Izmir) in the 1090s similarly required coperation from local sailors. It was over a century before the Turks again reached the Anatolian coast and not until the start of the fourteenth century did they challenge Christian domination of the Aegean. Once they did so, however, the Turks sent raiding forces into the European mainland. Their fleets consisted of large numbers of small vessels, only the *beylik* of Aydin having war-galleys based at Izmir. These small ships successfully transported raiders and even siege equipment, but could not yet defeat

Christian galley fleets in open battle. The Turkish challenge in the Black Sea actually came earlier than in the Aegean, the Saljuq governor of Sinope sending a naval squadron to ravage the Byzantine ruled Crimean coast in 1220.

From the Steppes to the Baltic

The military history of Russia, Central and Northern Asia during the Middle Ages had been one of large-scale population movements, tribal migrations, cultural and linguistic assimilation as well as wars of conquest and religious conversion. During the tenth century the main thrust of Kievan *Rus* or Russian ambition had been southwards, seeking even closer links with Byzantium and attempting to control the isolated Russian principality of Tmutarakan on the Black Sea. After the Turkish Pechenegs and later the Kipchaqs won domination over the southern steppes in the eleventh century, Kiev continued to focus on this southern connection, though now largely via the principality of Galich in what is now the Ukraine.

Subsequently the Principality of Muscovy, which dominated Russia by the end of the Middle Ages, arose in a region which had once been purely Finn in population. The process whereby Finns were assimilated by a dominant Slav population was not a direct result of Russian conquest but was more closely connected with the spread of Christianity. For example, the Finnish Merya tribe was already culturally similar to its Slav neighbours and the Merya, like the Finnish Ves, become Christian between the tenth and thirteenth centuries. Other Finn peoples such as the Mordva remained independent and notably warlike for many years, but by the twelfth century most of the remaining Finnish-speaking peoples of Russia survived in isolated enclaves, as their descendants do to this day.

Far to the north, the remarkable Russian state of Novgorod was founded by Slavs, Finns and Balts. Still further north the sub-Arctic regions were inhabited by scattered Finn and Ugrian tribes, through the latter may have been pushed beyond the Ural mountains into the Ob river basin in the later Middle Ages. Many of the Ugrians had, like the Finns, originally been forest dwellers rather than nomads, and although these northern Ugrians were not a warlike people, they were primitive enough to terrify their medieval Slav neighbours who believed that God had locked the 'terrible' Ugrians behind the Ural Mountains until Judgement Day.

Far to the south, the steppes of what are now southern Russia and the Ukraine served as a corridor through which nomadic peoples migrated westward, pushed by more powerful nomads to the east. The most important were the Pechenegs, the Uzes (also known as Torks), the Kipchaqs and finally the Mongols. Some were driven further, crossing the Carpathian mountains into the Hungarian plain, into Wallachia in present-day Rumania, or into the forests north of the Carpathians. Though defeated by nomad rivals to the east, these largely Turkic peoples often assimilated into the dominant military élites of these areas or were recruited as frontier troops far to the west of their steppe homelands.

People of Norse Scandinavian origin had played a significant, though perhaps exaggerated, role in the creation of the first Kievan Russian state. The flow of Scandinavian, Varangian or Varjazi mercenaries through Kievan Russia to the Byzantine Empire continued into the twelfth century, though few seemed to have been diverted into Russian service after the eleventh century. Instead Kievan Russian armies of the eleventh to mid-thirteenth centuries served ruling dynasties which were almost nomadic in their lifestyle, moving from principality to principality across huge distances. Each prince had a *druzhina* armed retinue, that of the Grand Prince being the strongest, whose members were bound by oaths of loyalty to their prince rather like those which cemented the armies of tenth century Middle Eastern rulers. Most were Slav, though Scandinavian Varangians, Ossetians (Iasy) and Kosogians (Circassians) from the Caucasus, Magyars, Turks and others were recorded in various *druzhinas*. In fact adherence to the Orthodox Christian Church permitted acceptance into the community of Rus whatever an individual's origins or language and these *druzhinas* would eventually form the basis of medieval Russia's *boyar* or aristocratic class, along with the existing landed, tribal and urban commercial élites.

As the years passed, the traditional Slav tribal levies were gradually replaced by urban militias from towns which emerged across the vast Kievan Rus state. Archery was still an infantry affair and archers were recruited from younger soldiers, most probably coming from urban militias. The ordinary *smerdi* or peasantry were only summoned in dire emergencies, yet in the twelfth century the southern steppe frontiers of Kievan Russia were already garrisoned by warriors who lived in virtually autonomous farming communities, like the later Cossacks.

Throughout this period, Turkish soldiers from the steppes played a vital role in Kievan Russian armies, sometimes as allies, sometimes settled in military colonies or garrisons along the steppe frontier. The *Chernye Klobuki* or 'Black Caps' (*Karakalpak* in Turkish) were recruited from tribes which had already been driven out of the steppes and into Kievan Rus. First recorded in the late eleventh century, many were given land along the Ros river in the Ukraine and further west in the Bukovina, where they retained their tribal organization and served in the armies of several Russian principalities. Following the Mongol conquest, many Kipchaqs similarly fled the steppe region to be absorbed into existing *Chernye Klobuki* communities. The isolated Russian principality of Tmutorokan, beyond the Turkish-dominated steppes on the shore of the Black Sea, also had its own *druzhina* in the tenth and eleventh centuries. Recruited from rather different sources it included many Kosogian Circassian troops from the Caucasus. In the far north the wealthy city of Novgorod would enlist warriors from neighbouring Finn tribes against Swedish and other Baltic Crusaders in the mid-thirteenth century.

By the early thirteenth century the Russian *druzhinas* were in many ways comparable to the armoured cavalry retinues of Western European princes, while the tribal *voi* had largely been replaced by urban militias. The fully developed Kievan *druzhinas* of the twelfth and early thirteenth centuries were in two parts, a 'senior' and a 'junior'; the former included high ranking officers such as the *ognishchanin* (bailiff), *koniushi* (master of horse), *tium* (steward) and *podiezdnoi* (adjutant), while the latter or *grid* consisted of household cavalrymen and servants. Meanwhile differences had developed in the military equipment used in northern and southern Russia, with far greater steppe influence upon the latter. Also, unlike the Western European feudal system, a *boyar* who left his ruler's *druzhina* did not forfeit his lands.

The most effective Russian urban militia was probably that of Novgorod, being organized and equipped by the city's almost autonomous quarters. These were similarly responsible for maintaining and defending their own stretch of city wall. The *veche* council of Novgorod selected the *tysiatski*, or militia commander, who also served as a kind of chief of police, while the *posadnik*, or 'mayor', of Novgorod was selected by the *veche* from amongst the local *boyars*. Novgorod also sent *posadnik* 'mayors' to subordinate cities, the most important of which was Pskov. The frontiers of medieval Russia, particularly those in the south, east and north, were often far distant from the chief city of the principality in question. Perhaps as a result, military structures comparable to the *limitanei* of the late Roman and Byzantine Empires emerged in Russia while largely disappearing from Western Europe. Generally speaking, however, Kievan Russia did not have enough troops to garrison its more distant southern conquests in the twelfth century and soon lost a great deal of territory to the steppe nomad states. In the far north, Novgorod faced little effective opposition from the scattered tribes of what came to be known as Novgorod's 'fur empire'. Consequently its little *pogost* trading, administrative and military outposts soon reached the Arctic sea and northern Ural mountains.

By the early twelfth century the élite of the Kievan Russian army was largely mounted and so was capable of taking the battle to the nomadic enemy, even catching the Kipchaqs encamped and unprepared for battle in 1103 AD. In the far north, meanwhile, Russian armies found that winter was the easiest time to undertake long-range campaigns, since they could move across the frozen swamps in sledges while using frozen rivers as ready-made highways deep into enemy territory. In the rarer summer campaigns the only way to transport large amounts of supplies or siege equipment was by boats along these same rivers. Spring and autumn were usually a wash-out, these being seasons of *rasputitsa* or roadlessness when the landscape disolved into mud and rain.

Russian armies had been almost entirely infantry until the tenth century and after that largely consisted of infantry archers with a small cavalry corps. From the late tenth century onwards this cavalry corps was increasingly armoured in central European or Byzantine style. Archaeological evidence also shows that Asiatic style horse-harness was gradually supplemented by more European forms during the twelfth and thirteenth centuries, at least by Russia's armoured close-combat cavalry. The oldest known Russian battle array was in five parts, astonishingly similar to the early Islamic *khamis*. When facing nomad foes, eleventh- to thirteenth-century Russian forces typically placed the low-grade infantry *voi* at the centre, infantry archers shooting from behind a shield-wall of perhaps-higher grade infantry with cavalry protecting their flanks, while large waggons like those of the nomadic peoples were used to carry supplies in southern Russia and the steppes.

Although the Russian military aristocracy adopted a chivalric code similar to that of Western Europe, the little that is known about military training suggests that it had more in common with the steppe cultures. For example, the ritual combats characteristic of pre-Christian Russia continued until the twelfth century, while huge and prolonged hunting expeditions had much the same training function as those amongst Central Asian nomadic peoples.

Very little is known about Russian riverine warfare, yet the numerous waterways of Russia provided arteries of communication in all directions. Here *ushkúynik* river pirates preyed upon riverborne trade and were a serious problem in many of the more remote areas of later medieval Russia. In response, and as a defence against nomad raiding, Russian princes stationed military units at the major portages between rivers as well as building wooden roads along these portages. In the deep south the rivers provided Cossack-like *brodniki* communities of Slav settlers with security as well as food, while in these people also kept the rivers open for merchants and *druzhinas*.

Christian Iberian Armies of the Reconquista

The term *Reconquista*, meaning the military, cultural and religious struggle between the Christian northern and Islamic southern states of the medieval Iberian peninsula is misleading as it assumes that the northern states really were 'retaking' areas which they or their ancestors had 'lost' when Islam became the dominant culture in what are now Spain and Portugal during the eighth century. An alternative interpretation maintains that the peninsula was not 'occupied' by Islamic forces in the early eighth century, but that the early medieval Germanic Visigothic kingdom of Iberia and southern France was merely taken over by a new Islamic ruling élite which then established a provincial government on behalf of a vast Islamic Caliphate whose capital was currently in Syria. One thing which is clear is that the culture which developed in al-Andalus, the Islamic-ruled regions of the Iberian peninsula, drew upon existing Iberian traditions and populations as much as it did upon the small number of newly-arriving but politically, culturally and religiously dominant Islamic settlers.

From the eighth to tenth centuries the army of the Christian kingdom of Asturias maintained some Visigothic traditions from pre-Islamic Iberia but was also strongly influenced by Islamic Andalusian military influence. A rather different army then developed as Christian forces pushed southward, with urban cavalry and infantry forces undoubtedly existing alongside those of a quasi-feudal aristocracy by the tenth century. In eleventh-century Castile the powerful magnates, or *ricos hombres* served as regional governors and military attendants for the king, some *ricos hombres* having their own *masnada* military retinue, while a lesser aristocracy of *infanzones* consisted of warriors like the Spanish epic hero El Cid. Urban militias were meanwhile divided into *caballería* (cavalry) and *peonía* (infantry). During the early years of Portuguese history, comparable *cavaleiros vilãos* were provided by richer but non-noble families while the *peões* (infantry) were drawn from poorer families who nevertheless owned their own land.

Normans, Flemings, Burgundians, Bretons, Poitevans, Angevins and others played a notable role in the early campaigns of the *Reconquista* but the Christian states of northern Iberia got much less help from north of the Pyrenees after the mid-twelfth century, most Crusaders being lured to the Middle East. Meanwhile in the fertile Ebro valley much of the Islamic rural population remained under new Christian rule, though the Islamic urban élites mostly left and were replaced by Christian military and ruling aristocracies. The Islamic Andalusian troops who remained to serve Christian rulers in several areas were listed as non-noble *cavallers*, or horsemen.

Each Christian state also differed. In the late thirteenth century

County of Barcelona, the greater lords continued to have strict feudal obligations to the crown of Aragon, whereas in Aragon the unreliability of most quasi-feudal forces obliged King James I to raise a loyal force mostly related to the ruling family and known as *mesnaderos*. Meanwhile a thirteenth-century rural *sometent* peasant militia was expected to maintain the peace in the countryside, an urban *sometent* or *somatent* becoming a vital source of trained infantry in the fourteenth century, often recruited from or organized around the craft guilds.

The *almogavars* of Aragon clearly included Muslims; their name coming from the Arabic *al-mughawir* meaning 'raiders'. Recruited from non-feudal mountain pastoral communities, these *almogavars* formed the backbone of the thirteenth-century Aragonese army, serving as light cavalry and infantry. Members of the old Islamic military élite who had been evicted from the towns during the Christian conquest also remained a potent military force in the mountains, particularly around Valencia where some still held castles, retaining a quasi-noble status and fighting as mercenaries for both Aragon and Castile. Navarre was squeezed out of the process of *Reconquista* at an early date. It had limited manpower, made regular use of mercenaries and as late as the fourteenth century the local *mesnaderos* still included Muslim soldiers from around Tudela.

Castile would become the most powerful state in the Iberian peninsula. Here, despite the importance of the Crusading Military Orders, urban militias played an increasingly sigificant military role from the early twelfth century onwards. Similarly, herds and flocks were so important that herdsmen were exempt from military service. At the same time Muslims were sometimes accepted as *mauri pacis* ('pacified Moors') and in thirteenth-century Avila such *mauri* provided a military unit of seventy cavalry plus five hundred infantry. One reason why such Muslims could feel loyal to Christian rulers was their widespread dislike of the North African who, though fellow-Muslims, had taken political control of twelfth and thirteeenth century al-Andalus. Meanwhile the sole remaining Islamic state of Granada survived as a vassal of Castile, sending cavalry to the Castilian army when required. Of all the Christian Iberian states, Portugal was the least influenced by French military systems. Here a new military aristocracy was largely drawn from those who took part in the conquest of the south. At the top the *ricos-homens* were mostly of foreign origin. Then came the *ingénue*, or old families of free men, the *infações* or *cavaleiros* (knights) and *escudeiros* (squires).

Temporary military *confraternities*, or 'brotherhoods', were seen in Iberia well before the development of permanent Military Orders in the Crusader States of the Middle East. Thereafter the establishment of specifically Iberian Military Orders provided a vital source of highly trained troops and, like other Crusading Military Orders, those in Spain and Portugal became more class conscious in later years. Perhaps as a result, the *Real Confradía de Santísmo y Santiago* was set up to satisfy the non-noble *caballeros villanos* who wanted a military order of their own.

Two basic characteristics distinguished the military organisation of twelfth and thirteenth-century Christian Iberia. The first was a relatively loose command structure and a lack of discipline compared with the Islamic forces of the south. The second was the substantial amount of conquered land which was handed over to the Spanish Military Orders as the Christian frontier pushed southwards.

In Aragon, many if not most soldiers were now paid professionals, the largest number being urban militias. Castles were held by *bailiffs* and *castellans* of the king or his leading barons, the latter also having their own paid professional armies. However, during the chaos which followed a decline of royal authority in the second half of the thirteenth century, the towns formed their own *hermandades* or 'police forces', rather like Islamic *shurtas* to maintain local law and order. Such urban forces increased in importance during the fourteenth century, often being based upon craft or merchant guilds, each city or region also having its own *deputation* which collected taxes, recruited, equipped and paid the troops.

The newly conquered south was organized along similar lines, though the rugged mountain territory inland from Valencia remained a problem. Though divided into military zones based upon small towns, it was still dominated by a free and warlike Christian and Muslim peasantry who provided infantry and cavalry to the Aragonese army.

Castile and León were less sympathetic to the rise of urban militias than was Aragon. Nevertheless urban forces continued to play a vital role. By the fourteenth century a *hueste*, or major expedition led by the king, necessitated urban militias assembling according to their *collación* quarter under the *juez* or town leader appointed by the crown. Each *collación* also elected its own *alcalde*, though this was an administrative rather than command function. The inhabitants of the southern towns were, in fact, largely descended from troops who had conquered them and then been encouraged to settle the new territory. Nevertheless much of the Islamic rural population remained, the Islamic kingdom of Granada was only a short distance away and the Marinid rulers of Morocco continued to send military expeditions across the Straits of Gibraltar. As a result these southern towns were given virtual autonomy when it came to defence, some coming together in *hermandad* mutual aid agreements, not only against Granada and Morocco but during internal Castilian civil wars.

Crossbowmen were the most important infantry forces, often being mentioned in city charters. In late thirteenth-century Castile an *almocadén* (commander of infantry) was distinguished from an *adalid* (commander of cavalry), each type of soldier having his own training systems and specified kit according to King Alfonso's *Siete Partidas* book on government. These militias selected their own *talayeros* scouts who had the best available horses and additional pay, *guardadores* who looked after prisoners and *pastores* who looked after the animals. In fact the organization of the Castilian frontier under the Crusading Military Orders and local forces mirrored the *thughur* military provinces on the Islamic side of the border. In the thirteenth and fourteenth century the *almogavar* mountain troops of Castile had a well defined ranking system, most of whose titles again reflected their Arab-Islamic origin, the *sencillo* (ordinary soldiers) being led by an *almocaden* under the command of a senior *adalid*.

Until the fourteenth century, Portuguese military organisation remained very traditional, the only consistent rank being that of *alférez môr* or army commander in charge of both administration and operations. Big changes then came in the wake of English and French involvement in Iberian affairs in the late fourteenth century. In 1382 the entire military system was overhauled, the old *alférez môr* being replaced by a *Condestabre* and a *Marichal* in the more typical Western European manner.

Ecological factors played a major part in strategies developed by the Christian Iberian states from the twelfth to fourteenth centuries. Control of winter and summer pastures was economically important for both Christian and Islamic frontier communities, thus leading to specific forms of small-scale raiding. In November cattle and sheep would be assembled at an agreed location, then in December one *esculquero* guard would be put in charge of each herd of cows, with three guards for every flock of sheep. These *esculqueros*, who did not act as herdsmen themselves, then elected a leader before moving south into the plains. They and the animals returned in mid-March, the guards being disbanded while the herds were driven to summer pastures in the high Sierras with a smaller infantry escort provided by the villagers themselves.

A comparable system was used by the Muslims who came up from their winter grazing in the southern Sierras and there were frequent clashes along important migration routes known as *cañadas*. In fact, large-scale cattle rustling almost seems to have been invented in twelfth-century central Spain.

Offensive warfare in the Iberian *Reconquista* largely consisted of small-scale raids and larger campaigns of conquest, operations being carefully planned and usually occurring in the dry summer and autumn. The *Reconquista* was also channelled along major roads, bridges and passes. As a result major river crossings were defended by castles or fortified towns. Meanwhile raids could take place at almost any time of year, the main concern for those taking part being to keep their own escape route open.

A remarkable early-fourteenth century book on military affairs by Don Juan Manuel indicated that this raiding strategy still had a major part to play in undermining the enemy's economy and reducing his garrisons to starvation. Don Juan Manuel similarly emphasized the importance of espionage to sow dissention within enemy ranks, good defensive positions while moving through enemy territory, and special large lanterns for night marches. The guerrilla tactics used by Aragonese light cavalry to defeat a French invasion in the late thirteenth century similarly seem closer to Byzantine and Islamic 'shadowing warfare' than to Western European strategy.

Christian Iberian battlefield tactics during the early period used *turna-fuye* tactics of repeated charges and withdrawals like those of Islamic Arab *karr wa farr* cavalry warfare. Subsequently tactics were a combination of French influences from the north and Islamic from the south, being characterised by large numbers of relatively light cavalry operating from strongly-fortified encampments defended by large numbers of crossbowmen.

The military sections of the mid-thirteenth century *Siete Partidas*, by King Alfonso el Sabio, were more than merely an updating of the late-Roman author Vegetius, being remarkably similar to the tactical advice by the tenth-century Byzantine Emperor Nicephorus Phocas. For example Alfonso advocates a wedge-shaped cavalry formation when attacking superior numbers. Over a century later the Spanish knight Don Juan Manuel maintained that Andalusian Islamic tactics were more pragmatic and scientific than those of Christian armies, but he also listed some cavalry formations which showed the influence of Islamic *furusiyah* military theory. These included *el haz*, 'the closely packed bundle', which was defensive and probably lay behind the *herse* formation used by English armies during the Hundred Years War. Though Christian Iberian tactics had been successful against French invaders in the thirteenth century, they proved unable to break the increasingly professional French and English armies which subsequently intervened in Iberian affairs. One of the main lessons learned from the defeat at Najera in 1367, for example, was never to attack a French or English army when it had dismounted and prepared.

The majority of fourteenth-century Spanish cavalry generally seem to have been lighter than those of France, and were trained as cavalry skirmishers *a la jineta* rather than heavy cavalry fighting *a la brida*. In this respect they were influenced by Granada and Morocco, the term jineta stemming from the Berber Zanata tribe which was famous for such light cavalry tactics.

The effectiveness of Iberian *almogavar* fighting skills was well illustrated by an event in thirteenth-century Crusader Greece when a captured unarmoured *almogavar* was made to fight a fully-equipped Angevin knight. The *almogavar* awaited the knight's charge and at the last moment hurled his javelin into his opponent's horse, dodged the latter's lance then jumped on the unfortunate knight as he fell from his wounded horse. At that point the duel was stopped, the *almogavar* being released with suitable gifts.

The Christian conquest of Almeria in 1146-7 required maritime help from Genoa, Pisa and Barcelona. Most such operations involved the use of barge-like coastal vessels to transfer men and goods ashore from larger ships. During a mid-fourteenth century Castilian naval attack upon Barcelona, the defending fleet's larger ships lined up alongside a sandbar from where their crossbowmen and stone-throwing machines could shoot at the attacking vessels while their smaller ships were drawn up on the beach with 'their keels outwards', apparently to form a barricade.

Although the Christian states of Iberia's Atlantic coast inherited their Islamic predecessors' experience of sailing the Atlantic, the first thirteenth-century Castilian navy was built in Galicia with Genoese help from Italy. By the fourteenth century the best Castilian sailors and galley-oarsmen came from Seville in Andalusia, Castilian galleys now being the largest and most effective warships in the Atlantic. Their design was based upon Genoese galleys, though they were larger and had a significantly higher freeboard to deal with Atlantic waves. It was, of course, a Castilian galley fleet which destroyed an English fleet off La Rochelle in 1372, during the Hundred Years War.

Ambitions to conquer Morocco had been one reason why Seville was developed as a naval base shortly after it was siezed by the Castilians in 1248, while the economic expansion of Morocco's Atlantic coast since the tenth century also attracted Castilian or Portugese naval raiders by the thirteenth century. The Christians also dreamed of reaching the sources of slaves and gold which came across the Sahara from West Africa.

Portugal came relatively late to Atlantic navigation and the first Portugese navy was again established by the Genoese. Nevertheless the Islamic maritime traditions of Lisbon and the Algarve were not broken by the Christian *Reconquista*. The Algarve may also have been the birthplace of the *caravo*, *caravela* or *caravel*, a ship which had once been a small Arab fishing craft but which evolved into the sturdy ocean-going vessel which took Columbus to America. More significant was the store of geographical knowledge which the Portuguese conquerors inherited from their Andalusian predecessors, knowledge which included the concept of a spherical world, the fact that it was possible to sail south around Africa and that there were real rather than mythical islands out in the Atlantic.

Although the Genoese were the first Christian mariners known to have reached the Canary Islands in 1312, the Portugese tried to occupy them a generation later. Pope Clement VI then declared the establishment of a Kingdom of the Fortunate Isles and, in 1344, invited the Spanish prince Luis de la Cerda to conquer both them and the neighbouring Islamic coast of Africa.

The Armies of al-Andalus

Within al-Andalus itself Islamic civilization was on the defensive by the twelfth century. It then collapsed in the thirteenth but survived in the small *amirate* of Granada through the fourteenth and most of the fifteenth centuries. The army of the Andalusian Umayyad Caliphate, and that of the *wazir* al-Mansur, who reduced the last Umayyads to little more than figureheads, was as mixed as those of the eastern Islamic dynasties, but was drawn from very different sources. In the early days a slave-recruited but non-Turkish *mamluk* élite formed the professional core based in Cordoba. Around this an army of free Andalusian *iqta'* estate-holding troops of largely Arab and Berber ancestry assembled. To these were added mercenaries, religiously-motivated volunteers and urban militias. The freeborn local elements were, however, severely downgraded in the late tenth century to be replaced by expanded *mamluk* and mercenary units when al-Mansur recruited large numbers of Berbers. They retained their separate identity when the Umayyad Caliphate of al-Andalus finally collapsed a few decades later. Meanwhile, the descendants of the first Arab settlers were still organized into provincial *jund* armies which, despite having been downgraded by al-Mansur, remained as a substantial body of local Andalusian troops.

In fact Andalusian Muslims were of very mixed origins, including families descended from converted Iberian Christians and Jews, from mercenaries or military slaves drawn from many lands, and of course the original Arab or Berber conqueror-settlers. Meanwhile an aristocracy of *Mozarab* or 'Arabized' Christians played some military role, usually in inaccessible or frontier regions, and were quite prepared to fight alongside their Muslim fellow-Andalusians against external 'barbarian' Christian invasion from the north.

The collapse of the Caliphate of Cordoba in the early eleventh century was followed by al-Andalus fragmenting into an array of states known as *taifa* kingdoms. Although most were too small to maintain large armies, their recruitment patterns generally reflected the origins of their competing dynasties; Arab, Berber, Slav or those claiming pre-Islamic Andalusian descent. Some feared to recruit Berbers, others enlisted

Christian mercenaries while a few relied on local urban militias. The army of Granada under the Zayrids, for example, was initially dominated by a small corps of Sanhaja Berbers, plus a small number of *abid* ('white slaves'), *wusfana* ('black slaves') and mercenaries. An early and quite successful commander of this polyglot army was the Jewish poet Samuel Ha-Nagid who was the ruler's *wazir* or 'chief minister'.

A link between military obligation and the possession of land seems to have characterised al-Andalus to a greater degree than elsewhere in the medieval Islamic world. Nevertheless, fortresses and fortified towns formed the basic framework around which Andalusian military organisation was built, the Umayyad rulers of Cordoba having generally adopted the military systems of the Abbasid Caliphs who had overthrown their Umayyad predecessors in the Middle East.

The Andalusian army consisted of *junds*, each based in a *kura mujannada* (military province) and supported by units based in the capital. One important *jund* provincial force was that led by the *wali* or governor of Seville, who had a force of around five hundred regular cavalry with their main base at Carmona, and other provinces may have been similar. The command structure was much like that of the Abbasid army. As in Abbasid Iraq, the government stables near Cordoba were a huge and complex organization reputedly housing 2,000 war horses, tended by units of one hundred horsemen each commanded by an officer of *arif* rank. The pay of Andalusian *jund* cavalry remained high and they seem to have evolved into a provincial aristocracy maintained by *iqta'* fiefs, organized into squadrons and operating alongside an army of infantry volunteers. *Ard* reviews were as important in al-Andalus as elsewhere, these being organised by a specially commissioned officer who also arranged large-scale *buruz* military parades before important military expeditions.

The Umayyad Andalusian frontier which faced the increasingly aggressive Christian states of northern Iberia was structured along much the same lines at the Abbasid frontier facing the Byzantine Empire with militarised *thughur* provinces facing each Christian state or group of states. In the tenth century each had been governed by a *sahib al-thughur* whose status and function was different to that of the governors of a central province, being senior to other military commanders, leading his own forces and in some cases having a fleet under his control. However, urban *futuwwa* or *ahdath* military organizations only developed in belated response to the massive Christian conquests of the late eleventh and twelfth centuries.

There were basically two types of *taifa* state in fragmented eleventh-century al-Andalus. Relatively large ones emerged in sparsely populated *thughur* regions close to the Christian frontier, while much smaller city-states appeared in the densely populated and urbanised south. Some were ruled by descendents of those *qa'ids* who had governed *thughur* frontier provinces and had effective military forces but others had virtually no army at all. None were capable of resisting the Christian advance, except for the Hudid rulers of Saragossa who survived until 1141 AD, resisting both their Christian neighbours and the African Murabitin who crossed the Straits of Gibraltar to save Andalusian Islam at the end of the eleventh century.

The military organisation of indigenous rather than occupying North African forces in Islamic al-Andalus already had several features in common with their Christian neighbours, but Andalusian society was not so class differentiated as that of the Christian states. Instead it consisted of extended family networks and alliances which ran across categories of wealth. As a result poorer soldiers or militiamen tended to garrison a castle held by someone richer or more powerful to whom they were distantly related through shared clan or tribal origins.

There was a second, briefer *taifa* period of small independent statelets between the collapse of Murabitin domination and the imposition of North African Muwahhidin domination in the mid-twelfth century. This second *taifa* period was also characterised by remarkable alliances between Andalusian Muslims and northern Iberian Christians against North African rule. During this period most local Andalusian troops appear to have been professional mercenaries, large parts of the country-side now being in the hands of an Islamic military aristocracy. To further confuse the issue, some of this Andalusian élite were *Mozarab* 'Arabized' Christians, one such family becoming vassals of an independent Islamic ruler of Valencia in the mid-twelfth century, before declaring their in-dependence and then falling under Aragonese domination. Thereafter they remained locally powerful well into the thirteenth century.

A third *taifa* period following the collapse of Muwahhidin domination was stifled by the rapid Spanish conquest of all Andalusia except the *amirate* of Granada. Nevertheless Andalusian military systems during this brief period already had more in common with those of Christian northern Iberian than with fellow-Islamic North Africa. Local military obligations appear to have been assessed on a family basis and were in-herited by the following generation. The Nasrid Kingdom of Granada actually resulted from a native revolt against North African rule, its first army consisting of the ruler's own family or clan and its political clients. Additional troops included refugees fleeing Christian conquest and Berber volunteers or refugees from Morocco. Political refugees also moved from Granada to Morocco, including the Arab *Banu Ashqilula* who had played a major role in defence of Granada's frontiers until they quarrelled with the Nasrid rulers in the late thirteenth century. Larger numbers of infantry and mounted crossbowmen were meanwhile recruited in the Alpujarras Mountains southeast of Granada.

Friction between Berber volunteers and local Andalusian militias who formed the *thagri* frontier defence forces led Muhammad V of Granada to reduce the numbers of North Africans in the mid-fourteenth century. Nevertheless, religiously motivated volunteers continued to play a significant role, particularly in defence of Granada's coast against Christian piracy and garrisoning many coastal *ribats*. More unusual, perhaps, was Muhammad V's bodyguard of Christian renegades called *ma'lughun* plus *mamluks* drawn from younger Christian captives who were trained to form a high-status light cavalry regiment.

The register of military obligations was similarly overhauled in mid-fourteenth-century Granada, resulting in separate Andalusian and North African Berber divisions under their own leaders. That of the North African volunteers was known as the *shaykh al-ghuzat* who was usually related the ruler of Morocco, while local provincial units were now under commanders called *shiyakha khassa*. The *thughur* frontier provinces were initially garrisoned by *murabit* religious volunteers – not to be confused with the Murabitin ruling dynasty of the twelfth century – organised under their own leaders, but this system proved inadequate and was soon backed up by eleven major provincial military bases with *jund* forces.

Similar strategies were used by Islamic armies in North Africa and al-Andalus, both relying on superior mobility compared to their Iberian Christian foes, but by the later-medieval period Granada had to rely on counter-raiding rather than full-scale invasions of its now much more powerful Christian neighbours. According to their enemies the Muslims of Granada were particularly effective in *cabalgada* raiding by light cavalry at night, favoured economic targets being orchards or mills. In defence the Islamic *amirate* of Granada reverted to guerrilla strategy, at most seizing isolated mountain castles to threaten enemy communications.

The most important example of theoretical military literature from the Islamic west was a treatise of archery written by Ibn Maymun in thirteenth-century Morocco, which argued in favour of traditional archery and against the increasingly popular crossbow. Another treatise written in later fourteenth-century Granada repeated the classic view that the defeat of the wings was unimportant if the centre held, and that it was risky for the centre to attempt a feigned flight in order to lure the foe into an ambush by the flanks. However, according to fourteenth-century Spanish sources the light cavalry of Granada would launch repeated attacks in an *esplonada* or 'spur' formation and made considerable use of feigned or false retreats. These troops were also said to be highly effective in close-combat despite using lighter arms and armour than the Christians.

During the late twelfth to early fourteenth centuries the élite of Islamic Andalusian cavalry were equipped much like their Christian Iberian opponents, having two warhorses and being supported by squires. Perhaps this reflected a desperate attempt to meet Christian knightly cavalry on equal terms at a time of military setbacks. These horsemen also adopted the couched lance with a deep saddle and long-legged riding position while, in contrast, even the highest status North African Berber horsemen remained lightly armoured.

In the mid-fourteenth century, however, just as light cavalry *a la jineta* were spreading amongst the Spaniards and Portuguese, the horsemen of Granada abandoned the Western European fashions which had failed to stop the Christian *Reconquista* and adopted a slighter heavier version of Berber-style weapons and harness. Though this light cavalry included very few horse-archers, its tactics of harrassment and rapid flank attacks had a great deal in common with those of the Islamic Middle East. The main difference was that Granada made considerable use of crossbows, both on foot and on horseback, and used slightly heavier armour than their North African counterparts.

Infantry remained relatively more important in North Africa and Granada than they did in the Islamic Middle East. Those of Andalusian origin in fourteenth-century Tunisia included a majority of archers, while infantry crossbowmen of Andalusian origin were also prominent in Morocco. A variety of skills was clearly expected in professional troops in both North Africa and al-Andalus. Here, as in the Middle East, the problem of fear was faced in a more matter of fact manner than in medieval Christian Europe, a fourteenth-century Andalusian military scholar named Ibn Hudhayl advising that swords should not be drawn until the last moment to avoid making their users nervous. The same practical author cautioned against swinging a weapon too wildly as this could lead to one's own horse or even one's own foot getting hit. When it came to crossbow shooting this commentator stated that archers should be trained to use ranging shots, 'bracketing' the target and hopefully then achieving a bullseye.

Islamic Armies of North Africa

The military history of Morocco from the decline of the Abbasid Caliphate to the rise of the Murabitin in the eleventh century is little known compared to that of what is now Tunisia and Algeria. Here in the *Maghrib al-Aqsa*, the 'far West' of the medieval Islamic world, the most powerful group was the Sanhaja tribal confederation, whose military élite were described as spear-armed horsemen. On the Atlantic coast of

Morocco the Baghawata were a powerful sub-tribe of the Masmuda Berbers but had long been regarded as heretics, eventually being declared 'infidels'. Nevertheless they survived, largely as a result of their numerous and effective cavalry, until crushed by the Murabitin in the eleventh century.

The Murabitin themselves created one of the most extraordinary empires in medieval African history, a state that included half of the Iberian peninsula and was thus a 'sub-Saharan African empire in Europe'. The first Murabit army was recruited from a Berber tribal confederation, including Jazula, Lamt, Zanata and Masmuda. As the state expanded, so its army became more sophisticated and varied with large numbers of slave-recruited 'black' African troops, of whom the *hasham* formed a cavalry guard unit, alongside a small élite of Christian Iberian captives and mercenaries. Though the Murabitin army which conquered most of al-Andalus in the later eleventh century remained largely Saharan Berber it soon also included men from northern Morocco, naval archers of Sabta (Ceuta) who later became even better known as naval crossbowmen, and eventually Spanish, Catalan and French Christian mercenaries who formed one of the Murabit ruler's guard units.

The army of the Muwahhidin rulers who overthrew the Murabitin and inherited the northern part of their empire was more a Moroccan than a Saharan tribal levy, relying primarily on men from the Lamta, Zanata and Masmuda tribes of the Atlas mountains. At the same time it also included slave-recruited African soldiers, former Murabitin troops, an élite training unit consisting of the sons of tribal leaders destined for government or officer roles, Spanish Christian prisoners-of-war and, once again, a guard formation of Iberian Christian mercenaries. Further east the twelfth-century Zayrid rulers of Tunisia drew upon a small number of refugees from Norman-ruled Sicily including Christians whose fathers had been Muslim and who now returned to that faith, as well as Christian mercenaries.

Following the collapse of the Muwahhidin state, recruitment into Marinid armies in Morocco largely reverted to the ruler's own Banu Marin tribe or other tribes allied to the dynasty. Each province was governed by a member of the ruling family who had his own locally-recruited army. There was nevertheless an élite of Andalusians, some of whom had been *Mudejars* or 'Muslims under Christian rule' in Spain. They enjoyed a privileged position, being free from the local loyalties which divided Moroccan tribes. According to one source, the fourteenth-century Marinid army also included 1,500 Ghuzz Turkish cavalry, 4,000 European cavalry, 500 European horse-archers who had converted to Islam, plus infantry archers as well as Andalusian infantry and mounted crossbowmen. Muslim Andalusians were similarly renowned as siege engineers and for establishing a naval arsenal at Sala on the Atlantic coast.

While the Marinids now dominated Morocco, the Hafsids dominated Tunisia and much of Algeria where they maintained Muwahhidun military traditions throughout their history. Though local Arab tribes were generally unsympathic to the Hafsid dynasty, some urban militias defended their own towns. More significant, perhaps, was a loyal guard of Andalusian refugees who contributed to the defeat of St.Louis' Crusade against Tunis in 1270. More exotic were the Hafsids' *janawa* black guardsmen from Guinea in West Africa.

Between the Hafsids and Marinids lay the territory of the Ziyanids whose army was largely a Berber tribal force, plus a regiment of Ghuzz Turks inherited from the Muwahiddin and some more recent Kurdish arrivals. More remarkable were the Turkish *mamluk* soldiers who, purchased as slaves in Cairo, formed a guard unit in fourteenth-century Mali, south of the Sahara Desert.

Little is known about the military administration of North Africa following the decline of the Abbasid Caliphate. The *iqta'* system was clearly introduced to Islamic Sicily, the western part of this land also being divided into *iqlim* districts each with a *jund* territorial army before the Norman conquest. In Morocco political fragmentation reached a peak in the early eleventh century, small states comparable to the better documented *taifa* states of the Iberian peninsula dominating at least northern Morocco before the whole area fell to the Murabitin in the late eleventh century.

The organisation of armies in late medieval North Africa continued to reflect the Muwahhid period, fiefs comparable to the *iqta's* of the Middle East becoming a common feature. The Hafsid army of Tunisia, for example, was commanded by the ruler or a *wazir al-jund* 'minister of war'. Other officers included a *sahib al-ta'im* in charge of equipment and supplies, several *qa'id* in command of separate sections of the army including the cavalry, with *a'rif* and possibly *muharrik* junior officers in charge of smaller operational units. Tactics similarly seem to have been simple and old-fashioned with evidence from mid-eleventh century Tunisia suggesting that an army was vulnerable at the moment of *nuzul* or halting and reassembling, and that North African armies tended to march with their infantry at the centre, protected by a screen of cavalry.

The early Murabitin who, as an essentially Saharan military force, consisted of camel-mounted infantry with very few cavalry, introduced significant changes to warfare in North Africa. Their discipline was proverbial and they would reputedly neither advance nor retreat, however strong their enemy. In such formations spear and shield-armed men and standard-bearers formed the front ranks, supported by men carrying several javelins. It was said that if their flag fell, such would simply sit down where they were rather than flee.

Even though North African tactics evolved in response to current conditions, they remained old-fashioned. For example, twelfth- to four-teenth-century North African Arab nomad tribes used tented encampments, erected at night and containing herds of animals as well as families, as field fortifications. From these cavalry launched repeated attacks and withdrawals. Such Arab tribal forces also used infantry and cavalry mixed together, which was regarded as unlike other armies. The role of infantry and camel-riding mounted infantry had been paramount in Murabitin forces since the late eleventh century and this resulted in very defensive tactics. A small number of horsemen again made controlled charges from behind a shield-wall of foot soldiers, the latter having been specifically trained to open their ranks obliquely left or right.

On the other hand, Murabitin infantry armed with very large leather shields and javelins were perfectly capable of advancing from their field fortifications to attack Spanish cavalry and panic their horses, as they did at the Battle of Zallaca in 1086. The Murabitin reliance on infantry was further developed by the Muwahhidin who reportedly arrayed their foot soldiers in an open ractangle rather than a solid phalanx, placing their more abundant cavalry in the centre but again attacking through gaps opened by the infantry.

Around 1295, the Spanish scholar Raymon Lull admitted the greater discipline of the 'Moors' and the effectiveness of their light cavalry tactics, still using javelins. In broader terms Hafsid strategy was one of move-ment and siege warfare, avoiding major battles and reportedly being able to cover thirty kilometres a day in flat country. The skills required were reflected in what little is known about military training in medieval North Africa. Much the same forms of training schedules developed here as in al-Andalus. During the twelfth and thirteenth centuries, for example, the Muwahhidin trained specially selected youths called *huffaz* to ride, shoot, swim and row. The latter skill was not included in the military training schedules of most medieval Islamic states and probably reflected the importance of naval warfare in these regions.

Islamic Sea Power in the Western Mediterranean and Atlantic

Islamic sea-power endured for longer in the western Mediterranean than in the eastern, particularly amongst the eleventh- and twelfth-century Murabitin. The Nasrid kingdom of Granada subsequently maintained a small but effective fleet long after the rest of Islamic Andalusia had collapsed and may, in fact, have been stronger at sea than on land during the fourteenth century. Almeria served as Granada's main arsenal and naval base, the rest of the coast being defended by a series of fortified *tali'a* watch towers. The navy itself was organized in *ustul* squadrons, each under a *qa'id* officer. On board ship a *ra'is* was in charge of manoeuvering the vessel while a junior *qa'id* commanded the marines whose main strength lay in archers and crossbowmen.

Three-masted and two-decked ships were almost certainly being used by Andalusian Islamic fleets much earlier than by Byzantines or Italians. These may have come to be known as *qarqura* which were probably the ancestors of the later *caracca* or *carrack* in which Columbus and his contemporaries explored the oceans. Contrary to popular opinion, Islamic fleets soon ventured into the Atlantic and the Andalusian Umayyads developed several large Atlantic naval bases. An Umayyad squadron actually defeated the fearsome Vikings in at least two significant sea battles off Silves in what is now southern Portugal in the tenth century and Andalusian merchants or fishermen returned with descriptions of whales being hunted off Ireland, Britain or Iceland in the eleventh century. The extraordinary story of the *Adventurers of Lisbon* has proved more difficult to interpret; however these sailors made several ocean voyages, bringing back stories of islands far out in the Atlantic, some inhabited by fair-skinned men with long hair and no beards, but having ships, cities and a king whose interpreter already spoke Arabic. These were probably the British Isles or Ireland rather than North America as some romantics have suggested.

Nevertheless, the mariners of Morocco and al-Andalus certainly knew about the Canary Islands and claimed to have sailed sufficient degrees westward to reach Madeira, though not the Azores. Other evidence indicates that Islamic mariners habitually sailed to Cap Blanc on the Saharan Atlantic coast of what is now Mauretania and may actually have reached the Cape Verde Islands.

Little is known about the ships operating from medieval Morocco's Atlantic coast, though a late fourteenth-century graffito from Malaga shows an advanced form of galley which has features in common with the *xebecs* in which sixteenth-century Moroccan 'Sally Rover' pirates raided as far as the British Isles. A petraglyph drawing in south-western Morocco shows a similar vessel but it is unfortunately undated. Of the five major ports on Morocco's Atlantic coast, only two were protected by stone walls in the eleventh century. The threat posed by Christian piracy to the northern part of a rich trans-Saharan caravan route along the coast lay behind the new naval arsenal built at Sala by Andalusian refugees in 1314/5, and for the erection of coastal watch-towers from Asfi to Mazjanna in the mid-fourteenth century.

A Christian fleet which tried to blockade Ceuta in the thirteenth century was driven off by a naval sortie which captured one ship whose rigging had been jammed by arrows. The Marinids practically wiped out the Castilian fleet off Algeciras in 1340 as a result of their superior archery and seamanship, there being two hundred crossbowmen and archers aboard each of their larger vessels. These would clearly have been capable of continuing the Muslims' existing tradition of Atlantic voyages. The contribution of African Muslims to Atlantic exploration has not been fully studied. However, the expedition sent out into the Atlantic by Sultan Mansa Musa's father, the ruler of Mali early in the fourteenth century, probably set sail from what is now Senegal and may have been heading for the Cape Verde islands. None of its vessels reportedly returned, but the very fact that it set out incidates that local sailors, perhaps fishermen blown off course, knew that there was something out there to find.

Elsewhere, the thirteenth century saw a decline in North African naval power, though it revived when the Hafsids of Tunisia counter-attacked Christian pirate lairs in Sicily, Malta and elsewhere. According to a Portugese observer in 1428, most Hafsid vessels were galleys of twenty-five to thirty rowing benches, though the fleet also included seven great horse-transport galleys capable of carrying one hundred animals each.

The Mongol Onslaught

The last and most devastating Central Asian invasion of the Islamic Middle East and Russia was that by the Mongols during the thirteenth century. The Mongols do not, however, seem to have been interested in conquering Europe. Their objective was to dominante the steppe peoples and those neighbouring states who might be rivals for such domination. Nor were the Mongols strictly nomads by the time they invaded Russia. Like the Huns long before, they had evolved into what could be described as 'dominant predators' whose power was based upon the extortion of tribute. By the mid- and late thirteenth century the Mongol ruling and military élites had also been strongly influenced by Chinese culture while the most sophisticated aspects of Mongol warfare had a distinctly Chinese character.

The armies of the Mongols were much larger than those of their Middle Eastern and European foes and even under Genghis Khan, during the initial decades of the Mongol 'World Empire', conquered Turks were recruited in substantial numbers to supplement an always-limited supply of ethnic Mongols. Numerous ex-Chinese soldiers were soon similarly being enlisted, particularly as infantry and specialist siege troops. The Mongol habit of transferring part of various conquered communities to distant provinces resulted in Orthodox Christian, Iranian-speaking Alans as well as Russians serving in eastern Mongol armies. Some of these Russians later returned home, presumably having learned advanced military ideas from the Chinese.

The bulk of the army with which Genghis Khan's grandson, Hülagü, conquered much of the eastern Islamic Muslim world was no longer strictly Mongol but included many Kipchaq Turks and Chinese siege machine operators. Amongst those Mongol troops who did accompany Hülagü were Oirats, a forest tribe from west of Lake Baikal. Some remained in the Middle East but substantial numbers deserted Hülagü's descendants, the Il-Khan ruling dynasty, to fight for the Mamluk Sultanate of Egypt and Syria. Other Oirats remained on the steppes of Central Asia, adopting the new name of Kalmuks, becoming dedicated enemies of Islam and eventually converting to a warlike form of Buddhism.

The various Mongol successor *khanates* which dominated the steppes from the Pacific to the Black Sea following the breakup of the Mongol 'World Empire' were all similarly organised, with conquered peoples at the bottom rungs of society. Various Turkish and Finno-Ugrian tribes came into this category, whereas the Russian principalities were regarded as tributary states. Next came previously dominant élites while superior status went to those Mongol tribes who provided the Great Khan and his subordinate *khans* with their military and administrative aristocracies.

The Mongol armies were themselves characterised by more cohesive command structures than those seen in Europe, though not necessarily as sophisticated as those of the Byzantine Empire and Islamic world. The legitimacy of military leaders depended on their membership of the ruling 'Cingisid' family descended from Genghiz Khan, and proven military success. Devotion to Mongol tradition meant that the old *yasa* tribal law attributed to Genghiz Khan remained the basis of military organization and government even after the Mongol conquerors of the Middle East and southern Russia largely converted to Islam. Later Mongol forces were, however, bound by personal allegiance to a leader or a ruling family rather than to any abstract concept of Mongol domination.

Traditionally, Mongol tribal cavalry needed five horses per man. In the Middle East, however, they are said to have had up to eight, which gave Mongol armies extraordinary strategic mobility and speed. The basic Mongol military unit was the *tümen* theoretically consisting of 10,000 men and, whereas the Mongol Yüan dynasty in China rapidly became Chinese in all but name, the Mongol Il-Khan dynasy in Iran and Iraq retained traditional Turco-Mongol military structures even after becoming Muslim at the start of the fourteenth century. For example the *amir* of an *ulu* frontier or 'marcher' province was called a *berlerbey*, as was the commander of the army as a whole. The Arabized *tuman* version of the basic Mongol military unit still meant 10,000 men but also came to refer to the province which supported such a force. In fact the new *tuman* was little more than the old Islamic *wilayat* province renamed.

Instead of declining over the years, the Il-Khan army was considerably increased by Khan Ghazan at the end of the thirteenth century, along with the reintroduction of the earlier Islamic *iqta'* system of military fiefs. Unlike previous *iqta's*, however, those of the Il-Khan state were largely hereditory, apparently mirroring the *hazara* 'units of 1,000' and their smaller subdivisions. Other *iqta's* were allocated to increasingly important Persian infantry.

Mongol strategy was essentially the same as that of the preceding Huns and Central Asian Turks, though with greater sophistication as a result of Chinese influence. Even in peacetime Mongol horsemen may have changed horses three times a day to avoid tiring the animals. Care for their enormous horse-herds was paramount and on most campaigns the main forces were preceded by scouts who rode several days ahead, looking not only for the enemy but for adequate pasture for the army's horses. The availablity of grazing had a clear strategic impact upon Mongol campaigning in the frequently hot and dry climate of the Islamic lands. Fertile regions served as bases from which to launch major campaigns. The problems faced by Mongol cavalry in Syria in the late thirteenth and early fourteenth centuries further highlighted the unsuitability of their breed of horses, and their method of feeding them, when campaigning in these arid areas. In 1300 AD, for example, a Mongol army was accompanied by huge numbers of camels carrying fodder for the horses. Nevertheless so many horses starved that a large part of the Mongol army ended up on foot.

It may have been the iron discipline of the early Mongols which made them such formidable foes. This also enabled their commanders to remain behind the fighting line rather than getting involved in combat, and thus retaining a wider view of what was happening. Mongol horse-archers generally shot their arrows in charges by repeated waves of horsemen aimed at different parts of an enemy line. These probably involved a single shot from quite close range rather than the long-range and prolonged harrassment 'shower-shooting' preferred by Middle Eastern forces. The small number of heavily-armoured Mongol cavalry protected these horse-archers from counter-attacks and would eventually make a final charge with close-combat weapons to complete the enemy's discomfort. A more novel feature may have been the Mongol habit of opening up a gap, once they had surrounded an enemy, seemingly to allow him to escape but in reality forcing him down a corridor of murderous archery.

The Mongols were also noted for their use of imaginative battlefield ruses, though most of these were not new. For example, putting straw dummies on the backs of their many spare horses to make an army look several times larger, as done in Afghanistan in 1221 and later in Hungary, was merely a variation on a long-established ruse. Turco-Mongol horses, though smaller than European and slower than Arabian horses, were more resilient than their stall-fed rivals. They also appear to have been better at climbing, jumping, swimming and enduring cold climates. Large-scale and prolonged hunting expeditions played a major role in military training, though they were more important in improving a commander's ability to coordinate widespread forces. The only other known forms of 'exercise' were horse-riding ceremonies which took place at the accession or death of a ruler.

Chapter 3
Expansion and Survival

The Northern Crusades

Germany was the powerhouse of the Northern Crusades, although Denmark and Sweden also played a significant role. Meanwhile, Norway remained primarily concerned with the North Atlantic throughout the Middle Ages.

Following the fragmentation of the Carolingian Empire in the late ninth century, Germany emerged as the centre of what would eventually become known as the Holy Roman Empire. This huge, rambling state was normally known simply as 'The Empire' by medieval Europeans. Within a few decades Germany felt the brunt of attacks by Scandinavian Vikings and Magyars or Hungarians while the German Empire also expanded its control over several Slav peoples along its eastern border. The raising of sufficient troops to meet threats and carry out ambitions remained a problem for German emperors, though the aristocracy, Church and peasantry all had military obligations. Relatively poor and backward regions such as Thuringia continued to provide *inermes*, or largely-unarmoured horsemen, for many decades; nevertheless the fully equipped *milites* had become the dominant military arm by the eleventh century.

Another distinctive military group was meanwhile emerging. Rarely seen elsewhere in Western Europe, these *diensleute* or *ministeriales*, non-noble or even serf cavalry, may have evolved out of the serf or even slave-origin guard units recruited by some German magnates in the eleventh century. Although the lower social classes were gradually being excluded from warfare in most parts of Germany, except in defence of the country's few towns, infantry still had a role in relatively poor Saxony and Thuringia. Rural peasant militias were only summoned in response to specific emergencies, though the *dithmarschen* peasant infantry of the bleakest parts of northern Germany were an exception, remaining an effective though localised force to the end of the fifteenth century.

Although urban militias began to appear in economically developed regions, many of the 'imperial' cities dotted about Germany were isolated from one another by the great baronial realms that lay between. Such 'imperial' cities theoretically still provided the Emperor with knightly cavalry, though in reality few were doing so by the early fourteenth century. Instead, the emperor relied on taxation from these cities and other sources agreed by the *Imperial Diet* or parliament; money with which to hire mercenaries.

Another distinctive characteristic of medieval Germany were the 'leagues' which initially consisted of cities which pooled resources and hired cavalry forces known as *knechte der freiheit*, or 'knights of freedom', to defend their interests. A particularly powerful and virtually permanent example was the Hanseatic League which consisted of cities involved in overseas trade through the Baltic and North Sea.

On the other side of the Baltic Sea, Prussian tribal troops would serve as auxiliaries and as guides during Germanic Crusader campaigns against the still-pagan Lithuanians, while to the north of Lithuanian territory, Estonian, Semigallian, Kur, Liv and Lett tribes played a similar role. Whereas the Estonians often rebelled, the last such uprising being in 1343, the Livs and Letts were the most loyal to their new rulers, it largely being from these two previously-weak and oppressed tribes that the modern Latvian people evolved during the fourteenth century.

The breakup of the Carolingian Empire had also seen Germany develop its own distinctive military systems, with some of the pre-Christian tribal regions re-emerging in the form of *Duchies*. The new German emperors next set about restructuring the military system, above all by creating an essentially cavalry force of *milites* led by Dukes, Counts and frontier marcher lords known as *Margraves*. As in northern France, the local knights, or *miles armatus* were supported by *benefice* estates, though in the newly-conquered Slav areas of what is now eastern Germany they were maintained by a subject population.

Throughout the twelfth and well into the fourteenth century, Germany was an exporter rather than an employer of surplus military manpower. This had a profound impact upon the success of the Baltic Crusades and of German settlement in what had been Slav or Balt territories. However, the concept of knighthood came late to Germany where it remained rather different from the knighthood of northern France or England. In the early twelfth century the German term *riter*, which is normally translated as 'knight', appears to have meant 'one who went ahead' – not even necessarily a horseman – and sources written in Latin similarly included references to *milites pedites* or *infantry knights*. Yet by the early thirteenth century the *riter* was clearly part of the military élite and the term would gradually come to mean a member of a new German military aristocracy which had evolved from the minor vassals of earlier years and even from the originally unfree *ministeriales*.

While the west of the German Empire gradually adopted socio-political structures similar to those seen in France, more old-fashioned feudal forms of military organisation continued to exist in the eastern provinces of Germany well into the fourteenth century. The élite armoured cavalrymen also came to be known as a *panzerati* or *renner*, 'men-at-arms', rather than *knechts* or knights which eventually came to mean a military servant. Such armoured horsemen were normally organised into *gleven*, which were comparable to the *lances* of France and Italy, and as such formed the smallest cavalry 'unit'. This initially consisted of the man-at-arms and a following of three armoured sergeants, but later the following usually involved either *diener* lightly-armed servants or three hired mercenaries.

The towns which developed in newly conquered eastern and Baltic lands, including those of the Crusader Teutonic Knights' territory, were organised in much the same way as those in Germany itself. Here urban militias played an increasingly important military role as the German part of the Empire fragmented into minor principalities, Church estates, free and 'imperial' cities. Such towns were usually divided into quarters, each with its own gate to guard and the militiamen were led by a *viertelmeister* appointed by the city council. He in turn could be supported by other officers, a trumpeter, perhaps semi-professional watchtower guards and, towards the end of the fourteenth century, a *buchsenmeister* or 'master gunner'. As elsewhere, the richer citizens served as cavalry and were organised into *gleven* units, particularly when supplemented by professional mercenaries.

Because the emperors were themselves so often preoccupied with maintaining their crumbling authority in the 'imperial' territories of Italy, they played much less of a role in the Northern or Baltic Crusades than might have been expected. Here, from the late thirteenth century onwards, campaigns against the pagan Lithuanians largely consisted of rapid raids or *reysa* deep into the other's territory. The Lithuanians and others responded with comparable retaliatory raids. For both sides rivers were vital as communications routes to and between a series of relatively small fortifications, most of which were actually built along the most important such rivers.

In more general tactical terms, German armies employed essentially the same battlefield manoeuvers as did other Western European forces, often trying but only rarely succeeding in luring their more nimble Baltic foes into close combat. By the eleventh century German warfare was almost entirely dominated by men on horseback, either as mounted infantry or as proper cavalry. It is often difficult to distinguish between the two during the early period, but where mounted archers were concerned these were almost certainly mounted infantry as there was no tradition of horse-archery in Germany. It is also worth noting that, even when cavalry came to dominate in Germany, Byzantine observers still regarded the Germans, and above all the Saxons, as sword-fighters, while the French and Normans operated as lance-armed horsemen.

Before the Vikings erupted out of Scandinavia in the centuries before the Crusades there appears to have been relatively little naval warfare in these northern seas. There would, however, clearly be a vital naval element to the Northern or Baltic Crusades and the ships concerned soon included large vessels, especially those commissioned by the German Crusading Order of 'Sword Brothers' in the early thirteenth century. Generally speaking, however, northern German cargo ships were smaller than those of the Mediterranean, while galleys were far fewer and generally less suited to northern conditions. When *trebuchets* were occasionally mentioned, they were almost certainly being transported rather than being for use on board. Great crossbows were mentioned rather more often from the early fourteenth century onwards, along with the torsion powered *espringal* or *spingarda*. The ferocious winter climate of the Baltic also ensured that naval warfare remained a summer occupation for German mariners during the Northern Crusades.

In Denmark the *liedang* levy of men, ships and military equipment had emerged during the tenth century and was based upon the expectation that all free men should help defend an area. In Norway a complete levy was only summoned in defence, though a half-levy could be called up for offensive operations. Throughout this early period Scandinavia had been an exporter of military manpower, but from the mid-eleventh century there was a small but influential influx of foreigners. Among the most significant were Anglo-Saxon refugees from those once-élite families who had lost their military role as a result of the Norman Conquest. Some served the Norwegian king though a larger number went to Denmark.

The twelfth and thirteenth centuries were a period of considerable change in Scandinavia. During this period Denmark, Sweden, Norway and even to some extent Iceland, were drawn into the mainstream of Western European culture. Meanwhile a simple form of feudalism, largely based upon that of Germany and the Low Countries, spread across Denmark and the more densely inhabited southern parts of Sweden and Norway. All these regions remained, however, old fashioned compared to the rest of Western Europe.

Even in the early twelfth century the Danish military aristocracy was still similar to that of the preceding Viking period. Yet the Viking Age had ended, and there were fewer outlets for the Scandinavians' warlike energies. At first these focused on resisting a series of ferocious naval raids by Slav peoples of the southern Baltic coast or finding a military role as mercenaries in Russia and the Byzantine Empire. Even the Christian Slav ruler east of Lübeck, in what is now northeastern Germany, recruited

Danish and Saxon mercenaries during this period; but in the mid-twelfth century Scandinavian Christianity took the offensive against the remaining pagan Slavs of what is now northern Germany and northern Poland. At the end of the twelfth century this offensive turned against the pagan Balts and Finns of what are now Lithuania, Latvia, Estonia and Finland.

The forces involved in these lesser-known Crusading enterprises were organised along essentially German lines. This was particularly the case in royal armies of Denmark and to a lesser extent of Sweden. Meanwhile, rural militias continued to play a role, notably on the island of Götland which, though technically part of Sweden, remained largely autonomous. Götland was, in fact, only required to contribute six or seven ships to the defence of the Swedish kingdom and even then only for campaigns against heathen rather than Christian foes. Urban militias also developed in some merchant cities, a classic example being prosperous Wisby on the island of Götland.

By the late eleventh century the ruler of Denmark had also become a territorial monarch rather than merely 'king of an army' as in the Viking era. As a result the twelfth-century Danish crown began recruiting and organising an army like those of the rest of western Christendom. A similar process was seen in Sweden, though generally half a century later. Norway was even more backward, while distant Iceland, though not completely isolated from military and cultural trends within Europe, was the most archaic of all. Virtually nothing is known of the military organisation of the well-established Norse colonies in Greenland and on the edge of the North American continent. Here recent archaeological evidence indicates close but generally hostile relations between the settlers and the *Skraelings* or Inuit Eskimos. In the far north of Scandinavia itself the Nordic peoples also had other neighbours, the Lapps who were at a similar level of development to the Inuit *Skraelings*.

Although the Norwegians reportedly made the greatest use of bows, archery was a major aspect of warfare in other Scandinavian and Baltic countries, especially in areas which lacked substantial cavalry forces until the twelfth century, and in naval clashes. Naval warfare had been so important in tenth- and eleventh-century Scandinavia that the entire military system of a country like Denmark was geared to warfare at sea. Naval conflict, however, may have differed in certain details between the Scandinavian countries. For example, archery seems to have been particularly important at sea in Sweden, wheras in Norway it might have been more important on land. Everywhere, however, it seems that the term *stafnbúi* or 'stem man' referred to one of those élite troops who stood at the prow of a ship in naval confrontations because sea battles largely consisted of boarding and then close fighting.

Although naval warfare was less advanced in northern waters, some similarities with the Mediterranean emerged during the twelfth and thirteenth centuries. For example, she sturdy but slow merchant *cogs* were often converted into warships, many perhaps having permanent wooden 'fighting castle' structures on their prows and sterns. When used as warships, vessels seem to have been lightened to ride higher in the water because this gave their crew an advantage when boarding or shooting down at an enemy, though it would also have made them less seaworthy.

Despite the fact that Danish ships could still only carry a small number of horses, this capability did give them a significant strategic advantage over their Baltic Slav rivals whose ships remained smaller. In other respects naval warfare remained remarkably traditional in Scandinavia and the Baltic until the early fourteenth century when German, or more specifically Hanseatic League, ships and tactics began to have a major influence upon those of Denmark, Sweden and even Norway.

South of the Baltic Sea lay the extensive territories of the western Slavs. Here the military situation had remained relatively unchanged until the later tenth and eleventh centuries despite the emergence of Poland as an independent though still poor and rather backward kingdom. While the Poles became Catholic Christian, the Slav tribes of what is now north-eastern Germany remained fiercely pagan for many decades. Here the high priest of the god Svantovit at the pagan shrine of Arkona was said to have had a war-band of three hundred dedicated horsemen. After the Slav rulers of Rügen and Mecklenburg converted to Christianity, they and their troops soon joined in the Northern Crusades against pagan peoples farther east and north. However, during the twelfth century the Slav peoples of the southern Baltic coast still made great use of infantry archers, though their bows were increasingly outclassed by the crossbows of the Danes and Germans.

Further south, in Poland itself, the archaeological record suggests that warfare was dominated by spear-armed infantry until the tenth century, when there seems to have been a rise in the importance of archery. The ruler of Poland now had a small élite *druzyna*, part of which was mounted and, like comparable royal forces to the west, could form the core of a larger levy. Nevertheless, armoured horsemen remained rare until the eleventh century while the great majority of Polish warriors remained unarmoured infantry well into the twelfth century.

The fact that the majority of Polish cavalry still apparently did not use spurs in the twelfth century was evidence of continuing influence from eastern European and more particularly steppe traditions of horseman-ship. Even in the thirteenth and fourteenth centuries, the Poles' rare use of full Western European forms of armour might have reflected a tactical need for large numbers of light cavalry in the forest warfare of the Baltic region. From the mid-thirteenth century onwards some eastern regions of Poland, such as Mazovia, came under stronger Eastern and even Mongol military influence, though this was more apparent in military equipment and tactics than military organisation.

Military recruitment in medieval Poland seems to have been almost entirely internal and rural, there being few towns; its armies continuing to be drawn from a large but often poor aristocratic class. During the early fourteenth century, Poland came under pressure from the increasingly aggressive Margrave of Brandenburg in northeastern Germany; so much so that the Poles summoned help from traditionally rival neighbours such as the Baltic Lithuanians in the east and semi-autonomous Ruthenians to the south. In other respects the most significant change in Polish tactics or military recruitment may have been a rise in the importance of infantry during the mid-fourteenth century, but quite why this occurred in a part of Europe otherwise dominated by cavalry remains unclear.

The pagan Baltic peoples who were the primary targets of the Northern Crusades were tribal societies in which each free man was an active warrior. In Prussia and what is now Estonia and Latvia a large proportion of the indigenous population continued to live in a traditional manner even after being forcibly converted to Catholic Christianity, their warrior élites providing auxiliary troops to the Crusading Order of Teutonic Knights which now ruled over them. Between German-ruled Latvia and German-ruled Prussia lay the territory of the Lithuanian tribes. This subsequently evolved into the Grand Duchy of Lithuania and not only survived constant military pressure from its Christian neighbours, both Catholic Westerners and Orthodox Russians, but went on to carve out its own huge empire during the fourteenth century.

The Lithuanian *karias* or army consisted of local *boyars* or warrior noblemen who eventually included aristocrats of Lithuanian, Belarusian 'White Russian', Russian, Polish and Ukrainian origin. In addition the Lithuanian *karias* relied upon the Grand-Duke's own castellans (castle governors) plus local levies from these disparate regional powers. During the fourteenth century Lithuania was reorganised as a *diarchy*, that is two separate regions with their own governments but forming one state. The western half gradually adopted many Western European systems of military recruitment and organisation while resisting German Crusader and Polish aggression. In contrast the eastern half was able to conquer vast areas of what had been Russian principalities, reaching the Black Sea during the early fifteenth century. An Act of Union with Poland in 1356 then created the largest single state in medieval Christendom, with the possible exception of the sparsely inhabited Russian republic of Novgorod. This Act of Union also brought pagan western Lithuania into

Catholic Christendom, the eastern half having already largely converted to Russian Orthodox Christianity.

The Estonian peoples south of the Gulf of Finland had developed their own rudimentary tribal military systems by the eleventh century. Beyond the Gulf of Finland, in what is now the state of Finland, the southern and southwestern coastal peoples also appear to have become tribally organised, though this political structure may only have been been relevant in times of war. During the thirteenth century southwestern Finland was occupied by Sweden, but it remained a poor and backward reflection of an already poor though not necessarily backward Sweden. Here only a tiny Finnish military élite fought on horseback, the rest remaining on foot. Meanwhile, the Karelian Finns to the east and the Lapps in the far north remained a nomadic and essentially 'pre-tribal' or clan-based society with no identifiable military aristocracy.

Thereafter more rigid social and military divisions developed as the Baltic peoples resisted efforts by their Christian neighbours to impose their own cultures upon what would remain the last bastion of paganism within Europe. The Prussians were conquered before they achieved a unified national state. That of the Lithuanians was forged during exceptionally ferocious guerrilla warfare against invading Crusader forces from Scandinavia and Germany in the twelfth century. During the thirteenth century, efforts by the rulers of the emerging Lithuanian state to change the land's tribal landowners into feudal landholders who owed military service led to civil war in the mid-thirteenth century. However, once an essentially Western European style of government and military administration had been imposed, Lithuania was ready to counterattack.

The first wave of German and Scandinavian Northern Crusader assaults achieved relatively easy conquests, but as Lithuanian resistance stiffened the invaders adopted much the same strategy of raid and ambush as their Baltic opponents. In such circumstances the troops of all sides remained vulnerable when returning home laden with booty, captured cattle and prisoners. By the thirteenth century the Crusaders had also developed a sophisticated system of small stone fortifications or blockhouses from which they could ambush enemy raiders, launch their own raids and gradually consolidate their hold on captured territory. In response the twelfth- and thirteenth-century Prussians, Lithuanians and other indigenous peoples used light cavalry guerrilla warfare in the extensive marshes and forests of these regions. These tactics were known as *latrunculi* or *strutere*, banditry or destruction, and were again employed by both sides.

Winter offered certain advantages to the Crusaders' armoured cavalry, especially against the pagan Lithuanians when the frozen ground was more suitable for their heavily-laden horses. In contrast the Lithuanians' own light cavalry preferred the summer when the vast swampy forests hampered their enemy. The little that is known about Lithuanian combat skills suggests that, at least in the mid-thirteenth century and probably much earlier as well, they fought much like Mongol cavalry except that they harassed their enemies by throwing javelins from horseback rather than using Turco-Mongol horse-archery. Further north, the nomadic Karelian Lapps were more noted for their skill in winter raiding, small groups of warriors wearing skis attacking isolated enemy outposts though not the more densely populated centres in western Finland.

Western Slav fleets were raiding beyond the Baltic by the early twelfth century, even reaching out into the North Sea. They were formidable naval foes but as their coasts fell under the domination of German or Germanised rulers and the Crusading Order of Teutonic Knights, the naval history of these peoples was absorbed into that of Baltic northern Germany. By the eleventh century several other Baltic peoples also had fighting ships comparable to those of the Vikings. These Baltic seafarers included the Curonians and Prussians but their coastline had again fallen under the control of the Teutonic Knights, Denmark and Sweden by the later thirteenth century. Consequently the indigenous Baltic and Finnish peoples of this area lost their independent maritime heritage.

Islam Looks South:

Military developments in medieval sub-Saharan Africa stemmed almost entirely from contact with the Islamic world. The spread of Islam into sub-Saharan Africa was first seen on the eastern coast, with a chain of Islamic trading settlements eventually reaching southern Mozambique though there was no attempt to control the hinterland. In the Horn of Africa the Somali people may have originated in southern Ethiopia and northern Kenya before migrating to their present homelands and gradually converting to Islam by the later-medieval period. From the thirteenth century onwards the longer-established Islamic merchant communities of the Somali coastal towns hired Somali warriors as *abaan* or 'protectors'. In fact the close cultural and economic links between the Horn of Africa, Arabia and Egypt had already led to the development of sophisticated Islamic urban centres which formed part of a network of trading relationships around almost the entire Indian Ocean.

Nevertheless these coastal communities remained culturally and politically separate from the interior until a broader sense of Islamic Somali identity began to appear at the end of the fourteenth and early fifteenth centuries, probably as a result of Christian Ethiopian expansion. By then the largely Islamic state of 'Awfat had also appeared in what is now central Ethiopia. It was a formidable military power with a large army consisting of roughly equal proportions of cavalry and infantry led by *amir* officers, though its military equipment was considered primitive by Muslim commentators from elsewhere.

Meanwhile, the Beja people of the western shores of the Red Sea, almost facing the Islamic holy land of the Hijaz on the eastern shore, remained largely pagan but formed a loose tribal state by the ninth century. Arab accounts from this period describe the Beja as warlike, organised in small family groups, fighting with bows and poisoned arrows but not carrying shields. A century later, Arab travellers described Beja warriors as camel riders equipped with spears and leather shields. They are also said to have had war-elephants which, according to the thirteenth-century Venetian traveller Marco Polo, were also used by pagan warriors armed with swords, spears and 'hand stones' along the late thirteenth-century East African coast. Most commentators dismiss this as a garbled second or third-hand report though African war-elephants had clearly been used in Ethiopia and the Sudan in the pre-medieval period – at least one having been taken to Yemen and used in an abortive Abyssinian attack on Mecca in 570 AD, the year that the Prophet Muhammad was born.

There had been urban as well as tribal civilisations in sub-Saharan West Africa since antiquity, the first to emerge into recorded history being the kingdom of Ghana in the eighth century. The next major cultural changes came with the spread of Islam during the tenth to four-teenth centuries which brought the sub-Saharan steppes from the Atlantic to the Red Sea into close political, cultural and military contact with long-established Islamic cultures to the north. Despite this seem-ingly widespread conversion to Islam, some of the states which now emerged were only superficially Islamic. Some were, however, hugely rich, especially Mali which controlled access to the gold mines that would soon lure Europeans into their great Age of Discovery.

The armies of pre-Islamic Ghana and pre-conversion Mali had a remarkably rigid social heirarchy, with the lower ranks being little more than slaves. On the other hand enslaved enemy troops could be enrolled in these armies and some went on to reach high rank. Most early West African warriors were infantry, but one of the most dramatic changes to follow conversion to Islam was the rise of cavalry organised along tradi-tional Islamic lines and including a significant number of North African mercenaries.

Pre-Islamic West African kingship held a semi-divine status while ethnic, tribal and clan divisions tended to be very rigid, each with their own established hierarchies. The pre-Islamic armies of states such as Mali probably reflected this strictly hierarchical system but the coming of Islam led to profound social changes while the ruling élites now looked to North Africa and Egypt for their political and military models. Islamic

Mali included large areas under vassal rulers while others were under governors sent from the centre, each local authority apparently having their own military forces which, by the mid-fourteenth century, included cavalry units led by *amir* officers. The hugely rich king of Mali also had a guard regiment of Turkish and other northern *mamluks* purchased in Egypt. The next Islamic Empire to emerge in sub-Saharan Africa was that of Songhay, slightly further east. Its army is known to have been dispersed in strategic garrisons; each under a royal prince known as a *Kurmina Fari* or a member of the provincial aristocracy called a *Dendi Fari*. According to the remarkable North African traveller Ibn Battuta, each *farari* or commander in Mali was permitted horns or trumpets made of elephant tusks while other military instruments included calabashes and hollow reeds beaten with sticks.

To some extent North African tactics were also adopted south of the Sahara where cavalry had become the dominant arm by the late thirteenth century. However, this rise in the importance of cavalry was not always accompanied by the use of modern harness. For example, the Muslims of fourteenth-century 'Awfat in central Ethiopia still used frameless saddles, probably without stirrups, while the nominally Islamic peoples of the sub-Saharan region still supposedly rode 'bareback' in the twelfth and thirteenth centuries.

Meanwhile, infantry archers remained by far the most numerous troops throughout the sub-Saharan grasslands and forests and many used arrows poisoned with snake venom. Murabitin armies from Morocco suffered from these when attempting to invade Ghana in the twelfth century and, over two hundred years later, the first Portuguese explorers in these same regions faced similarly-poisoned weapons. The ebony maces noted by Arab geographers in the thirteenth century had, however, fallen from favour except in backward regions, though the pre-Islamic traditions of raiding along the great Niger river in great war-canoes was inherited by the Muslim warriors of both Mali and Songhai.

The indigenous Guanches of the Canary Islands were excluded from this spread of more advanced civilisations. They continued to speak Berber-Libyan languages while apparently remaining ignorant of iron-working or boat-building despite the fact that their islands were visited by sailors from al-Andalus and Morocco. Before the arrival of Western European Crusaders, conquerors and settlers at the end of the Middle Ages, there appear to have been several rulers on each island and society consisted of classes or groups whose names indicated their Berber-Libyan origins. However, the pagan Guanches, though virtually within sight of the Moroccan coast, were still only armed with stone knives, specially sharpened 'throwing stones' and small, hardened wood javelins when the first Europeans arrived.

During the early medieval period the Byzantine emperors had seen Christian Ethiopia as a rising regional power, potentially stretching from Africa to India, but these ambitions were snuffed out by the rise of Islam in the seventh century. From then on Christian Ethiopia was largely isolated from the rest of Christendom, although the *Negus* or King of Ethiopia continued to be regarded by Islamic rulers as the protector of Monophysite Christians throughout the Middle East. West of Ethiopia, in what is now the Sudan, the Nubians had converted to Christianity around the sixth century and recent archaeological discoveries support those tenth-century Islamic geographers who stated that the peoples of Kordofan and Darfur were 'subject' to Christian Nubia in cultural, if not political, terms.

The three original kingdoms of Nubia were reduced to two when the northern states merged as Makuria, with its capital at Dongola. Its relations with Islamic Egypt had been governed by a *baqt* (pact) since the mid-seventh century, though this was occasionally broken by frontier squabbles. The military organisation of Makuria was based upon thirteen sub-kings or *eparchs*. The most northerly and powerful had his capital at Faras or Qasr Ibrim. This *eparch* was, in fact, the inheritor of the defunct northern Nubian kingdom of Nobatia. Here the Nubian Nile was protected by an increasing number of castles, though these were probably intended more as a defence against Beja nomads than against Islamic Egypt. For several centuries Nubian infantry archers retained their reputation, using large bows of acacia wood similar to those of ancient Egypt, and even as late as 950 Nubian armies were strong enough to capture much of the population of Egypt's western oases.

For centuries these Christian Nubian kingdoms lived in relative harmony with their Islamic neighbours in Egypt, being more concerned with the warlike and still largely pagan Beja to their east. Despite the unexpected arrival of Armenian and other ex-Fatimid soldiers disbanded by Salah al-Din in the late twelfth century, the military effectiveness of the Nubian states was now in decline relative to their Islamic neighbours. For example, the once-renowned Nubian archers could no longer deal with armoured Mamluk cavalry from Egypt in the later thirteenth century. The mid-thirteenth century had also witnessed the arrival of Arab Bedouin tribes fleeing Mamluk persecution in Egypt. Nubian decline continued in the fourteenth century but it was Islamic *Fung* people from the west rather than north who destroyed the last Nubian state at the end of the fifteenth century.

Less is known about the southern kingdom of Alwa whose capital was at Soba, near modern Khartoum, than about Makuria. Alwa was closer to the pagan regions which were the source of the slaves who formed the major 'commodity' in Nubian trade, so Alwa's interests tended to be focussed southwards. By the eleventh century, Arab geographers were describing these savannah grasslands 'south of Nubia' as being full of warriors, many of whom served as mercenaries in Egypt. Most were spear and sword-armed infantry, not apparently using the bows which were characteristic of other sub-Saharan troops. According to Arab geographers, the *Ahadi* and partially-Christian tribes of Kordofan, west of the Nile, used weaponry and tactics similar to those of Saharan tribes south of Morocco, including large *lamt* leather shields and quilted armour.

Having lost control of the Red Sea coast by the ninth century, Christian Ethiopia turned away from Southern Arabia where its language and civilisation had originated and looked southward for future expansion. In the late tenth century pagan Agau tribesmen, led by a terrifying queen Judith who may have had some connection with the Jewish Falasha people of Ethiopia, devastated the Ethiopian kindom whose capital of Axum was destroyed. During the following chaotic decades Islam made great advances but the highlands remained largely Christian and the Agau were themselves converted to Ethiopian Christianity.

Surprisingly perhaps, the warriors of tenth-century Ethiopia were said to have no horses whatsoever, though this statement probably referred to the pagan rather than Christian or Islamic tribes. During this period, Arab geographers stated that the Ethiopians' principal weapon remained a simple all-wood longbow, sometimes with a cotton string, while long javelins were also used but only the élite possessed shields and swords. Cavalry were known in the eastern lowlands but remained rare. Furthermore their riders still used goat skins rather than wood-framed saddles.

Ethiopia remained a Christian kingdom but by now had a substantial Muslim minority and maintained reasonably good relations with the powerful Mamluk Sultanate of Egypt. The fourteenth-century Ethiopian army had no *diwan* or government department, as seen in Islamic states, but was based upon recognized *jund* territorial forces whose size was checked against a system of 'special stones' each time they were mustered for a review. Large-bladed javelins and large bows of simple construction remained the most common weapons while swords were reserved for a small élite.

Containing the Mongols

As the enormous Mongol 'World Empire' fragmented it was succeeded by smaller regional *Khanates* under the nominal leadership of the Great Khan of the Yüan dynasty in China. Those Khanates which ruled western Asia and eastern Europe, though they still bore the name of Mongol or Tatar, were soon overwhelmingly Turkish in speech and population, though their armies clung to many Mongol traditions. The most urbanised was the Il-Khan state centred upon Iran and Iraq. Even here, however, sedentarisation of the Turco-Mongol tribes was more common in central regions than on the frontiers where nomadism survived along with a warlike raiding mentality. By the fifteenth century the Mongol tribes of Transoxania, though still regarding themselves as Mongols, were fully Turkified and would form the backbone of Timur-i Lenk's (Tamerlane's) army.

Although Timur-i Lenk invaded the Mamluk Sultanate in Syria, the Qara Qoyunlu ('Black Sheep') and Aq Qoyunlu ('White Sheep') Turcomans of Azarbayjan and eastern Anatolia also became significant rivals, having emerged out of the collapse of Mongol authority. The Aq Qoyunlu went on to carve out a state that dominated several rich trade routes and cultivated an alliance with Venice because both feared the growing power of the Ottoman Turks in western Anatolia and Balkans.

The dominant non-Mongol Islamic power in Middle East was still the Mamluk Sultanate of Egypt and Syria where, in 1382 AD, the rule of the largely Turkish *Bahri* Mamluk Sultans was replaced by that of the nominally Circassian *Burji* Mamluk Sultans. The latter were, in fact, largely of European origin, mostly from Christian regions of the Caucasus and Russia but also from further afield.

Traditional Islamic military systems of recruitment reappeared in Mongol Il-Khan Iran and Iraq during the fourteenth century and there is evidence that attempts were made to recruit Western European crossbowmen before this date. In late thirteenth-century Mongol-dominated Anatolia some Islamic *sufi* religious fraternities known as *runud* already played a military role, while on the eastern frontier of the Il-Khan state a new group of fourteenth-century warriors called *qaraunas* may have been descended from Mongol fathers and Indian or Kashmiri mothers. The Jagatai Khanate of Central Asia was a regional rival of the Il-Khans and regarded itself as the guardians of true Mongol identity, retaining Mongol tribal organization and a nomadic way of life, though in reality again becoming largely Turkified. Here the *qautchin* élite guard formation evolved into a virtually separate tribe in its own right.

As the Il-Khanate of Iran and Iran fragmented during the fourteenth century, an array of relatively small successor states were characterised by a revival of the traditional Islamic military system of slave-recruited professional *ghulam* or *mamluk* soldiers and militias, many based upon *sufi* or *dervish* Islamic fraternities,. Among these the *sarbadars*, urban militias of late medieval Transoxania and eastern Iran, proved the most effective and gave their name to a ruling dynasty in Khurasan.

Meanwhile, warlike Afghan and other mountain peoples, most of whom had a longstanding infantry tradition, formed the garrisons of many cities in areas ruled by the Kart dynasty. The Karts similarly recruited Mongol allies to fight Mongol enemies at a time when the Mongol 'World Empire' was falling apart.

In western Iran and Iraq the Mongol Jalayrid dynasty still held sway, but their armies seem to have consisted of slave-recruited professionals rather than Turkish or Turco-Mongol tribesmen. In the mountains of Anatolia the Armenians had by now lost their independence and were caught between Timur and the Qara Qoyunlu Turcomans. The Georgian kingdom was devastated by several Timurid invasions and gradually sank into anarchy, though the Georgians were nevertheless able to maintain close military links with the Byzantine 'Empire' of Trebizond on the Black Sea.

In late fourteenth-century eastern Anatolia and western Iran the Aq Qoyunlu and the Qara Qoyunlu Turcomans were at first confederations of small nomadic Turcoman groups, Kurdish clans, Arab tribesmen and refugees from Ottoman Turkish expansion. Each of these constituent peoples formed a distinct group within the Aq Qoyunlu and Qara Qoyunlu armies. In 1475 a Venetian ambassador also reported the presence of many Persian foot soldiers in one Aq Qoyunlu army. A year later, at the height of Aq Qoyunlu power, a review held in southern Iran was described in a document called the *Ard-Namah*. This text stated that there were three grades of troops: the *pushan-dar* who wore full armour, the *tirkash-band* horse-archers who formed the bulk of the army, and the *gullughchi* 'servants'. Precedence was, however, given to religious leaders and religiously motivated volunteers who, like the ordinary soldiers, had their own flags, banners and drums.

The numerous camp followers who accompanied Aq Qoyunlu armies were also described by Venetian visitors; one named Barbaro writing that the army had 6,000 tents; 20,000 cavalry horses of whom 2,000 were armoured; 42,000 assorted baggage animals, 25,000 horsemen, 3,000 infantry most being archers, 15,000 women and 11,000 children. The camp-followers included cobblers, smiths, saddlers, fletchers, assorted victuallers and apothecaries.

Despite the re-emergence of Islamic systems of recruitment, the military structures of the eastern Islamic world and Middle East had been deeply influenced by the Mongols. Yet this influence left plenty of scope for variation. For example, the nominally 'Mongol' Timur-i Lenk adopted classic Islamic principles by keeping the bulk of his forces under his own direct command in Transoxania and permitting only small units to his provincial governors. In contrast the armies of the avowedly Turkish Aq Qoyunlu and Qara Qoyunlu were organised along more Mongol lines, consisting of the ruler's own warband supported by those of his leading tribal vassals. Archaic Mongol military terms survived though the Mongol language itself had disappeared from most parts of the Islamic world. For example daytime guards were called *turghaq*, night guards being known as *kebte'ül*; and the heterogeneous clans who made up the Aq Qoyunlu Turcoman confederation were known as *boy*.

Despite the Mongols' astonishing military success, their influence upon Islamic strategic thinking was patchy. While the Karts consciously avoided excessive ruthlessness, relying on good intelligence sources and being primary concerned to control centres of trade, the Aq Qoyunlu sometimes resorted to Mongol ruthlessness, leaving dead captives along their route to demoralise pursuers. The Aq Qoyunlu were similarly willing to adopt new tactical ideas and weapons, soon recognising the need for modern firearms. An attempt was therefore made to obtain artillery from Venice in 1471, via the small Anatolian emirate of Karaman which similarly feared Ottoman expansion. According to Venetian records, guns and 'one hundred artillerymen of experience and capacity' were sent to the Aq Qoyunlu seven years later.

Timur-i Lenk and the Fragmentation of the Mongol 'World Empire'

Timur-i Lenk's army was supposedly built upon forty clans who claimed Mongol origin, though in reality Timur tried to break up the old Turco-Mongol tribal structure as a precaution against rebellion. The forty privileged clans nevertheless provided agreed contingents from which the ruler's personal guard regiments and larger regional forces were drawn. The latter could also be summoned by the ruler without reference to the local governor. Timur and his fifteenth-century successors habitually enlisted defeated enemy troops, despite Timur's advice to his descendants not to trust those who had not fought loyally for their previous leaders. Large numbers of Iranian-speaking troops and even a few Western Europeans clearly got caught up in Timur's devastating campaigns around the eastern Mediterranean and Black Sea. Further to the northeast, out of reach of Timur's ability to conquer (though not to raid), the Uzbek Turks were as yet still divided into many small and nomadic tribes which would only be welded into a unified and powerful fighting force in the the later fifteenth century.

In strategic, tactical and logistical terms, Timur-i-Lenk's armies combined the traditions of Mongol and Middle Eastern Islamic civilisations but it was Timur's massacres, on a scale which would have daunted even the ruthless Genghis Khan, that chroniclers most remembered. Cavalry dominated open battle, yet even here Timur's infantry had a role. When facing the Golden Horde leader Toqtamish deep in the forests of what is now eastern European Russia, Timur abandoned the normal battle plan of the period and instead divided his troops into seven divisions, with the centre and wings each having their own vanguard plus a strong reserve hidden behind the centre. This enabled Timur to drive off a Golden Horde force which broke through his left and then attacked it from the rear.

When fighting the Delhi Sultanate's army in northern India, Timur's troops secretly placed large spiked caltrops ahead of their position. Next day Timur's cavalry attacked through lanes left in this medieval 'mine-field' then retreated in apparent flight, pursued by the enemy's elephants. These great beasts then panicked when several of their number trod on the giant caltrops, fleeing back into their own ranks followed by terrified camels whose howdahs had been filled with some form of inflamable material by Timur's men. Elephants played a minor role in some later Timurid forces and, according to visiting Europeans, each elephant had a howdah on its back carrying four or five soldiers, plus the mahout. These fighting elephants attacked in a series of short forward rushes, sweeping upwards with their tusks while the men on their backs shot at the enemy.

The Later Mamluk Sultanate

Throughout these tumultuous centuries Egypt and Syria were ruled by the remarkably enduring Mamluk Sultanate. The fact that the Mamluk state remained so powerful and stable was testament to the long-established earlier-medieval Islamic military and bureaucratic traditions which it had inherited. During the fourteenth century there were, in fact, few changes to the military systems of those parts of the Islamic world which escaped Mongol conquest. These had evolved over a long period and continued to prove their worth. Nevertheless, most of the Islamic world was entering a period of conservatism that lasted almost until modern times.

The direct Mongol threat to the Mamluk Sultanate had been defeated in the late thirteenth and early fourteenth centuries, as was the threat posed by Timur-i Lenk in 1394-1401. Even so, internal rivalries were undermining the Sultanate, along with lax military training, disobedience and weakened loyalty. Although the Mamluk Sultanate had been amongst the first Islamic states to use gunpowder and cannon, firearms were not adopted in any numbers, hand-held guns being particularly resisted by *mamluk* cavalrymen who regarded them as dirty and degrading.

Significantly, many Turkish or Circassian women from the same linguistic groups as the *mamluks* themselves arrived in the wake of military recruits, either as slaves or free women and bringing with them some of Central Asia's traditions of sexual equality. The bonds of loyalty that kept the *mamluk* military class together were still based upon the *khushdash*, a group of men recruited, trained and released as members of a military élite who subsequently served together. On the other hand, the bonds of a *khushdash* were always based on mutual self-interest and agreements sealed with money. If the master or leader of a *khushdash* died or was disgraced, the members simply looked for a new leader and ambitious *amirs* had to keep in mind the aspirations of their followers if they wanted to retain their loyalty.

In terms of strategy, the later medieval Mamluk Sultanate largely continued that of the early Mamluk Sultanate and the Ayyubid rulers. The Crusaders were gone but the threat from the sea remained. Western European mariners and pirates now dominated the Mediterranean, so the Sultanate had to pay greater attention to the defence of a coastline which now stretched from Cilicia in the north, through Syria and Egypt towards Libya. Existing fortifications were strengthened and new ones built. For example, Sultan Bars-bay's early fifteenth-century fort at Burj al-Tina on the northern coast of Sinai was garrisoned by ten cavalrymen and fifteen infantrymen supported by local Bedouin auxiliaries. When Burj al-Tina was rebuilt by the penultimate Mamluk Sultan to counter Christian piracy and the Ottoman threat, it was given an unusual double-octagon plan, probably with guns mounted on both the inner and outer walls. A new threat to the Red Sea coast suddenly emerged at the start of the sixteenth century with the arrival of the Portuguese.

In general, fourteenth-century Mamluk military writers repeated what had been accepted practice since Abbasid times. However, such advice was so firmly based upon earlier traditions that it may not, in reality, have reflected current warfare. During the fourteenth century gunpowder artillery was used in several Mamluk citadels but only came into more widespread use after the Mamluks suffered a disastrous defeat at the hands of the Ottoman Turks in 1516. The following year the Sultan gathered all available artillery from Mamluk fortifications and assembled the few hand-gunners who had not already been sent against the Portuguese in the Red Sea. At Raydaniyah, outside Cairo, in 1517, the Mamluks constructed a strong defensive position with artillery in stone emplacements behind a ditch and a wooden palisade, hoping that the Ottoman Turks would break themselves against these field forti-fications. They also had about thirty ox-drawn waggons carrying light guns, as well as camel-riding handgunners. Nevertheless, the heavier Ottoman guns won the ensuing artillery duel and the Mamluks' position was outflanked. The following day, the Ottoman Sultan, Selim the Grim, entered Cairo and for the next four centuries Egypt and Syria formed part of the vast Ottoman Empire.

Military training in the Mamluk Sultanate had been very traditional, though it resulted in exceptionally high standards of skill. At least one mid-fourteenth century training manual included a cavalry exercise called 'playing the Frank' and appears to be based on the jousting so popular amongst the Western European knightly aristocracy. However, there were 129 other ways of handling the lance, plus twenty-one dis-engagement exercises or parries and thirteen unit manoeuvres in this training manual alone. Practice with the sword was almost as compli-cated, various sword-strokes being made against a target made from multiple layers of wet felt on a heap of wet clay. A few exercises even involved two swords, as in some Far Eastern martial arts, while other manuals dealt with the use of maces, javelins, large daggers, lassos and incendiary weapons.

The last forested areas of Egypt were cut down for agriculture during the Mamluk period, making Egypt even more dependent on imported timber for shipbuilding. Despite the fact that their Genoese allies provided a vital maritime link between the Mamluk Sultanate and the Mongol Golden Horde in southern Russia, which was the source of the slaves who replenished the Mamluks' own ranks, the Mamluks had a generally negative attitude towards the sea. Fleets were manned by low-grade troops and even the commanders of the main ports were local men rather than Mamluk officers. On the other hand, the Mamluks' distaste for the sea may have been exaggerated by chroniclers and the abundance of surviving information about naval matters suggests considerable interest amongst some senior men. One Mamluk fleet raised for an abortive attack on Cyprus included elite *nafata* fire-troops as well as religiously motivated volunteers who mostly came from Lebanon and Syria. In contrast, professional sailors and marines normally included North Africans, Turcomans and men from Upper Egypt, perhaps because the latter had experience of service on the Red Sea.

The most famous Mamluk book on naval tactics focussed on operation by small squadrons rather than large fleets, describing both compact and looser formations as well as the tactic of feigned flight, just as used on land. Though partially based on Byzantine naval treatises it updated traditional information for current conditions, for example discussing the new stern rudder. Mamluk texts dealing with fire-weapons indicate that the Mamluks used, or at least experimented with, advanced naval pyrotechnics which even included a rocket-powered torpedo described as an 'egg which moves itself and burns'.

The Survival of Mother Russia

The Golden Horde was the westernmost of the Mongol successor *khanates*, initially holding sway from the Altai mountains northwest of China, westwards to include most of the Russian principalities. During the second half of the fourteenth century the Russians achieved autonomy if not yet independence, and a Muscovite Russian victory over Khan Mamai at the Battle of Kulikovo Field in 1380 is widely regarded by Russians as marking their country's 'liberation from the Tatar yoke'. A few years later Timur-i Lank invaded the Golden Horde, winning a crushing victory at Kunduzcha, yet the Golden Horde was still able to crush attempts by some of its Russian vassals to rebel. It is also significant that the Russian princes generally remained loyal to the Golden Horde and many of their troops continued to serve in Mongol armies.

During the fifteenth century Russia grew steadily stronger while the Mongol Golden Horde declined and eventually fragmented; subordinate *khanates* appearing in the Crimea, along the Volga river and at Ryazan southeast of Moscow. The latter, known as the Khans of Qasimov, were now vassals of the Grand Prince of Moscow, inverting the long established power relationship between Mongols and Russians. In 1480, a stand-off across the Ugra River between a Russian army with large numbers of firearms and the army of Khan Ahmad of the Golden Horde ended with a Mongol retreat. This effectively removed the Mongol-Tatar 'yoke' and Russia became a fully independent state under Czar Ivan III Vasilievich. He and his successors won strong support amongst their *dvor*, courtiers or gentry, and the sons of the *boyar* provincial aristocracy, which enabled them to begin a process of Muscovite Russian expansion which only ended in the twentieth century.

Under Mongol Golden Horde rule, Russian military recruitment and organization changed significantly. During the later thirteenth and fourteenth centuries, Russian armies still consisted of professional *druzhinas* plus the *dvorjane* court and provincial élite. The latter provided the *bojarskye deti*, young aristocrat warriors led by older, more experienced noblemen, plus the *gorodskoe opolchenie* urban militias and mercenary units. Meanwhile, the Mongol tradition of demanding military service from the entire male population meant that the rural peasantry of Russia once again became involved in warfare and, as Mongol power declined, the Russian princes took over this right of general conscription. Similarly, the Cossacks of the later medieval period, whether serving in Russian or Polish-Lithuanian armies, originated in steppe regions which had formed a vital part of Golden Horde territory. They were of mixed ethnic and cultural origins but became some of the fiercest proponents of Russian Orthodox Christianity.

At first the rulers of the Orthodox Christian Russian principalities, including Novgorod in the far north, were under the watchful eyes of Mongol *bashaks*. These Mongol officials were stationed in the main cities to oversee the collection of taxes and the raising of militias, ensure the loyalty of Russian princes and to offer them military assistance where appropriate. The *bashaks* may also have had their own units of Mongol and Russian troops. While Russian princes often called upon Mongol aid during their own rivalries, princely *druzhinas* would take part in Mongol campaigns thousands of miles away. On major campaigns these thirteenth- and fourteenth-century Russian *druzhinas* were joined by the military aristocracy, the younger *boyars* and sometimes the urban militias, though the latter were now declining in importance. Meanwhile the *druzhinas* changed from being almost free associations of warriors into something similar to a Mongol ruler's *ordu*, with much stronger ties of loyalty to its prince. The term *druzhina* also fell from use to be replaced by *dvor*, meaning princely retinue, whose members were bound to their prince for life or for a fixed contractual term.

From the thirteenth to fifteenth centuries, warfare in Russia increasingly focussed upon the conquest and annexation of territory. As a result fortified centres rose in importance and approximately a third of campaigns involved attacks upon, or in defence of, towns. Different methods of defence also emerged, reflecting differing local circumstances. For example, along the northwestern and western frontiers, where the neighbouring Teutonic Knights and Lithuanians made considerable use of siege machines, there was a significant programme of fortification and of assembling stone-throwing siege engines. As defences of timber and earth became obsolete, many were replaced by stronger stone structures. New fortified towns were similarly established in strategically vulnerable regions. In the later fourteenth and early fifteenth centuries, firearms began to be used in attack as well as in the defence, though older forms of siege weaponry continued to be used alongside. Even so, Russian fortifications and siege techniques remained old-fashioned compared to those of Western Europe.

By the end of the fifteenth century the whole northern territory as far as the Arctic coast had been incorporated into an expanding Muscovy. Nevertheless, raids by neighbouring tribes made fortresses necessary even in this remote region, while fortified monasteries, small *ostrogs* and *pogosts*, or administrative outposts, provided defence in depth. One of the earliest examples was the northernmost *ostrog* at Kola, which had first been mentioned in the thirteenth century. Another feature of military architecture in northern Russia was that many fortresses with stone inner walls also had timber outer walls, one such being Novgorod itself. Russian expansion eastward towards Siberia really began during the fourteenth and fifteenth centuries and here small *ostrogs* were again built to defend newly- acquired territory. They and the comparable *sloboda*, fortified winter encampments, gradually increased in number, continuing to serve as military-administrative and trading centres well into the eighteenth century.

Changes in Russian tactics under Mongol domination indicated military influence from both east and west. In the later thirteenth and fourteenth centuries Russian cavalry, for example, increasingly adopted Turco-Mongol forms of weaponry including curved sabres, lamellar armour, helmets with face-covering mail aventails and light, round shields. Meanwhile some Russian infantry began using Western European forms of crossbow and operating in disciplined ranks while light infantry skirmishers continued to use lighter, supposedly 'oriental' composite bows.

A battle between Muscovite and Novgorodian armies in 1455 has been described as the last major Russian combat in which spear-armed cavalry played the leading role; the sabre thereafter becoming the primary cavalry weapon. Meanwhile Russian horse harness had changed with the adoption of lighter, taller Asiatic saddles, whips replacing spurs and shorter stirrup leathers enabling a rider not only to turn more easily in his saddle but also to use a bow.

Nevertheless, the most significant development in later-medieval Russian tactics was the adoption of firearms in the second half of the fifteenth century. Various types were recorded by the end of that century, including the *arquebus* which could be carried on a soldier's back, the *samopal* which was another kind of hand gun, and the *ruchnitsa* which was a form of long-barrelled musket. Such weapons were not yet very accurate but their fire caused panic amongst Mongol opponents who were not used to such weapons.

The Decline of the Golden Horde

The later medieval period may have been one of relative decline for the Mongol Golden Horde, yet it remained a very important military power even in the fifteenth century. Subordinate peoples who served in Golden Horde armies included Muslim Turkish Bashkirs from the Ural mountains and Christian Slav Ruthenians from the Carpathian mountains. Western European mercenaries were recruited from the mid-thirteenth century onwards, including crossbowmen and perhaps Genoese marines. Ossetian and Cherkess troops from the Caucasus had served in Mongol Golden Horde forces for a long time but the presence of Islamic militiamen from Golden Horde towns probably showed that Khan Mamai, the ruler of the Golden Horde, could no longer rely on adequate support from Turco-Mongol tribes.

The Golden Horde remained more traditional in both social and military organisation than did the fellow-Mongol but rival Il-Khanate of Iran and Iraq, even after largely converting to Islam. On the other hand it could be misleading to regard the Golden Horde simply as a tribal state. Instead four of five élite, 'ruling' clans or families dominated both the ordinary tribes and the conquered peoples.

Membership of these 'ruling clans' was remarkably fluid, kinship bonds being little more than nominal except within the ruling dynasty. This tribal aristocracy provided the administrative and military élite, including many of those *bashaks* who supervised non-Mongol rulers such as the princes of Russia. Furthermore the traditional Mongol 'four bey' or four senior governors system continued to exist, being known as the *qaraçi* system within the Golden Horde. It also remained in place within the lesser *khanates* which emerged, often out of the original *qaraçi*, following the fragmentation of the Golden Horde in the fifteenth century.

The *beylerbeyi*, overall army commander, was probably also the senior *qaraçi bey*, while the other *qaraçi beys* or *ulu beys* (frontier beys) probably commanded the flanks. Lesser officers were given the Arabic, Turkish and Persian titles of *amir*, *bey* or *mirza* depending on the regions which they governed. As Golden Horde power declined, so the *bashaks* who had been stationed inside the Russian principalities were withdrawn, to be replaced by *daruga* officials who, while still having basically the same tasks, were now based on the lower Volga River and only visited their regions of responsibility when necessary.

Chapter 4
The Later Crusades

The Completion of the Reconquista

Throughout the later thirteenth and fourteenth centuries the balance of power between the Iberian states remained largely unchanged; the last Islamic realm of Granada was now a vassal of Castile, while Aragon carved out an empire in Italy and Greece. The fifteenth century then saw the early stages of a Portuguese empire beyond the boundaries of Europe and ended with the discovery of America on behalf of the rulers of Castile and Aragon, just over nine months after the surrender of the remaining Andalusian Islamic bastion of Granada.

In North Africa the fall of the Muwahhidun in the mid-thirteenth century had been followed by another period of fragmentation before a new dynasty, the Marinids, rose to dominance though they were never as powerful as their Muwahhid or Murabitin antecedents, being unable to stop the Portuguese occupying parts of northern Morocco during the fifteenth century. This assault upon the African mainland then prompted the development of religious movements under the leadership of *shaykhs*, some of whom claimed descent from the Prophet Muhammad. The development was similarly linked to a revival of *sufi* Islamic mysticism and the building of *zawila* religious centres which served as centres of resistance to Christian invasion.

The final Spanish campaign against Granada drew men from all sections of society, being motivated by religious enthusiasm as well as the epic traditions of the so-called *Reconquista*. During the resulting war some Christian commanders consciously immitated the behaviour of heroes from the epic *El Cid*, but, for most men with a claim to noble status, fear of *Vergüenza* or 'shame' to one's family or lineage was enough to inspire courage and loyalty. Surprisingly perhaps, *Mudejars*, or Muslims living under Christian rule, also played a role, mostly as waggoners, muleteers, smiths, armourers or vetinary experts. Others were temporary 'allies' from amongst Granada's fractured political élite.

The majority of those who volunteered for this campaign seem to have been unemployed labourers and craftsmen whose enthusiasm cooled after months of getting no pay. There were also *homicianos*, criminals offered a pardon in return for military service. Meanwhile the bulk of the Castilian infantry were still recruited via the *Hermandad* system of urban militias. The *Hermandadas* of Toledo and Ciudad Real had also been the first to include *espingerderos*, hand-gunners, though guns rapidly spread to other cities during the 1480s.

The *Santa Hermandad* established in 1476 was a separate system which to some extent unified the older local *Hermandadas*, almost like a royal conscription in which all registered urban tax-payers either paid a contribution or served in the ranks. Additional infantry were recruited and organised by royal *continos* or agents from rural areas.

Perhaps the most unexpected members of the Castilian army during these years were Guanches, natives of the still not-completely-conquered Canary Islands, the majority apparently being slaves in the service of various noblemen. On the other hand some of these Guanches were clearly soldiers, including a certain Juan Doramas who was awarded a coat-of-arms for his efforts in the concluding siege of Granada city.

The armies of Aragon were different from those of Castile in several respects, knights normally having small fiefs and often paying taxes like other members of society. Aragonese urban militias felt no social or military inferiority to the knightly aristocracy and beyond the cities there was a form of rural militia called the *sometent*, though this maintained law and order rather than taking part in wars of conquest. A significant part of the Aragonese king's own forces included paid professional mercenaries, noble and non-noble, Christian and Muslim, plus troops from Sicily which had long been under Aragonese rule. The role of foreign volunteers was important in this campaign for religious and propaganda reasons, amongst the more distant being Lord Scales from England, who was a distant relative of Queen Isabella of Castile.

The organization of the Castilian armies changed considerably during the fifteenth century, though retaining many medieval features. The artillery seems to have been the only autonomous unit within what might be called the Royal Army and there was as yet no *Guardas Reales* or 'Royal Guard', this being created shortly after the fall of Granada. The bulk of the Royal Army nevertheless consisted of heavy cavalry men-at-arms, ten times as many light cavalry *jinetes* and assorted infantry. The feudal retinues of the higher Spanish nobility included the same sorts of troops, generally with a larger proportion of cavalry and lacking the artillery. The Iberian Crusading Military Orders of Santiago, Calatrava and Alcantara still provided well-trained and highly-motivated contingents, of whom the Knights of Santiago were considered the best.

The southern frontier facing Granada had a military organisation with the cities serving as base areas, while numerous fortresses guarded the border. Mobilisation and military reviews were taken very seriously, being held three times a year in Seville even in peacetime. One, drawn from the Seville area in 1406, listed 142 royal knights, 964 other men-at-arms, 1,276 crossbowmen and 3,720 halberdiers, plus 1,904 soldiers from neighbouring villages. Nevertheless, Spanish armies still seem to have been inferior to their Islamic Moorish foes in terms of adminis-tration, communication and, above all, medical support. Ferdinand and Isabella were aware of these limitations and in 1477 established a tribunal to find out how many qualified doctors and surgeons were available. The new-style European wars of the fifteenth century were hugely expensive and, although Castile had much greater resources than Granada, it was the southern provinces of Andalusia which served as the Castilian armies' main arsenal and granary. Castilian forces to the east, in Murcia, had far fewer resources.

The Spanish artillery already formed an élite and Queen Isabella recruited gunners from all over Spain, plus France, Germany and Italy. Some of the biggest guns had handling crews of two hundred men, though there were said to have been only four professional artillerymen in Castile-Aragon in 1479, rising to ninety-one over the next six years. Because the war for Granada proved so protracted and expensive, financial planning became vitally important. Money came from Papal gifts, enforced 'loans' from the *Hermandadas* as well as the Jewish and *Mudejar*-Islamic communities, plus smaller amounts stemming from the sale of property confiscated from those convicted of heresy by the Inquisition.

Although Islamic territory was now limited to the *amirate* of Granada, the traditional strategy of raiding and ravaging remained central to Christian Iberian warfare, still being dictated by the relatively few *puertos* or passes through the rugged Sierra mountains which surrounded Granada's heartland. In such circumstances both sides used early warning systems with fortified hilltop observation towers, particularly near the vulnerable passes. Fire or smoke beacons hopefully gave the inhabitants time to move themselves and their livestock out of harm's way while also summoning defensive forces to deal with smaller raids. One of the biggest problems faced by Castilian armies operating inside Granadan territory was feeding their own men. Not only had the local Islamic population usually fled, taking available food resources with them, but the Spaniards' tactics of devastation often led to a lack of avail-able food. Consequently convoys carried wheat to an army in the field so that it could bake bread, this then being sold to the soldiers at half its normal price.

In other respects siege warfare remained paramount, with fortifications vital as bases for attack and defence. Efforts to sow dissent within the enemy camp and to have an efficient intelligence network were considered standard practice. Raiding economic targets such as crops, orchards and mills was regarded as the best way to undermine an enemy's ability to resist while a field army also needed plenty of defensive crossbowmen in case the cavalry suffered a setback. On campaign Castilian forces were still divided into traditional *battallas*, or 'battles', for tactical purposes. In combat the heavily armoured Spanish man-at-arms usually seems to have fought individually, with his squire in close support, unlike the situation in France where heavy cavalry *lances* were tactical battlefield units. The light cavalry *lanzas a la jinete* may have been real tactical formations, Castilian *jinetes* having been assembled into squadrons in imitation of their Moorish foes since the late fourteenth century.

Later-medieval Spanish armies continued to place great emphasis on field fortifications, particularly when facing highly manoeuverable Moorish foes, and the Castilians used light anti-personel cannon to defend such field fortification during the war for Granada. The Spaniards were also skilled in using field fortifications to secure a bridgehead following a naval landing, this proving effective during their conquest of the Canary Islands. It would subsequently be brought to perfection when the *Conquistadores* invaded America.

In open battle late-medieval Spanish cavalry used several tactical formations, some of which reflected Arab-Islamic influence while others were a result of more recent Italian and French tactical ideas, particularly in Aragon. Consequently a *batalla* now often consisted of ten *cuadrilla*, or squadrons, each of around fifty men and led by a *cuadrillero*. Ideally five *batallas* of 500 men each were supposed to form a division, though in reality such divisions had no standard structure. During the conquest of Granada there was, however, a reduction in the number and importance of fully armoured cavalrymen and a corresponding increase in other arms, especially artillery. The disadvantage of this development was that surprise was now virtually impossible because huge numbers of labourers, defended by cavalry and infantry, had to be sent well ahead of an army to clear the roads and passes so that heavy artillery could get through.

The struggle for Granada also showed that heavy cavalry were rarely able to hit nimble Moorish light cavalry and infantry. Consequently light cavalry *a la jinete* increased in numbers and importance, despite the fact that many contemporary writers dismissed them as 'unarmed' or 'naked'. Other, perhaps more forward-looking, authors celebrated the use of a crossbow on horseback and other 'unknightly' methods of combat.

Lessons learned during the conquest of Granada would subsequently make Spanish infantry the first real gun-armed foot soldiers in European warfare. The tactics of these Iberian foot soldiers had much in common with those of fifteenth-century Italy, emphasizing the offensive use of light infantry including skirmishers operating out of strong field fortifications, often in close cooperation with their own cavalry. Their confidence when facing enemy horsemen was summed up in the early-sixteenth century Spanish saying: *'Muerto el caballo, perdito el hombre d'armas'* – 'When the horse is dead, the man-at-arms is lost'. Although the training of the Spanish knight was similar to that of his northern counterparts there were also distinctive Andalusian light cavalry *jinete* games called *juegos de cañas* with light spears or javelins. Other cavalry training included a form of mounted bullfight comparable to that still seen in southern Portugal.

There was no real naval warfare during the conquest of Granada but naval landings and the supplying of armies by sea play a major part. Here crossbowmen and archers were the decisive factor. Gunpowder artillery would not have much impact on galley warfare until the sixteenth century, though handgunners were significant in defence of merchant ships. Galleys rowed so close together that they almost collided and ships involved in naval landings tried to reach the shore at the same time. Once they were close inshore the oarsmen backed water and turned their vessels around in order to beach stern first. Trumpets recalled shore raiders to their ships and a withdrawal in the face of the enemy was a dangerous moment. Consequently planks were placed between the galleys so men could clamber aboard any vessel before crossing to their own.

The Last Armies of al-Andalus

Differences between the armies of Islamic al-Andalus and those of Islamic northwestern Africa had been considerable since at least the tenth century and during the later-medieval period the armies of Granada continued to differ from those of Morocco. The Nasrid ruling dynasty of Granada sprang from a family of Andalusian frontier soldiers and local troops continued to dominate the Granadan army until the fall of the *amirate* in 1492, the majority being recruited in a traditional manner through the *Diwan al-Jaysh*, or Army Ministry. In addition there were always Berber *ghuzat*) (singular *ghazi*), volunteer 'fighters for the faith', from North Africa who came to take part in the lesser or military *jihad* in defence of this last Islamic state in the Iberian peninsula. So many originated from the Zanata tribe that they gave their name to light cavalry warfare *'a la jinete'* – 'in Zanata style'.

Part of the local Granada militia known as the *jundi mutadawwan* served in return for regular salaries, but it is unclear how effective these troops were by the late fifteenth century. A more obviously military élite was the ruling *Amir*'s guard of *mamluks*, also known as *ma'lughun*. Recruited from young Christian prisoners converted to Islam and trained in the Alhambra palace in Granada, they remained few in number and were regarded as *renegados* or traitors by the Christian Spaniards. They were also noted for strict discipline and military training. These men could also expect their own sons to reach senior military positions, unlike the situation in the Mamluk Sultanate of Egypt where only first-generation *mamluks* could progress within the military structure.

Ordinary local or regional militia came from cities, towns and the countryside, the high Alpujarra valleys southeast of Granada being noted for their infantry crossbowmen. Other frontier forces had different specialist skills. These *thagri* 'frontiersmen' formed a distinct military group with their own leaders, officials dealing with central government, and included *dalil* 'guides', known to the Spanish as *adalides*.

The motivation of Granada's military personnel was a mixture of traditional religious commitment and a code of personal honour comparable to the concept of 'chivalry' seen on the Spanish side. Both sides' armies employed recognised champions who sometimes fought duels before the start of a battle. Granadan armies were traditionally accompanied by *sufi* Islamic mystics who inhabited frontier *ribats* and took part in frontier raids, but as the final crisis loomed so religious motivation grew even stronger. In fact during the last battles for Granada, Spanish chroniclers stated that their Moorish enemies no longer fought for booty or ransoms but only to kill or wound their enemies, seemingly caring nothing for their own lives.

While North African *ghazi* volunteers included those who only came to Granada for one campaign as well as those who settled in the *amirate* and dedicated their lives to *jihad*, Granadan troops continued to serve in various Moroccan garrisons. During the fifteenth century such crossbowmen defended Tangier and Qasr al-Saghir against the Portuguese, being welcome because North African armies were still largely based upon tribal contingents consisting almost entirely of light cavalry.

The size of Granada's army varied according to the wealth of the *amirate* at any given time, as well as its political circumstances, and Moorish troops were almost invariably outnumbered by their Spanish foes. The local Andalusian part of the Granadan army was commanded by a senior officer known as the *wali* who was often a close relative of the ruling *amir*. Similarly the North African volunteer *ghuzzat* were commanded by their own *shaykh* who was usually related either to the *amir* of Granada or the *sultan* of Fez in Morocco. The professional core of the army largely consisted of cavalry based in various fortresses, the largest of these being under the ruler's direct control in Granada city.

Here there were also barracks, armouries and stables under the *Qayid al-rawi*.

Comparable, though smaller, facilities existed in other cities, there being thirty military regions, thirteen having large fortresses. In addition the many lesser castles were often linked militarily and administratively with one of the main bases, some being supported financially by the rents of mills, shops and kilns in these cities.

Fortifications were sited to provide defence in depth against the frequent Spanish raids, with larger fortresses being in close communication with smaller castles and observation towers. Enemy raiders could be harrassed from such castles while the fortresses served as bases for counter-raids. Castles not located on the main invasion routes tended to be associated with villages in the *vegas*, fertile or irrigated regions around the main centres of population. The more fertile parts of the *amirate* also had many fortified hilltop enclosures where local inhabitants, their livestock and moveable possessions could find refuge.

The Amirate of Granada was, in fact, strongly fortified with many of the major structures being greatly strengthened during the fourteenth and fifteenth centuries. Most of the cities had also grown considerably because of the influx of Muslim refugees from regions conquered by the Christians. Some, like the Albaicin quarter on the northern side of Granada city, were now enclosed by concrete ramparts strengthened by rectangular towers. Many also had *al-barrani*, external towers attached to their main walls, which had been a feature of late-medieval Andalusian military architecture, the Alcazaba fortress overlooking Granada city being given three massive semi-circular artillery bastions in the late fifteenth century. Elsewhere, the fortifications of the Amirate of Granada continued to rely on the height and strength of their increasingy old-fashioned walls though some also had a *suluqiya*, a lower secondary exterior wall.

Light anti-personnel cannon had been used very effectively in the defence of Antequera in 1410 but from the mid-fifteenth century onwards it seems that virtually all Granadan firearms were captured from the Christians rather than being made by the Muslims themselves. Nevertheless, the armies of Granada used handguns, light anti-personnel artillery and even a few larger cannon in the final war against the combined Castilian-Aragonese armies, many reportedly being operated by *renegados*.

On those few occasions when Granadan forces were obliged to confront the Spaniards in open battle, their tactics remained traditional. Infantry adopted as strong a defensive position as possible, while the cavalry mounted repeated but limited charges to wear down and hopefully break the enemy. According to Don Juan Manuel, writing in the fourteenth century, Moorish horsemen were exceptionally hardy, enduring long marches with little food, and fighting with javelins and swords. They charged with a great deal of noise and made multiple attacks, sometimes with feigned flight to lure the enemy into ill-advised pursuit. If this failed to break the Christian ranks, the Moors would then attack *en masse*. These tactics were still seen at the Battle of Higueruela in 1431. On this occasion the Spaniard raiders did not go home with their loot, but instead threatened the orchards close to Granada city. The Granadan army drew up in an irrigated area of small fields, hoping to lure the enemy into a frontal attack in an area unsuitable for Spanish heavy cavalry. When this failed, the Granadans were obliged to block the Spanish advance in less advantagous terrain where the Moorish infantry formed traditional ranks supported by light cavalry. This time the Spanish heavy cavalry did attack, breaking the Moorish infantry which had to seek refuge in fortified farmsteads, castles and the city of Granada.

Moorish cavalry tactics were based upon those developed over many centuries in the Middle East, though in Granada and North Africa javelins were used instead of bows. Granadan cavalry did use crossbows on horseback during the fourteenth and fifteenth centuries, though these remained more important as infantry weapons. Advice on the use and maintainance of crossbows could, in fact, be obtained in certain mosques while military exercises using blunted javelins on horseback developed into something of a spectator sport.

Having lost control of the sea, the Amirate of Granada's interest in naval warfare focussed on defence of its exposed coastline. In most places this was backed by rugged mountains which almost isolated the fertile coastal enclaves from the interior towns. Consequently it was defended by large, permanently garrisoned *alcazabas* or fortresses at Malaga and Almeria, plus smaller castles and a host of watchtowers. This system was so effective that, despite their domination of the seas, the Spaniards only won control of Granada's coastline by invading from the landward side.

The End of Byzantium

The final decline of the Byzantine Empire of Constantinople began in the later thirteenth century. Nemesis would eventually come in the form of the Ottoman Turkish Sultanate, but the Byzantines also faced a deadly rival on their western frontier where a rapidly expanding Serbian state seemed to promise a new Orthodox Christian empire. However, this proved fragile and soon fell under Ottoman rule. The sudden eruption of the Ottoman Turks into the Balkans stimulated a series of Later Crusades. Here the increasingly isolated Crusader States in Greece endured until they too fell before the Ottoman onslaught, leaving only the Crusading Military Order of the Hospitallers on Rhodes and the colonial outposts maintained by Venice and Genoa, some of which survived long after the end of the medieval period. Meanwhile the only Middle Eastern Crusader State to survive was the Kingdom of Cyprus. The Kingdom of Cilician Armenia also endured for a remarkable time but became increasingly vulnerable to Turcoman raids from central Anatolia and Mamluk pressure form Syria.

Mid-fourteenth-century Byzantine forces still included a remarkable variety of linguistic groups from Europe, the Balkans, Turkish Anatolia and the steppes. The increasing importance of Turks went beyond the army, the general population of the lowland regions of the southeastern Balkans soon including many people of Turkish origin though now of Orthodox Christian faith. Amongst Greek-speaking troops, the best were infantry archers from Paphlagonia in Anatolia while Macedonian soldiers from the Balkans were less regarded. Cretan and other refugees from Venetian-occupied parts of the Aegean were similarly settled in Anatolia in a vain attempt to restore the old system of frontier *akritoi* warriors.

Following the Byzantine reconquest of much of southern Greece, the Despots of this area recruited almost as widely; Albanians played a particularly important role. Many of these troops were subsequently moved to defend Constantinople, which the Emperor regained in 1260, though the most numerous forces defending fourteenth-century Constantinople were the *mesoi*, or middle class, who probably formed an urban militia.

Part of the now largely-Islamic Ghuzz Turkish people had fled from the Mongols, from the steppes into the Danube Delta region where they converted to Christianity. Some Muslim Saljuq Turks similarly fled from the Mongol invasion of Anatolia, crossing the Black Sea to settle in the Byzantine-ruled part of the Crimean peninsula where they too became Christian. The Byzantine term *tourkapouli*, 'sons of Turks', probably distinguished these Christianised resident Turks from other Islamic Turkish mercenaries, while the *Mourtatoi* were now an infantry guard unit recruited from converted prisoners and renegades.

The Iasians were pagans or heterodox Christians originally from the northern Caucasus who had been allied to the Kipchaq Turks. Following the Mongol assault the Iasians, too, migrated, some being recruited by Hungary. The Alan tribes who suddenly appeared on Byzantium's north-western frontier at the start of the fourteenth century were probably another part of the same group, large numbers then serving in the Byzantine army. Numerous Western European mercenaries similarly became available in the late thirteenth and early fourteenth centuries as a result of the fall of the Crusader States in the Middle East, many ex-Crusader troops plus Catalan and Italian sailors and marines, then appearing in Byzantine service.

The soldiers who accompanied the Emperor John VIII to Italy in 1437 included armoured *stradiotti* light cavalry and even more-lightly equipped *gianitzaroi*. Powerful Byzantine noblemen also had military followings and those Byzantine soldiers who were *pronoia* fief-holders still formed a local élite. Many of them were of non-Greek origin including Slavs, Albanians and descendants of Latin Crusader or Italian colonial settlers. During the final siege of Constantinople in 1453 a list of defenders drawn up for the Emperor gave a total of 4,973 Greeks, both professional soldiers and militiamen, plus 200 permanently resident foreigners. Giacomo Tedaldi was also present during the siege and subsequently wrote a report for the Cardinal of Avignon that reported: 'In the city there were altogether 30,000 to 35,000 men under arms and six to seven thousand real soldiers'.

In terms of military organisation, little changed after the Palaeolog emperors regained Constantinople. By this date Byzantine military titles may have reflected status rather than military function, though the *Megas Adnoumiastes* was still in charge of training and military equipment. The commander of the Varangian Guard still had a Grand Interpreter to help him, suggesting that he or some of his men might still have been of English origin. Though the *pronoia* cavalry now formed a local aristocracy, they were not a provincial force because they were still registered as part of the central imperial army. During the late fourteenth century they were organized into *allagia* or larger *megalla allagia* regiments which appear to have served both as tactical and administrative formations. The term *allagia* was similarly applied to infantry and lower-grade frontier forces.

Though the Byzantine Empire was shrinking at an alarming rate it still had provincial forces under some degree of central command, though the title of *Dux* gave way to that of *Kephale* or 'head' of provincial civil and military administration in the late thirteenth century. Meanwhile the separate army of the Byzantine Despotate of the Morea in southern Greece seems to have consisted of troops in the Despot's immediate entourage plus those of senior vassals. The cavalry were divided into *allagia* regiments, the foreign mercenaries having their own commanders while the tribal Albanian or Slav auxiliaries were under their own chiefs.

The Anatolian border between the Byzantine Empire and various Turkish *beyliks* now consisted of a wide no-man's-land with Christian *akritoi* frontier warriors on one side and Islamic *ghuzat* on the other. Elsewhere Greek crossbowmen sometimes organised themselves into 'brotherhoods' similar to the rival Islamic military-religious associations. In the countryside Orthodox monasteries hired paramilitary guards, particularly if they were in exposed regions.

Even after the Byzantines regained Constantinople from the Crusader Latin 'Empire of Romania' their Emperors were fearful of further

Western European invasions and so concentrated the larger part of their forces in the Balkans, thus further weakening the eastern frontier. At the same time, in Albania the success of light cavalry and infantry archers against Western European heavy cavalry from southern Italian suggests that the Byzantine army was not as enfeebled as sometimes thought. A similar strategy was used successfully against the Crusader States in southern Greece. Byzantine tactics now reflected a variety of influences, most notably Western European and Turkish. For example, during a battle in 1345 some of the Byzantines' perhaps-armoured cavalry were placed on the defensive left wing, with allied Turkish horse-archers on the offensive right wing, while the best cavalry and infantry were placed in the centre.

By the fourteenth century Byzantine armies were usually small, which would fit the Italian-educated Byzantine prince Theodore Paleaologus' assertion that if a force was caught by surprise it should not waste time trying to form divisions but should gather into one large formation. Other interesting oberservations made by Theodore were that natural obstacles such as rivers and passes should be defended from a slight distance, rather than too close, and that some of the enemy should be permitted to cross such obstacles before being attacked, presumably before they had time to reform.

By the time of the final siege of Constantinople in 1453 the defenders of that city clearly had firearms, though these weapons were smaller than the Ottoman Turks' 'great guns'. The massive land walls of Constantinople had also been improved but their layout remained essentially the same except that a low wall or breastwork had been built along the inside of the moat in 1341. This seems to have been updated shortly before the final siege. One of Constantinople's main assets was, however, its size. The walls enclosed so much open space that the city's now-reduced population could grow much of its own food. There was even space to graze animals, while abundant fish could be caught in the waters outside.

During the twelfth century there had been an emphasis on Western European cavalry skills, though new recruits still played the eastern cavalry training game of *tzykanion* or polo. A Western European form of tournament was held in Byzantine territory in 1332, but for the rest of the fourteenth and fifteenth centuries cavalry training was increasingly Turkish or Islamic in style. On the other hand the cavalry training and 'games' witnessed by the Burgundian squire Bertrandon de la Broquière in the 1430s were remarkably similar to those of light cavalry *a la jineta* in the Iberian peninsula.

The last real Byzantine fleet had been crewed by men from both Byzantine and Crusader-ruled southern Greece, plus Russian, Spanish,

Catalan and Italian mercenaries. Early in the fourteenth century, however, the remnants of the Byzantine navy were disbanded, the majority of the crews transferring their allegiance to the Turkish *beyliks* of the Aegean coast. Perhaps as a result the Byzantines had to rebuild a small fleet at Gallipoli to stop the Turks from crossing into Europe. In this they failed and the lack of a proper navy would be a fatal handicap for the last defenders of Constantinople.

The only remaining Byzantine territory in Asia, apart from the little port of Sile which fell to the Turks in 1396, was the 'Empire of Trebizond' where a branch of the Comnenid imperial family seized power with help from the neighbouring Christian kingdom of Georgia following the Fourth Crusade. Hidden behind the densely forested Pontine mountains, a sub-tropical coastal strip was defended by fierce mountain folk armed with composite bows and crossbows. However, the only 'empire' that Trebizond controlled was an even more isolated Byzantine province in the Crimea on the northern side of the Black Sea. Even this was lost to Genoa after 1265, though Trebizond itself survived until conquered by the Ottomans eight years after the Great City of Constantinople had fallen.

During its two and a half centuries of independence the Comnenid 'Empire of Trebizond' could recruit from those of the Byzantine military aristocracy who fled those areas which fell to the Fourth Crusade or the advancing Turks. While such Greek *stradiotti* may have dominated the army of Trebizond, the bulk of the local population were warlike Laz and Tzan tribesmen, closely related to the neighbouring Georgians and Iberians who also fought as allies or volunteers for the Comnenid rulers.

Byzantine naval power faced fewer challenges in the Black Sea than in the Aegean or Mediterranean. The navy of thirteenth-century Trebizond remained a small but for many years an effective force under a Grand Admiral who, unlike the similarly entitled officer in Byzantine Constantinople, continued to have a fleet of large *katerga* galleys well into the fifteenth century. The Emperors of Trebizond also made great efforts to stop the Anatolian Turks reaching the coast. Once they did, however, they found rich pickings along the trade route linking Trebizond with the Crimea.

Meanwhile the cavalry of Georgia and Cilician Armenia were both increasingly influenced by those of neighbouring Turco-Islamic regions. The little that is known about Armenian military training in the thirteenth and fourteenth centuries suggests that it had more in common with the *furusiyah* exercises in the neighbouring Mamluk Sultanate than with cavalry training in Europe. In fact, warlike 'games' involving teams armed with maces featured prominently in the late medieval Armenian epic of *David of Sassoun*.

The Christian Balkan States

The military systems of the Balkan Christians developed along different lines. Bulgaria had lost territory to both Hungary and the Byzantine Empire in the later thirteenth century, the authority of the ruler was weakened and divisions between a common people, who were influenced by Bogomil (Dualist) religious teaching, and a military aristocracy maintained by conscripted labour widened. For several decades much of Bulgaria also had to accept Mongol overlordship and, although the Bulgarian army was helped by Mongol, Alan, and Wallachian allies, it was defeated by the Serbs at the Battle of Kyustendil in 1330. Macedonia was lost, most of the Black Sea coast returned to Byzantium and the rest of Bulgaria was split into three principalities. One of these, Dobrudja in the northeast, built a Black Sea fleet which challenged the Genoese and even intervened in the affairs of the Byzantine 'Empire' of Trebizond. When the Ottomans invaded in the 1360s, some areas were immediately annexed while others accepted Ottoman suzerainty until persistent revolts led the Ottoman Sultan to impose direct rule over Vidin, the last autonomous Bulgarian principality, in 1396.

Serbia's rise to local domination started in the late thirteenth century when increasing wealth from mining enabled the country's rulers to recruit mercenaries and import modern military equipment from Western Europe. The core of the Serbian army still consisted of horse-archers equipped in essentially Byzantine or Mongol style while the crossbow became the most important Serbian infantry weapon during the fourteenth century.

Since its foundation, the Serbian kingdom had looked south to the Byzantine Empire as the source of its Orthodox Christian civilisation and later as an arena for expansion. The victory over Bulgaria at Kyustendil highlighted interesting differences between Bulgaria, which was under powerful Eastern military influence, and the Serbian army which reportedly included some 1,000 Spanish mercenaries, perhaps actually Catalan veterans of Byzantine service. Serbian expansion continued under Stephan Dusan who eventually proclaimed himself 'Emperor of the Serbs and Greeks', to which he later added 'Bulgarians and Albanians'.

In its final form, Stephan Dusan's imperial army was built upon the existing Byzantine military administration. The levy of peasants was rarely used and although Dusan disbanded the Vlach cavalry of Thessaly he did recruit Albanians and Greeks as well as Serbian feudal forces. Nevertheless, the increasing Westernisation of the local military aristocracy deepened the gulf between nobility and commoners, weakening Serbia as it faced a new challenge from the expanding Ottoman Sultanate.

Most Serbian fortifications had been of timber and earth, though a few stone structures existed in the ex-Byzantine south and on the Adriatic coast where Serbia had won a small outlet to the sea. By the end of the fourteenth century, Serbia was dotted with stone fortresses and fortified monasteries, but, they were still built in the old Byzantine style with high walls and rectangular towers rarely capable of resisting cannon; this despite the fact that gunpowder artillery became increasingly common in late fourteenth- and fifteenth-century Serbia. Cannon were, in fact, soon being made in Serbia, though it was the Turks who benefitted most; gunners from the now-vassal state of Serbia fighting for the Ottoman Sultan in Anatolia in 1390 and 1402.

Bosnia, to the east of Serbia, emerged from tenuous Byzantine domination late in the twelfth century when the local *zupe* chieftains accepted the leadership of a regional *ban*. Lower, or northern, Bosnia soon consisted of two Hungarian duchies serving as outposts against Serbia while Upper, or southern, Bosnia generally retained an anarchic independence. Militarily the Bosnians were similar to the neighbouring Serbs, their light cavalry using kite-shaped shields which, by the mid-fourteenth century, evolved into the distinctive *scutum bosniensem*. Another characteristic of this area was the Bogomil Dualist heresy which survived persecution and Crusader attack from Hungary but disappeared with the coming of the Ottoman Turks. Most Bogomils apparently converted to Islam, a faith which shared their egalitarian outlook. Meanwhile, Bosnian light cavalry continued to serve under a Turkish banner and became the most effective raiders along the still-expanding Ottoman Balkan frontier.

Throughout the Middle Ages the Albanians were divided into numerous mountain tribes or clans, some being Catholic Arbanites while others were Orthodox Epirots. A limited degree of independence followed an Angevin invasion from southern Italy in the later thirteenth century which established a local sub-kingdom, but the Angevins rarely controlled more than the narrow coastal strip and local lords were taking over from Italian governors even before a general anti-Angevin revolt.

The Italian Angevins returned in strength in 1304 but this time they allowed greater autonomy to the Albanian leaders. Cities developed along Italian communal lines while most of the mountain people remained semi-nomadic, thousands then migrating south into Greece when famine struck in the fourteenth century. There the Albanian newcomers competed with the existing semi-nomadic Vlachs for grazing land while Greek-speakers were forced to the coasts where their fighting men sought service as mercenaries for anyone able to pay.

An independent Albanian enclave north of Naupactos (Lepanto) in Greece survived well into the fifteenth century, by which time Albanian resistance to the Ottoman conquerors had become an inspiration for a

Christian world reeling before the Turkish onslaught. From 1443 to 1468 this defiance was led by George Kastriotes. He had been educated at the Ottoman Court where he had converted to Islam and took the name Iskander or Alexander. Iskander Beg, better known as Skanderbeg, later reverted to Christianity but, from his base at Kroia in northern Albania, Skanderbeg attacked his Venetian neighours almost as often as he did his Ottoman overlords. After his death in 1468 Albania fell firmly under Ottoman control, a majority of its population eventually converting to Islam.

During the early Middle Ages the Romanian-speaking Vlachs were a semi-nomadic tribal people who built temporary villages and spent part of their year in the high pastures of various upland regions, most notably the Carpathian Mountains. The history of those Vlachs who inhabited the western slopes in Transylvania was linked to that of Hungary, but those of the eastern and southern slopes largely remained beyond direct Hungarian rule. Many years would pass before the first independent Vlach, or Wallachian, principality emerged where the river Olt bursts through the Carpathians. The origins of this Oltenia are obscure, but it was probably founded when members of the Orthodox Vlach warrior aristocracy of Transylvania moved into this region to escape Catholic Hungarian pressure in the thirteenth century. Here they joined the local Vlachs, nomadic Turks and Mongols, Saxons of German descent, and Hungarian *székels*, while the military styles of Oltenia clearly reflected Mongol influence.

By the late fourteenth century the Ottoman Turks were nearing the frontiers of Wallachia and Mircea the Old, whom the Turks called 'the most courageous and shrewd among the Christian Princes', defeated Ottoman raiders no less than four times. He was, however, then caught up in the catastrophic defeat of a massive Crusading army at the Battle of Nicopolis and, in 1417, Wallachia had to accept Ottoman overlordship. Of the many Wallachian princes who seized power during the fifteenth century, one, Vlad Tepes, known as 'the Impaler', stands out for a variety of reasons. Legendary for his sadistic cruelty as well as his determination as a military leader, Vlad Tepes entered legend as Dracula. Partly because of the efforts of rulers like Vlad, Wallachia survived as a separate Christian entity, never being wholly swallowed by the Ottoman Turks.

North of Wallachia, the plains and hills between the Carpathian Mountains and the River Dnistr had sometimes been under the political influence of Kievan Russia or its southwestern principalities. Here the plains were largely dominated by semi-nomadic Turkish peoples such as the Pechenegs and Kipchaqs, while Slavs inhabited some of the northern foothills and Vlach *voivodates* gradually developed under Hungarian suzereinty in the high valleys. The Vlach principality which emerged in this area as the Mongol 'World Empire' fragmented and the Golden Horde *khanate* declined would be under stronger military influence from the steppe than was Wallachia. When the Black Death undermined Mongol power, Moldavian feudal lords helped by Hungarian *székels* seized the foothills, later pushing into the plains towards towns which had developed under Mongol rule. The main local Mongol base had, in fact, been on the coast at 'White Castle' – 'Aq-Kerman' in Turkish, 'Cetatea Alba' in Rumanian and now 'Bilhorod Dnistrovskyi' in Ukrainian.

An event shrouded in Moldavian patriotic legend was the *descalecat* in 1359, when the Transylvanian *voivode*, Dragos of Maramures, supposedly led his followers over the Carpathians to establish the first Principality of Moldavia. The reality is less straightforward, and although Dragos did become the Hungarian *voivode* of Moldavia around this time, he did so while bringing a rebellious region back under Hungarian control. In the late fourteenth century Moldavia won access to the Black Sea and the river Danube, giving it control of one of Europe's richest trade routes. Throughout the fifteenth century, Hussites and Orthodox Vlachs continued to flee to Moldavia from Hungarian Transylvania, having considerable impact upon its military development.

The most famous of the princes of Moldavia was Stephan the Great (1457-1504) who led resistance to the Ottoman Turks but saw Catholic Poland as a greater threat and eventually accepted Turkish overlordship. The remarkably successful armies of fifteenth-century Moldavia were organised along similar lines to those of Wallachia. Permanent forces had appeared in the late fourteenth or early fifteenth century, as they had in Wallachia, but these were organised like the earlier *dorobanti* feudal formations and levies under local *boyar* noblemen. Meanwhile there were references to foreign mercenaries and new types of militia. Any permanent units now formed part of the *Oastea* whose name, stemming from the Western European term 'host', probably reflected Hungarian influence. The aristocracy, as provincial governors or *voivodes*, also raised a general levy when required; this being known as the *Oastea cel Mare* or 'Great Army'.

In the later fifteenth century, Stefan cel Mare of Moldavia recruited cavalry from outside the traditional class of noble *boyars* and put considerable effort into training the foot soldiers who still formed two-thirds of most Romanian armies. In this Stefan had learned both from his western neighbours, where Hussite infantry had upset the traditional military systems of central Europe, and from his Ottoman foes with their famous *Janissary* infantry. Even so, Moldavian and Wallachian foot soldiers proved more effective in the forested slopes of the Carpathian Mountains than in the neighbouring lowlands.

The Crusader States in Greece faced similar problems to the Balkan states and reacted to them in a variety of ways. For example, the Catalan mercenary army which dominated much of the Aegean region during the fourteenth century often had remarkably good relations with the Islamic states. This was probably a consequence of their own cultural background in the Iberian peninsula. Meanwhile the Italian élite which now dominated most of Latin Greece was essentially mercantile rather than feudal, living in the coastal towns and using its rents and taxes to hire mercenaries, feudal service gradually being replaced by an *adoha* tax with which to pay such professional soldiers.

The Military Orders played less of a role on the mainland of Crusader Greece than they had in Syria and Palestine, while a serious shortage of military manpower in the Greek Crusader States led to a gradual integration of existing ex-Byzantine *archontes* into their military structure. In Achaia, during the later thirteenth and fourteenth centuries, many such *archontes* became Latinized in culture though not in religion, in feudal and military terms ranking alongside non-noble sergeants and squires. From the mid-fourteenth century onwards indigenous Greek crossbowmen were enlisted to defend the Aegean islands while the *gasmouli* of mixed Latin and Greek parentage were highly regarded as marines.

The Catalan Grand Company which conquered Crusader Athens organised itself and its territories like an autonomous military corporation under a civil *vicar general* and a military *marshal*. When Catalan Athens subsequently accepted the distant suzereinty of the Aragonese Spanish rulers of southern Italy these two governing officials were imposed from outside, though the marshal was always selected from the ranks of the Catalan Grand Company. The tactics used by Latin forces in Crusader Greece mirrored those of the countries from which they had come; the French and Burgundians operating as their cousins back in France would do, and the Catalans continuing to use the tactics which served so well in the Iberian peninsula and Sicily. In naval warfare, attempts to resist a landing on the beach were rare but not unknown. During the Crusader assault upon Izmir in 1344 AD, for example, the defending Turkish cavalry rode into the shallows to fight the Crusaders as they emerged from their ships.

The Rise of the Ottoman Turks

Militarily, one of the most significant periods in the history of Anatolia and the Aegean region was the later thirteenth and early fourteenth century, which saw the collapse of the Saljuq Sultanate of Rum, the emergence of numerous small Turkish states known as *beyliks*, and the rise to domination of one – namely the Ottoman Turks. There seem

be no references to Western European mercenaries in Saljuq Rum
following the Mongol conquest. Instead the armies of the small *beyliks*
largely relied upon tribal Turcoman cavalry and infantry. Once some of
these states broke through to the Mediterranean, Aegean and Black Sea
coasts they developed small raiding fleets which not only attacked the
neighbouring islands but also the Balkan mainland. As Byzantine
authority collapsed, much of the remaining Byzantine military establishment transfered its allegiance to these *beyliks*, most converting to Islam
though some retained their Christian faith.

Many of the *ghuzat*, or 'fighters for the Faith', who typified this period
formed *futuwa* religious brotherhoods linked to urban militias or guilds
and characterised by an egalitarian spirit. Some of their elaborate
initiation ceremonies were similar to those of the Crusading Military
Orders. Some of the fleets of those coastal *beyliks* were an extraordinary
amalgamation of Muslim *ghuzat*, Orthodox Christian Greek sailors and
Western European pirates. They proved so effective that by the 1330s
the inhabitants of some islands close to the Anatolian coast were recognised as *illik kafirleri*, 'infidel frontiersmen' who payed tribute to the
neighbouring Turkish *beylik*.

The rapidly increasing power of the Ottoman *beylik*, which later rose
to become an *amirate* and finally a *sultanate*, was built upon military
systems that proved to be extraordinarily adaptable. A remarkable degree
of religious toleration also characterised the Ottoman state from the very
start. Indeed, for various largely-financial and political reasons the
Ottomans almost discouraged conversion to Islam while welcoming military support from their expanding subject population, both Muslim and
Christian.

Nevertheless, the earliest Ottoman armies were largely traditional,
consisting of a majority of Turcoman tribal cavalry, a tiny élite of *ghulams*
recruited from slaves or prisoners, and some ill-trained, if enthusiastic,
infantry. The early *ghuzat* may later have evolved into the light cavalry
akinji 'raiders' and *deli* 'enthusiasts' of the Balkan frontier, though many
of these fearsome warriors appear to have been recent converts from the
previous Christian indigenous military aristocracies.

Ottoman rulers then broke with tradition, or perhaps more accurately
modified it, to establish a dramatically new form of Islamic army – one
that would eventually march to the gates of Vienna. The first of these new
forces were *müsellem* cavalry recruited from both Islamic and Christian
mercenaries supported by fiefs. The first properly trained Ottoman
infantry were the *yaya* or *payadeh* recruited from free Muslim and
Christian peasants who formed a territorial defence force in return for
cash grants, tax exemptions or plots of land and fought alongside short
term volunteers known as *azabs*.

The most famous Ottoman military formation was, of course, the Janissaries or *Yeni Çeri, New Army'*. The earliest *Yeni Çeri* were apparently drawn from the Sultan's one-fifth share of prisoners-of-war during the reign of Murat I. Like later *Yeni Çeri* recruits they are said to have been sent to work for farming families in Anatolia to learn Turkish and the basics of the Islamic faith before returning to the Sultan's court. At that point they were given their distinctive tall white cap and were enrolled into the *Yeni Çeri* corps. Though the *Yeni Çeri* were within a long-established Islamic tradition of slave-recruited military élites, they soon differed by being recruited from 'enslaved' members of the Ottoman Sultan's own non-Islamic population which was strictly contrary to Islamic religious law. This considered a Muslim rulers' non-Islamic subjects to be *dhimmis* or 'protected people' who were excused military service but paid a special tax instead. However, the *devsirme* was still on a small scale and would not dominate the *Yeni Çeri* corps until the later fifteenth and sixteenth centuries.

The fourteenth-century Ottoman army was also characterised by its large number of high-status Christian troops. Whereas most of the Byzantine frontier aristocracy and *pronoia* fief-holding families who had previously tranferred their allegiance to the Turks in Anatolia converted to Islam, a substantial number who joined the Ottomans in the Balkans clung to their original faith and only converted to Islam after the second or third generation to confirm their position in the new military heirarchy. A distinctive Ottoman military class thus emerged in the European Balkan provinces, different from that of the Asian Anatolian provinces.

By the mid-fifteenth century and the final siege of the Byzantine capital of Constantinople, the majority of Ottoman professional soldiers were contractual *sipahi* cavalry or *Kapi Kulu* troops of slave or prisoner-of-war orgin. The former were greater in number and even in the mid-fifteenth century at least half of the *timariots* or fief-holding *sipahis* of the Balkan provinces were still Christian. Meanwhile the *Kapi Kulu*, especially those of the Sultan's own Household or Palace Regiments, formed an élite which was expensive to recruit, train and equip. Not all the youngsters forcibly recruited through the *devsirme* system entered the Janissary corps; the best being selected for goverment service or the *Kapi Kulu* Palace Cavalry. Under Sultan Mehmet II the ranks of *timariot* provincial cavalry were becoming filled with *Kapi Kulu* men.

Meanwhile the organization and command structure of the Ottoman army was the same in peace as in war. The heirarchy of command was unambiguous and military units were permanent formations, provincial contingents under the *Beylerbeyis* of Rumelia and Anatolia being as fully under the Sultan's command as were his own Palace Regiments. As a result the Ottoman army was probably the best disciplined and trained force of its day. The Ottoman Turks were also heirs to a variety of military traditions of which that of the Mamluk Sultanate of Egypt and Syria was the most important. The Ottomans then combined these elements to develop something awesomely effective.

At the very heart of the Ottoman army were the *silahdar*, 'guardians of ruler's weapons', who formed one of the six *gureba* or Palace Cavalry Regiments, each member of which had the status or rank of *ulufeci*. Quite when the two *Yeni Çeri* cavalry *ortas* or regiments were established is unclear, though another high status *Yeni Çeri* unit, the *Solak* infantry bodyguard, certainly existed from an early date. The *Sekbans* or 'Dog-handlers' were another early palace regiment whose reputation for discipline resulted in them being incorporated into the *Yeni Çeri* in the fifteenth century in an attempt to improve the latter's discipline.

Ottoman provincial forces were divided into European and Asian armies, those in the Balkans consisting of three *Uc* or frontier marches – left, right and centre – each under its own 'commander of *ghuzat*. Expansion eastwards and the forces of many of the Anatolian provinces were less clearly structured; the Ottoman state merely taking over rival *beyliks*. By the late fourteenth century the rapidly expanding Ottoman Empire was divided into *sanjaq* provinces, each of which was supposed to furnish a specified number of cavalrymen though the *timarli* fief-holders of these provinces were still under direct government authority. They were grouped into *alay* regiments under *alay bey* officers who were in turn led by the *sanjaq bey* provincial governor. Each group of *sanjaq beys* was commanded by the *beylerbeyi* of the wider *eyalet*, or military province. Meanwhile the auxiliary and largely Christian *yoynuqs* were commanded by *Çeri-basi* officers under the overall command of the *voynuq beyi*.

The classic form of Ottoman military structure probably existed by the time of the siege of Constantinople in 1453 AD. By then the Rumelian and Anatolian provincial forces consisted of three elements; the *toprakli süvarisi* fief-holding cavalry, the *serhadkulu süvarisi* frontier cavalry and the *yerlikulu piyadesi* local infantry. The structure of the Sultan's own Palace or Household regiments was similar, consisting of six regiments of prestigious *Kapikulu Süvarisi* cavalry, plus the *Kapikulu Piyadesi* infantry which included the Janissaries, the *Bostancis*, the *Sekban* 'dog handlers' and *Doganci* 'falconers' from the Sultan's militarized hunting establishment. In addition there were various small guard units, youngsters under training, armourers, other support formations and an increasingly numerous artillery corps. Nevertheless, the size of the Ottoman army was consistently exaggerated by its foes. In reality each *sancak* province supported around 400 cavalry while the Janissary corps grew from around 5,000 to 8,000 men under Mehmet II.

Joshua dressed as a high ranking soldier in a 10th century Byzantine wall-painting. The Prophet has a helmet decorated with pseudo-Arabic writing worn over a head-cloth. His armour is of the lamellar construction shown in most Byzantine representations of military saints or other warlike Biblical figures, while he is armed with a sword whose scabbard is slung from a baldric rather than a belt. He also has a spear.
(in situ Monastery Church of Osios Loukos, Greece; author's photograph)

Warriors in a panel of a Byzantine carved ivory box dating from the 11th or 12th century. Though based upon classical Graeco-Roman art, these two figures are also representative of their period in showing Byzantine light infantry with small round shields, a spear, a sword and with one man wearing a helmet.
(Hermitage Museum, St. Petersburg, Russia; author's photograph)

Some of the weapons recovered from a very early 11th century wrecked merchant ship, mostly carrying glass for recycling, at Serce Liman off Marmaris. The vessel itself is believed to have been from an eastern Mediterranean Islamic port, however pig bones in the wreck suggest the crew were Christian. The weaponry includes a remarkable array of very large spears or pole-arms, javelins, two swords, a boat-hook and what might be parts of a ceremonial parasol.
(Castle Museum, Bodrum, Turkey; author's photograph)

The carved capital of a doubled column in Moissac in southwestern France, dating from around the year AD 1100. The figure pulling back the stFring of an early form of crossbow is represented as a demon, to show that this weapon was regarded as potentially 'evil' in early medieval Western Europe.
(in situ Cloisters of the Abbey of St. Pierre, Moissac, France; author's photograph)

The carved lintel of a village church in western England was made shortly after the First
Crusade, and shows the Archangel Michael destroying a Saljuq Turkish army outside Antioch
while on the left the Crusaders kneel in prayer with their shields and lances behind them.
(in situ Church of St. George, Fordington, England; author's photograph)

This small carving representing Herod's
Guards at the Holy Sepulchre is located on
the inside of a structure itself symbolising
the Holy Sepulchre. The lower figure is
wearing an early form of coat-of-plates
secured by buckles on the man's back.
*(in situ Cathedral, Constance, Germany;
author's photograph)*

Most of the panels of the cast bronze 'Magdeburg Doors' in the Cathedral in Novgorod in north-western Russia were made in Saxony in the mid-12th century, including this scene showing Herod's soldiers at the Massacre of the Innocents. As such they would reflect German arms and armour, although other evidence shows that much the same military equipment was also used in this part of Russia.
(in situ Cathedral of Santa Sofia, Novgorod, Russia; author's photograph)

An archer using a recurved bow of composite construction and with an Asiatic-style quiver on his right hip, in a 13th century carving in Dalmatia, on the Adriatic coast of the Balkans. The Balkan peninsula, like this archer, used a great variety of eastern and Asiatic as well as western style military equipment during the medieval period.
(in situ facade of the Cathedral, Trogir, Croatia; author's photograph)

In this early 13th century north-eastern Italian wall-painting, the horse-archer shooting to the rear at an armoured knight who is pursuing him may represent a Hun, a Turk or some other type of 'infidel'. In reality his equipment and his horse's harness are likely to have been based upon those of the neighbouring horse-archers of medieval Hungary.
(in situ Crypt, Cathedral of Aquileia, Italy; author's photograph)

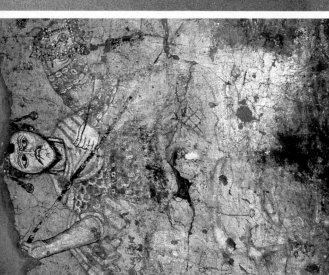

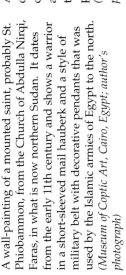

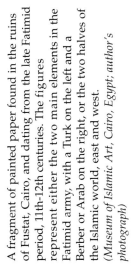

A fragment of painted paper found in the ruins of Fustat, Cairo, and dating from the late Fatimid period, 11th–12th centuries. The figures represent either the two main elements in the Fatimid army, with a Turk on the left and a Berber or Arab on the right, or the two halves of the Islamic world, east and west. (Museum of Islamic Art, Cairo, Egypt; author's photograph)

A wall-painting of a mounted saint, probably St. Phiobammon, from the Church of Abdulla Nirqi, Faras, in what is now northern Sudan. It dates from the early 11th century and shows a warrior in a short-sleeved mail hauberk and a style of military belt with decorative pendants that was used by the Islamic armies of Egypt to the north. (Museum of Coptic Art, Cairo, Egypt; author's photograph)

A ceramic grenade of the type used to throw naft or 'Greek Fire' in both naval and land warfare. It comes from al-Darb Ahaniyas in the Persian Gulf amirate of Ras al-Khaimah; a site inhabited from the 10th to 16th centuries, but this object is probably from the 10th to 13th centuries. (Al-Ain Museum, Abu Dhabi, UAE; author's photograph)

The 12th or early 13th century carvings on the massive medieval Islamic bridge at Ain Diwar in the north-eastern tip of Syria represent signs of the zodiac, astrology being taken very seriously by the ruling and military élites of the medieval Islamic world. This figure of a horseman is also interesting because he is shown as a heavily armoured cavalryman wearing a lamellar cuirass over a long-sleeved mail hauberk with a mail coif.
(in situ Tigris Bridge, Ain Diwar, Syria; author's photograph)

A mamluk cavalryman wielding a double-ended spear, riding a fully armoured horse and wearing a broad-brimmed helmet. Several examples of this form of helmet made of layers of hardened leather or reinforced with small blocks of wood and dating from the 13th or 14th century have recently been found in Damascus. The picture is on a silver inlaid bronze candlestick-base made in the Mamluk Sultanate in the late 13th or early 14th century.
(private collection; author's photograph)

Painted clay or stucco head of a guardian figure from a tomb in Chinese Turkestan. Made in the 12th or 13th century before the rise of Genghis Khan and the Mongol conquests, it shows a military figure wearing the quilted cap which was widely worn in Turkish Central Asia and was also adopted in much of the eastern Islamic world. *(Fogg Art Museum, Boston, USA; author's photograph)*

A sandstone relief carving of a warrior and two female figures from 10th century Rajastan in north-western India. In addition to his reverse-curved sword, the warrior has a dagger on his hip and rests his left hand on a rectangular shield. *(Harvard University Art Museum, Boston, USA; author's photograph)*

A battle scene in a page from a copy of the Shahnamah Persian epic, made in southern Iran or Iraq at the start of the 14th century. Some of the horsemen wear lamellar armour indicated by horizontal stripes, or probably scale-lined cloth-covered armours edged with rivets. *(Reza Abbasi Museum, Tehran, Iran; author's photograph)*

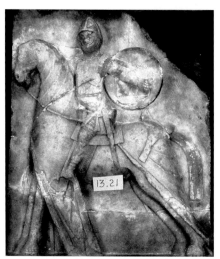

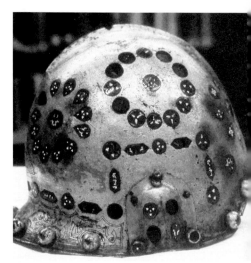

An early 14th century relief carving of an Aragonese or Catalan horseman from the Monastery of Poblet, near Tarragona. Several aspects of his military equipment distinguish this light cavalryman from what would have been seen in most other parts of Western Europe, most notably his round shield and open-faced conical helmet. *(Metropolitan Museum of Art, New York, USA; author's photograph)*

The 'Helmet of Boabdil' is believed to be a 15th century Italian or Spanish salet which has been modified, gilded and abundantly decorated for use in the last remaining Islamic amirate in southern Spain. Such a magnificent object may well have been owned by Muhammad XII Abu Abdullah, the last ruler of Granada. *(Metropolitan Museum of Art, New York, USA; author's photograph)*

The Christian hero Roland slaying the 'infidel' Faragut on a late 12th century carved capital in northern Spain. The conical but fully-enclosed helmets of both horsemen seem to have been unique to the Iberian peninsula and probably pre-dated the comparable flat-topped great helms of other parts of Western Europe by a few decades.
(in situ parish church, Rebolledo de la Torre, Spain; author's photograph)

A manuscript illustration from a little-known school of Islamic art which incorporated influences from as far away as China and Byzantium. It dates from the late 14th or early 15th century, perhaps being made in Central Asia during the reign of Timur-i-Lenk or one of his immediate successors. The writing is Persian but the armour of both men and horses is Turco-Mongol Central Asian while the massive weapons wielded by the warriors are clearly Chinese. (Fatih Album, Topkapi Library, Ms. Haz. 2153, f.87r, Istanbul)

Troops with a Mongol-style banner and wearing lamellar armour attack a 'Citadel of the Faith' in the early 14th century Russian chronicle. Though representing a Biblical subject, the Russian artist has clearly illustrated the 'enemies of the Faith' as Mongol or, more particularly, Golden Horde soldiers. (Chronicle of Georgi Amartola, Lenin Library, Moscow, Russia; via Alexander Matveev)

Relief carvings of light cavalry on a highly decorated mid-15th century Bogomil tomb from Donja Zgorsca in central Bosnia. Although the men's costume and their horses' harness were very similar to those seen in late medieval Italy, this form of light cavalry warfare had become typical of most of the Balkans. (*National Museum, Sarajecvo, Bosnia; author's photograph*)

Though carved by the Italian artist Bonfini around 1490 AD, this relief from the Palace of Matyas Kiraly in the fortress city of Buda, now part of Budapest, shows the sort of equipment used in 15th century Hungary. (*Budapest History Museum, Budapest, Hungary; author's photograph*)

'Dance of Death' showing a fully-armoured man-at-arms on a wall painting made in 1474 AD in the Istrian peninsula. The artistic style is primitive and the armour seems to have more in common with that of Germany than northern Italy. Within a few years this region where Venetian, Austro-German and Croat-Hungarian territory met would become a front line in the struggle against the advancing Ottoman Empire. (*in situ Church of St. Mary, Beram, Croatia; author's photograph*)

A typical 15th century Italian merchant ship on an alabaster relief carving which supposedly shows the Apostles fishing in the Sea of Galilee. There is an abundant store of javelins and shields in the crows nest, which would have been used to defend a ship if attacked by pirates in the war-torn late medieval Mediterranean. Made by Amadeo and Aiuto, it came from the Monastery of San Salvatore. (*Castle Museum, Pavia, Italy; author's photograph*)

The remarkable Tersane covered docks or slipways for galleys at Alanya are almost unique. Built by the Saljuq Turks of Rum in 1227 they were, however, simply the most sophisticated versions of the galley docks seen all around the medieval Mediterranean, Aegean and Black Seas. (*author's photograph*)

A *veuglaire* type of later 14th century cannon with a separate breech or powder chamber, from the castle of Lisieux. (*Historical Museum, Rouen, France; author's photograph*)

The fortified enclosure and gatehouse around the parish church at Blaj, west of Medias in Transylvania, dates from the 13th or 14th century. In this exposed frontier region of what was at the time the Kingdom of Hungary, small rural fortifications such as this provided refuge for the local population.
(Blaj, Transylvania, Romania; author's photograph)

One of the best-preserved late medieval towers of the Kremlin of Novgorod, dating from the 15th century. Before the stone fortifications were added at the end of the medieval period, Novgorod's defences largely consisted of timber on top of the earth rampart.
(Tower 14, Novgorod Kremlin, Russia; author's photograph)

The oldest part of the Toompea Castle in Tallinn is a simple but sturdy round tower. It was built by the Crusading Order of the Sword Brethren in the early 13th century but, like the rest of the fortifications of Tallinn, it was strengthened in the later Middle Ages. *Tallinn, Estonia; author's photograph)*

The 12th century city walls of Avila in central Spain are amongst the earliest and simplest yet almost complete urban fortifications in Western Europe. Their design was typical of the closely spaced towers and curtain wall which date from after the introduction of the stone-throwing traction mangonel but before the adoption of the more powerful counterweight trebuchet. *(Avila, Spain; author's photograph)*

One of the external towers of Trujillo castle in central Spain which is a characteristic examples of the *albarrana* or freestanding tower, attached to the main curtain wall by a removeable bridge which would originally have been made of timber. These Islamic defences date from the early 13th-century Muwahhid period and their name came from the Arabic *al-barrani* meaning 'exterior'. *(author's photograph)*

The single, well preserved corner tower in the outer walls of the small Crusader castle of Chastel Rouge, now Qala'at Yahmur, in Syria. Built of well cut limestone blocks but virtually lacking in decoration, it was held by the Templars and protected a very fertile coastal region south of Tartus.
(author's photograph)

Looking vertically up to the vaulted roof and five massive machicolations which protected the entrance to the gatehouse of the early 13th century Citadel of Aleppo. Built by Saladin's son, al-Ghazi, it was repaired by the Mamluks after the Mongol onslaught.
(Frederick Nicolle photograph)

The castle of al-Rahba, on the edge of the central Euphrates valley, was an important Islamic defensive outpost and communications centre mid-way between the major population centres of Syria to the west and Iraq to the east during the period of the Crusades. Subsequently it was the easternmost outpost of the Mamluk Sultanate, facing the Mongol Il-Khanate. Most of the existing castle dates from the 12th and early 13th centuries. *(author's photograph)*

The interior of part of the remaining medieval mud-brick city wall around Bukhara in Uzbekistan, dating from the 9th to the 16th century. This form of mud-brick fortification was used in Transoxania as well as several other parts of Central Asia and eastern Iran from ancient until early modern times. It was highly effective, cheap to build and easy to repair. But if the structure was not maintained regularly it gradually dissolved back into mud. *(author's photograph)*

The citadel of Harat in Afghanistan is the most impressive fortification from the 15th century Timurid period. One tower is decorated with blue and turquoise glazed bricks. Some surviving fragments suggest that similar glazed inscription may originally have run around the tops of the citadel's other walls. *(Geza Fehervari photograph)*

The castle of Anamur was one of the strongest on the coast of the Kingdom of Armenian Cilicia. The existing structure largely dates from the late 13th and 14th centuries and guarded the rout along the southern coast of Anatolia, facing the Crusader-held island of Cyprus. *(author's photograph)*

The interior of an upper chamber of a tower in the Romano-Byzantine land walls of Constantinople (Istanbul). Dating from the very early medieval period, this part of the fortifications had broad embrasures which were probably designed for the torsion-powered ballistas which fell out of use, to be replaced in the later medieval period by crossbows which required smaller arrow-slits. *(author's photograph)*

Firearms had been spreading across the Balkans and into Ottoman territory since the 1370s and by the time of the fall of Constantinople the Ottoman army was the most advanced in the Islamic world. The *Topcu* gunner corps and the *Top Arabaci* gun carriage drivers had both been created by Sultan Mehmet II's father whereas the *Cebeci* armourers were established by Mehmet the Conqueror himself. All formed part of the *Kapi Kulu* Palace Regiments while the Sultan also recruited gunmakers and engineers from abroad.

The Ottoman debt to the Mamluk Sultanate was clearer in strategic and tactical terms. Raids deep into the Balkans were clearly not spontaneous but formed part of a broad strategic plan and were followed up by further operations designed to seize territory weakened by raiding. The breadth of Ottoman strategic vision can be seen in the tasks of their three *Uc* frontier marches in the Balkans. The eastern or 'right' *Uc* under the Sultan himself aimed at the Black Sea coast to isolate the Byzantine capital of Constantinople; the central *Uc* pushed up the Maritsa valley through Bulgaria towards Serbia while the western or 'left' *Uc* followed the Aegean coast towards the Byzantine second city of Thessaloniki and Albania. It was, in fact, one of the most consistent examples of long-term strategy in medieval military history.

Ottoman battlefield tactics were again reminiscent of their Islamic and Byzantine predecessors. For example, at the Battle of Kossovo in 1389 the Ottomans were so concerned about dust blowing in their direction that they delayed their attack until the following day. The role of the *Yeni Çeri* infantry has, however, been exaggerated by most authors, and in reality *sipahi* cavalry remained the dominant arm. Most Ottoman cavalry would be placed on the flanks of a battle array, with regular infantry at the centre to provide a refuge in case the cavalry attacks failed. Here a small force of the best cavalry would also form a guard around the commander and serve as a reserve while irregular infantry and light cavalry were normally ahead of the main line as skirmishers. Most battles were fought in daylight, a defeated force then trying to escape under cover of darkness.

Ottoman military engineers are said to have learned much from their Hungarian foes during the early fifteenth century, but in fact the heritage of Islamic siege engineering was longer and more-sophisticated than that of Europe. Ottoman tactics were notably effective during the final siege of Constantinople though it was their artillery skills and an ability to combine operations on land and sea which brought success. By now Ottoman armoured cavalry made little use of bows and were just as skilled on foot as on horseback. Less is known about infantry training in the fifteenth-century Ottoman army but it clearly emphasized archery in the disciplined Byzantine and Arab-Islamic manner. An ability to cope with reverses was particularly emphasised in the training of *devsirme* recruits for the *Yeni Çeri* corps.

The Ottoman Turks were relative late-comers to naval warfare, only gaining a small Aegean fleet when they took over the Turkish *beylik* of Karasi on the southern side of the Dardanelles. Though this enabled the Ottomans to seize and hold part of the Gallipoli peninsula in the 1350s, their expanding European conquests remained highly vulnerable until they developed a full-scale navy in the fifteenth century. On board ship Turkish *azap* marines fought with crossbows and hand-held composite bows using *semberek* or *zemburek* arrowguides, though *tüfek* guns had also been adopted by the end of the fourteenth century.

The Ottoman fleet was a separate military arm by the mid-fifteenth century and probably already had its own dockyard and arsenal organization. With its main base at Gallipoli its initial role was to ensure that Ottoman armies could cross between Anatolia and Rumelia without hindrance. Nevertheless the size of the fleet which appeared outside Constantinople in 1453 came as a shock to the Byzantines and Italians, the Venetians having constantly underestimated the skill and initiative of the Ottoman navy. In fact the Ottomans had several nautical traditions to draw upon, including those of the Byzantines, the Turkish *beyliks* and the earlier Islamic Middle East. Since the Ottomans learned so much about land warfare from the Mamluk Sultanate of Egypt and Syria, it seems likely that they also had access to the Mamluks' advanced, if somewhat theoretical, nautical knowledge. If so, they made much more successful use of it than did the Mamluks themselves.

The Later Crusades in Southeastern Europe

One of the most ambitious, and most dramatically unsuccessful, of the later Crusades was the Burgundian-led expedition which came to grief in 1396 and came to be known as the Crusade of Nicopolis. Its composition, organisation and tactics reflected profound changes which were taking place within Western European society and its armies. By then the feudalism of the twelfth and thirteenth centuries had given way to so-called 'bastard feudalism' under which knights and squires of the feudal aristocracy served in return for payment. Warfare nevertheless remained a route by which the brave, capable and lucky could win social and economic advancement.

Burgundy was now emerging as one of the most powerful regions of Western Europe. Its duke rivalled the king in military might, and his acquisition of Flanders gave him huge wealth. Within Burgundy the duke's army was built around his 'household'. The nucleus consisted of heavily armoured, professional men-at-arms capable of fighting on horseback or on foot. There were also smaller contingents of mounted archers and crossbowmen, both of which were really mounted infantry, plus some light cavalry.

The current tactical emphasis on men-at-arms reflected Burgundian society where the old aristocracy remained deeply entrenched. Furthermore, the strongly aristocratic ideology of this Crusade discouraged the use of archers and crossbowmen, resulting in overwhelmingly offensive tactics which were ill-suited to cope with Ottoman warfare. Unfortunately many of the participants regarded both 'schismatic' Orthodox Christians and Muslims as their foes, and even the famous Italian humanist poet Petrarch had written:

> The Ottomans are merely enemies but the schismatic Greeks are worse than enemies. The Ottomans hate us less, for they fear us less. The Greeks however, both fear and hate us with all their soul.

The German contribution to the Crusade of Nicopolis has sometimes been overlooked. However, France was regarded as the fountainhead of chivalry and consequently the organisation of late fourteenth-century German aristocratic armies usually mirrored those of the French. An increase in the importance of infantry which had been seen earlier in the fourteenth century had, to some extent, been reversed by the 1390s, particularly in France, Burgundy and Germany. In these armies transport was supplied by large numbers of waggons which required an even greater number of waggoners. Nevertheless it was the river Danube which provided the Crusaders with their main means of transport while heavy siege equipment was to be brought by a Crusader fleet sailing up the Danube from the Black Sea.

A little over half a century after the Crusade of 1396 was crushed by the Ottoman army at the battle of Nicopolis, Western European volunteers were helping defend the Byzantine Imperial capital of Constantinople during the final Ottoman siege. They joined what remained of Byzantine forces to man the walls and also served as sailors or marines, the great majority coming from Italy. A population explosion in many Italian cities had resulted in an excess of young men, unemployed, unable to marry, often from prosperous or aristocratic families and available for adventure. In Constantinople in 1453 their leadership was largely drawn from Genoa and Venice, though there were also Catalans and others.

The Hospitallers

Unlike most other relics of the Crusades in the Aegean region during the fourteenth and fifteenth centuries, the Military Order of the Hospitallers based on the island of Rhodes remained dedicated to warfare against Islam. All Islamic states were, to some degree, regarded as the Order's foes and those Western European volunteers who joined the Hospitallers or fought alongside them for an agreed period saw themselves as Crusaders. However, the world from which these men were drawn was changing and this was reflected in Hospitaller recruitment. The prestige of the military aristocracy was under threat from a rising middle class while the fourteenth and fifteenth centuries also saw widespread criticism of a perceived decline in 'chivalry'. Given the resulting crisis of identity within the knightly élite, and a surplus of men compared to women in some parts of Europe, the motivation of Hospitaller recruits may have been mixed. Calls for a Crusade by those who spread stories of 'the terrible Turk' may actually have backfired, creating fear of the 'invincible' Ottomans, and it was not until the Hospitallers of Rhodes defeated a major Ottoman attack in 1480 that the Order witnessed a significant increase in recruitment.

On the headquarters island of Rhodes itself, the Order faced manpower problems during the mid-fourteenth century and there were so few men of recognised Western European origin that the Hopitaller Chapter ruled that those with Latin Catholic fathers but Greek mothers should be considered legally Latin. Nevertheless, when some local Rhodian Greeks requested permission to join in 1478 this was denied, indicating that Western prejudice against Orthodox Christians persisted almost to the end. Large numbers of European mercenaries who came to Rhodes included specialists such as the Englishman, Stephen Ward, who became master of the Rhodian arsenal in the mid-fifteenth century. Much of the fighting was, meanwhile, done by mercenaries in Hospitaller service.

Although the Military Order of the Hospitallers was extremely wealthy, it faced huge expenses, the cost of transporting food, raw materials, armaments and horses from Western Europe to Rhodes being immense, as was the cost of maintaining the island's fortifications. In 1409 a severe financial crisis was at least alleviated by the arrival of Venetian galleys bringing no less than 5,000 *ducats* from England. Of this 1,900 were spent on building the new castle at Bodrum on the Anatolian mainland, 1,000 on mercenary troops, 300 on stipends for the brethren and 600 for their food. All Hospitaller-held islands had castles of some kind and were dotted with smaller towers to provide refuge in case of Turkish raids. Other castles overlooked economic assets such as the salt-pans on Castellorizzo. The Hospitallers also maintained a remarkable chain of warning beacons stretching from Leros in the north, via Bodrum at least as far as Apolakia in southern Rhodes.

In 1375 the Hospitallers proposed a major Crusade in support of the

Crusader States of Greece. It was to consist of brethren from virtually all the Order's *Priories*, or provinces, in Europe, each brother to be accompanied by their squires. In the event the Order failed to assemble anywhere near the required number and the proposal was a dismal failure with little fighting against the Turks, except skirmishes which merely provoked the enemy and were stopped in 1409.

Despite such failures, the fanaticism of the Hospitallers meant that they killed almost all male Muslim prisoners except for children who were enslaved. Even the change of policy in the mid-fifteenth century probably reflected the Order's serious shortage of oarsmen for its galleys rather than a decline in its ferocity. As a result the Hospitaller fleet was the first, Christian or Islamic, to use large numbers of galley-slaves in its warships. The *servitudo marina* levy of Greek oarsmen was therefore abandoned and instead Turkish captives were used as oarsmen, along with the *buonavoglia* volunteers who enlisted to pay off their debts.

The Hospitaller fleet became a high quality force during the fourteenth century but it was so small that it rarely conducted independent action. After Smyrna (Izmir) fell to Timur-i Lenk in 1402, this fleet was enlarged and adopted an aggressive policy against Ottoman trade. The Hospitallers' new castle at Bodrum also gave the Order a strong outpost on the mainland which, with the Hospitaller-held offshore islands, enabled their galleys to attack passing merchant ships almost at will. Meanwhile the Hospitaller Master had spies in the main Ottoman naval base of Gallipoli and there was usually a Hospitaller patrol boat in the vicinity. This would hurry back to Rhodes with a warning if the Ottoman fleet emerged.

War galleys changed from the late thirteenth to mid-fourteenth centuries, and by the later fifteenth century it was traditional for Hospitaller galleys to be larger than those of most other fleets, enabling them to keep the seas for a longer period and in worse weather. The Hospitaller admiral, in charge of the Order's galleys and other ships armed for war, could also hire additional galleys. However, he and his fighting men were commanded by the marshal if the latter was present, and following a landing the knights were placed under the 'commander of knights'.

Armament aboard Hospitaller ships is likely to have been similar to that aboard other galleys. For example fourteenth-century Venetian galleys operating in the Aegean carried thirty to fifty men armed with swords and ten to twenty men with crossbows. Genoese naval regulations of around 1330 stipulated that a galley with a crew of 176 men included junior officers and twelve crossbowmen, four of whom were considered specialists with two weapons each. The ship was also 'armed' with twelve additional crossbows and 5,000 crossbow bolts, plus spears, javelins, bills and a certain amount of armour. By 1483 the weaponry aboard a pilgrim galley also included cannon. In galleys the forecastle formed the focus of both defence and attack, this being where most armoured men were stationed.

Service aboard ship was called *carovane* and was obligatory for all Hospitaller brethren. Naval tactics were based upon raiding enemy coasts and ambushing merchant ships. Good local knowledge was one reason for their success and this was obviously necessary when, as was normally the case, two galleys worked together. One would lie in wait behind a headland or small island while the second harried a victim into the jaws of this ambush.

Coastal raids could involve larger forces. The Turkish *Destan of Umur Pasha* described such a descent upon Izmir harbour by Hospitallers and others: 'Thirty galleys were sent to Izmir, all filled with men in full armour.... These inumerable Franks were dressed in iron from head to foot'. In a later verse the Turkish poet described the sound of the hand-guns or *tüfeks* in battle – 'shat! shat!'. Battles between fleets at sea were rare but when they did occur, galleys normally formed a loose line with larger transport galleys and sailing ships in reserve while small vessels carried messages from ship to ship. A disparity between the sizes, numbers and tactics of Christian and Islamic warships was again reflected in Turkish sources, the author of the *Destan of Umur Pasha* writing of the Christian vessels that 'their topsails are like fortresses. The cogs carry enemies without number'.

Meanwhile, the strongest Christian naval powers in the Aegean, as in the Mediterranean and Black Seas, were the competing Italian merchant republics of Venice and Genoa. More of their martial energies seem to have been directed against each other, or against the Orthodox Christian powers of the Aegean, than against the Muslims during the fourteenth century, but in the fifteenth century the rising power of the Ottoman Turkish Sultanate forced them to take Islamic naval competition more seriously.

The Venetian and Genoese Commercial Empires

Venice was unlike Genoa because its overseas possessions tended to be maintained by force whereas Genoa preferred to seek local support and maintain good relations with neighbouring states. Even in the twelfth and certainly in the thirteenth century the Venetian army had proved itself as effective as its fleet, despite jibes that the marsh-dwelling Venetians did not know how to ride their horses properly. During the fourteenth century Venice was unlike most other Italian states in still preferring domestic recruitment, conscripts and volunteers, rather than mercenaries.

Men chosen for the prestigious and lucrative role of crossbowmen aboard merchant ships and galleys were drawn from those who had shown their ability at various shooting ranges in Venice. The long Venetian tradition of military training and splendid tournaments stood Venice in good stead for many centuries. Archery butts for crossbow practice were dotted around the city and the Lido which separated the lagoon from the sea, generous prizes being given to the best shots. Other warlike pastimes included barely-controlled battles with staves and fists between the three eastern and the three western *sestieri* parishes of Venice. Sham sea fights and assaults on mock castles became a feature by the fifteenth century, as did *bagordi* light cavalry manoeuvres of attack and withdrawal inspired by Balkan or Islamic military practice.

The elite of Venetian infantry were drawn from the ranks of the *arsenalotti*, highly skilled and well-paid craftsmen who worked in the arsenal, which was itself a weapons factory and arms store as well as being the most famous ship-building yard in Europe. In the fifteenth century the *compagnie della calza*, or 'trouser clubs', similarly provided trained volunteers. Their peculiar name inevitably calls to mind the 'trousers ceremonies' which marked entry into Islamic *futuwwa* associations of a few centuries earlier and which often had a similarly military aspects.

The Ottoman advance across the Balkans and Greece in the fourteenth and fifteenth centuries resulted in Venetian colonial outposts filling with Byzantine refugees. Many came from the old military élite who now took service with Venice as *stradiottii* light cavalry. Armed with short lances or javelins, bows and light swords, they were recruited in Greece, Albania and Dalmatia. Their loyalty was rarely in doubt, their ferocity proverbial, and their habit of collecting the heads of slain foes never seriously discouraged.

Back in Venice itself, a standing army of *condottieri*, mercenary contract soldiers, emerged early in the fifteenth century, but its role was to defend Venice's expanding mainland territories, the *Terra Firma*, rather than its overseas possessions. Of the latter, Crete remained the most prized possession and to ensure its continued subjection the island was divided into six sections named after the six parishes of Venice. Here knights' *fees* and three times as many infantry *sergeantries* were mostly held by Venetian military settlers while fortifications sprang up all over the island, particularly along its northern coast.

The second-largest Venetian colonial possession in the Aegean area was the island of Negroponte, now Evvoia, which similarly bristled with fortifications. Only the most senior Venetian administrators could become *Bailie*, or governor, of Evvoia, whereas less important Greek islands were mere stops along the trade routes or bases from which to control piracy. A Venetian effort to drive the Ottomans out of the Peloponnese in southern Greece in 1463-4 with an army of *stradiottii*, Italian hand-gunners and *condottieri* heavy cavalry failed. Thereafter defensive operations were left to the naval and garrison infantry and to *stradiottii* who not only fought the Ottomans on their own terms but were much cheaper to maintain than Western European men-at-arms.

After the Fourth Crusade conquered Constantinople in 1204, Venetian merchants dominated the Black Sea. This dangerous area spanned the rich caravan routes from Iran and China and was also an important source of the wood from which crossbows were made, but when the Byzantines regained their imperial capital in 1261, Venice lost her dominant position to her rival Genoa, which was now a close ally of the revived Byzantine Empire. Despite the deep-seated hostility between these two Italian maritime republics, they occasionally co-operated in the hazardous environment of the Black Sea, particularly in the Crimea where a number of originally-Byzantine ports served as terminals for the trans-Asian Silk Roads as well as routes north into fur-rich Russia and Siberia.

The Crimea was itself a remarkably mixed area, with Armenians forming a majority in some trading towns while Christian Goths, descended from Dark Age Germanic and perhaps subsequent Anglo-Saxon refugee settlers, inhabited some coastal mountains. At Kaffa the Genoese even had a *Capitaneus Gothie* in charge of local troops, plus *castellani* and other full-time military officials. The Italians finally lost the Crimea to the Ottoman Turks in 1479 and within five years the Black Sea become an Ottoman lake in which the only Western European merchant vessels permitted to sail were from Venice's old Dalmatian rival Ragusa, now Dubrovnik.

Back in Italy, Venice had long been obliged to defend its independence from Italian rivals, German imperial armies, Hungarian and French invaders. By the 1470s, however, Venetian forces found themselves up against large-scale Ottoman Turkish raids deep into Friuli on the eastern edge of the *Terra Firma*, on what are now the borders of Italy, Slovenia and Croatia. This was an entirely new type of threat and, despite Venetian experience of war against Islamic Turks in overseas colonies, the defences of Friuli initially failed. The one major battle resulted in a serious Venetian defeat but, after assembling a much larger army, the Venetians beat off later Ottoman raids. It was this experience which convinced Venice to employ *stradiottii* colonial light cavalry on the Italian mainland, to improve its local military training and to overhaul the system of selective conscription.

At sea, Venetian and Genoese domination remained virtually un-challenged until the Ottoman Turkish Sultanate suddenly emerged as a serious rival in the second half of the fifteenth century. It was then that heavily defended, though bulky and unwieldy, merchant 'round ships' proved their worth against the fast and manoeuverable, but low free-board, traditional galleys preferred by the Turks. *Bombards* or cannon had been recorded aboard Venetian galleys in the 1370s and became standard armament during the fifteenth century. By then numerous small guns were also mounted on both galleys and round ships to cut down the enemy crew while a single larger cannon could be placed in a galley's prow to pierce the enemy's hull or topple his mast.

Hungary

While Venice eventually took the lead in the confrontation between Latin or Western European Christendom and the Ottoman Sultanate at sea, the Kingdom of Hungary did the same on land during the later decades of the fourteenth century. By then Hungarian forces had changed considerably from those that had faced the Mongols in the thirteenth century. The new ruling dynasty of Angevin kings, whose family origins lay in France and southern Italy, introduced Western European military systems with the existing Hungarian *banderia* baronial forces forming the basis of a new army. Relics of earlier military systems meanwhile survived, including the *insurrection* levy of the entire knightly class, various non-noble military groups who had traditonal military obligations and, in extreme emergency, a summoning of the entire male population.

The result could be a remarkably varied army which differed from those seen in Western Europe. Its aristocratic élite were armoured cavalry like those of Germany or France, but Hungary could also field large numbers of light cavalry, including horse-archers. Economic and cultural links with the steppes to the east remained strong and as a result the Hungarians often felt affinity with Turks and other steppe peoples. Western European feudal and chivalric influence was even weaker in Transylvania and the southern Slav provinces of the Hungarian state, where fighting forces largely consisted of rural militias of horsemen and foot soldiers under local *knez* leaders. It was, in fact, light cavalry that made Hungarian forces so distinctive. During the fourteenth century the bulk may have been drawn from the *szekelys*, a community divided into six clans and twenty-four lineages, each theoretically providing a hundred light cavalrymen plus a lower status militia.

Turkish Pechenegs had settled in Hungary in the later eleventh and twelfth centuries in small numbers that were soon absorbed. The Turkish Kipchaqs, or Cumans as they were generally known in Central Europe, arrived in larger numbers and had a profound military impact upon the character of later medieval Hungarian armies. Finally there were the Iasians, who were Iranian-speaking Ossetians or Alans rather than Turkish nomads. Such refugees and settlers served as horse-archers, though the feudalisation of their aristocracies led to a decline in their military importance by the late fourteenth century. Half a century later, the Burgundian squire Bertrandon de la Brocqière reported that the Hungarians

> use short strong lances . . . They joust one-to-one and always in pairs. In the border territory between Austria and Bohemia there are light crossbowmen. In Hungary there are archers with bows like those of the Turks, but they are not as good or as strong.

Most of the inhabitants of the eastern and southern frontier regions which faced the Ottoman Turks were non-Magyar, non-Hungarian; those in the Carpathian Mountains spoke Romanian, a language descended from Latin. Most of these Vlachs were Orthodox Christians and the status of their aristocracy had been eroded by Catholic Hungarian pressure. Nevertheless a Romanian military élite led by regional *voivodes* still existed in several other parts of eastern Transylvania, defending these regions against nomad infiltration. Hunyadi Janos, the great Hungarian hero and leader of the struggle against the Ottoman Turks, came from such a background. His father had become Catholic-Hungarian in culture; Hunyadi himself rising to power through military success and loyalty to the Hungarian crown.

Catholic pressure on the local Orthodox Christians, and on newly arrived Hussite refugees from Bohemia, grew stronger during the fifteenth century, yet this did not prevent Hussites from providing Hunyadi Janos with some of his most effective troops. Having learned his military trade as a young *condottiere* in Italy, Hunyadi used his own wealth to raise an efficient fighting force to face the Ottoman Turks.

Hunyadi's heavy cavalry largely consisted of mercenary German *ritters* while his light cavalry came from Hungary itself. The indigenous militias of fifteenth-century Hungary were recruited and organised in much the same way as those of independent or autonomous Wallachia and Moldavia. The foreign volunteers in Hunyadi's army regarded them-selves as Crusaders against the Muslim Ottoman Turks, the majority stemming from Prussia, Bohemia, Poland, Germany, Austria and Italy. Yet others came from regions which were already under some degree of Ottoman domination.

In 1458 AD, after another period of confusion and war, the fifteen years old son of Hunyadi Janos was elected as King Matthias Corvinus. Five years later the southern province of Bosnia was lost to the Ottomans and young Matthias not only faced further threats of invasion but the power of overmighty barons. He raised taxes and, building on his father's experience, recruited a standing army of Bohemian Hussites, German *ritters*, Polish and Serbian mercenaries loyal to himself. With this army King Matthias Corvinus tried to weld central Europe into a single empire powerful enough to confront the Ottomans. Numbering around 30,000 well-paid troops equipped in blackened armour, the 'Black Army' fought against Poland and Bohemia as well as the Ottoman Sultan, during which campaigns it gained a reputation for skill in winter warfare.

King Matthias Corvinus' central European empire collapsed shortly after his death in 1490. Baronial power revived and the Black Army was sent against the Ottomans with inadequate payment and supplies. Forced to rob the local inhabitants in order to survive, it was then crushed by a baronial force. All that now remained to face the advancing Ottomans were ill-disciplined private armies and poorly-led light cavalry which had, however, adopted many Turkish military styles. In 1514 a peasant uprising was ruthlessly crushed so that even the traditional *jobbágy* rural militia could no longer be relied upon. Their neglected potential was made brutally clear in 1527, a year after the disastrous Battle of Mohacs, when the peasant army of Ivan the Black, a fanatical self-proclaimed Serbian prophet, took part in the civil wars which tore Hungary apart.

The Kingdom of Croatia had been absorbed as a theoretically equal partner within the Kingdom of Hungary at the start of the twelfth century. Slav-speaking but Latin Catholic rather than Orthodox Christian, the Croats had drawn most of their military systems and much of their armament from Austria and Italy. Here the importance of light cavalry was initially a result of Croatia's relative isolation and mountainous terrain, but such troops would later prove their value against Ottoman raiders, their descendants being incorporated into the Hapsburg *Militargrenz* or Military Frontier Zone during the sixteenth century.

The similarly Hungarian-ruled province of Bosnia may have had more in common with neighbouring Serbia but in both Croatia and Bosnia, local forces came under strong Turkish light cavalry influence during the late fourteenth and fifteenth centuries, strengthening their existing light cavalry traditions. Meanwhile, little is known of their infantry except that many used rectangular *pavise* shields. One of the most important new forms of infantry weapon was, however, firearms, Ragusa (Dubrovnik) on the Adriatic coast of Dalmatia becoming a major entry point for such weapons into the Balkans as a whole.

The Struggle for the Indies

During the medieval period the Indian Ocean was a channel for peoples and ideas including new military technology. India itself lay at the hub of this network of cultural connections, as did the island of Sri Lanka which established trading and colonial outposts as far away as Burma (Myanmar) and the East Indies. Meanwhile, Indian influence was felt across a vast area, touching almost every coast of the Indian Ocean and spreading as far as Indo-China.

Others were also involved; the huge island of Madagascar, off the East African coast, being settled during the first millenium AD by people from what is now Indonesia and Malaysia. The Indonesian impact on the food plants of the East African mainland is clear and they may similarly have influenced its metallurgical skills. The presence of pre-Arab, in some cases even pre-Semitic, residual populations along Arabia's Indian Ocean coast could suggest ancient links with India, while commercial and settlement ties between the Arabian peninsula and East Africa go back almost to the dawn of Islamic history. Most dramatic of all, however, was the peaceful spread of Islam across southeast Asia, most notably in what is now Malaysia and Indonesia; a process which was under way by the thirteenth century. Similarly vast areas of what are now Myanmar (Burma), Indo-China (Thailand, Laos, Cambodia and Vietnam), Malaysia, Indonesia and even, to limited extent, the Philippines were influenced militarily as well as in more peaceful ways by the Hindu and Buddhist civilisations of India and Sri Lanka. The kingdom of Arimaddanapura in upper Burma was converted to Buddhism by Indo-Burmese missionaries from the south in the late eleventh and early twelfth centuries, while most aspects of Malayan material culture, as well as its concepts of royalty and government, stem from Indian civilization, despite conversion to Islam in the post-medieval period.

Since the eighth century AD, Islamic rule within the Indian subcontinent had been confined to a small part of what is now Pakistan, consisting of Arab-ruled *amirates* around Multan and Mansurah. Then, at the start of the eleventh century, the Ghaznawids pressed eastward from their Afghan mountain heartlands to conquer the Punjab and much of the Ganges plain. To this their Ghurid successors added the rest of the Ganges plain as far as the Gulf of Bengal, while also extending Islamic territory south towards the Deccan.

By the time that Mongol invaders raided but then withdrew in the thirteenth century, a *mamluk* dynasty similar to the Mamluk Sultanate of Egypt and Syria was already taking over the Islamic regions of northern India. These so-called 'Slave Kings of Delhi' and the two subsequent Turkish dynasties of the Khaljis and Tughluqids continued to push southward, dominating the entire peninsula except for its very southern tip, before a powerful Hindu reaction then emerged during the second half of the fourteenth century.

India already had its own distinctive military traditions based upon

Hindu religious principles. According to this ideology a powerful state should be aggressive while a weak one should be conciliatory and seek alliances, warfare being avoided if its outcome was unclear. Within India, competion for agricultural land between peasants and aboriginal forest tribes led to both being very warlike, despite a Hindu ideology which supposedly confined warfare to a warrior caste. However, there was virtually no coordinated resistance to Islamic encroachment.

Within Hindu India the caste system formed the foundation of military recruitment and organisation. Before the collapse of the Gupta state in the early sixth century, conscription may have been largely limited to the *kshatriya* warrior caste, but from then on the reality of military recruitment rarely seems to have reflected the theoretical ideal. According to this ideal, the *brahman* priests were of the highest status, followed by the *kshatriya* warrior and ruling caste, then the *vaisya* 'commoners' consisting of farmers or merchants, and finally the *sudra* serfs. Subsequent centuries saw this social structure being further subdivided, resulting in an extraordinary degree of social and ethnic segregation.

By the Middle Ages many or perhaps most of the *kshatriya* no longer worked the land as their ancestors had supposedly done in ancient Vedic times and many had their own armed retinues. Armourers were considered part of the *vaisya*, the free but supposedly non-military 'artisan caste', but the dividing line between *kshatriya* and *vaisya* was blurring. Both eventually included soldiers and administrators and could be involved in trade. Only in the later medieval period did the status of *vaisya* seriously decline.

Boys from the *kshatriya* were 'invested' into their caste between the ages of six and eleven but did not become full *kshatriya* until twenty-two when, like the priestly *brahmans* they were declared members of the 'twice born', or 'reborn', Hindu aristocracy. *Kshatriya* and *brahmans* were also excused taxation, being regarded as 'protectors' of the lower tax-paying castes. Others who became *bhrtya*, or 'soldiers', in royal service may also have been exempted from taxation.

The *Arthashastra*, 'Utilitarian Book', which was written in its existing form during the early medieval period, sheds light on the reality rather than the ideals of both recruitment and organisation. In this text an army was described as consisting of a *maula* 'hereditary élite', a term that recalls the *mawla* who entered the early Islamic military élite by being 'adopted' by higher-status Arab tribes. In addition there were *bhritaka* mercenaries, *shrenibala* short-term contingents from 'guilds', plus allies and 'non-Aryan' aboriginal auxiliaries. Apparently the bulk of early medieval Hindu armies consisted of lower castes and assorted foreigners, led by a *kshatriya* warrior élite, and perhaps as a result Hindu armies tended to be bigger than those of their Islamic foes.

Specific information about various military groups indicates that the Hindu warriors of the tenth-century Punjab were considered good cavalry, while the men of the Gauda area were described as infantry archers. By the eleventh century, northern Indian armies consisted of relatively small professional élites plus large numbers of assorted vassals and auxiliaries. For example, the Rajput Hindu army defeated by the Ghurids in 1192 included feudal levies and troops sent by allied *rajas* or local princes. The Rajputs themselves formed a military aristocracy claiming descent from the earliest, and thus 'purest', *kshatriya*. They existed solely for war and their younger sons tended to migrate to other parts of the country if they found no military role in their own territory. Meanwhile the military role of non-*kshatriya* declined in areas under Rajput control and so, when the Rajputs themselves were defeated, resistance collapsed.

Another distinct group were the Jats or *zutt* as they were known in Arabic who re-emerged in the eleventh century as a warlike community which now included both Hindus and Muslims. In fact, the apparent inexorability with which Islamic forces advanced southwards had the effect of loosening the rigid military system within Hindu territory. Almost in desperation some rulers of central and southern India recruited increasing numbers of warriors from previously despised Dravidian, aboriginal 'non-Aryan' hill and forest tribes.

The organisation as well as the recruitment of Hindu armies was supposedly based upon an ideal described in religious epics such as the *Mahabharata*. Once again the much later *Atharvaveda* text on government and administration gives a more realistic picture. Here the *sena* or army was commanded by the *senapati* and traditionally consisted of four arms; infantry, cavalry, chariots and elephants. In some areas a fleet and an armaments support system were also added.

Indian armies adhered to this basic pattern, as confirmed by foreign observers like the Chinese traveller Hiuen Tsang in the seventh century. He also noted the remarkably numerous support services and camp followers which continued to characterise Indian armies. Though well-organised and equipped, these medieval Hindu forces were comparatively lacking in mobility while infantry remained overwhelmingly more numerous than other troops. During the thirteenth and fourteenth centuries, Islamic pressure led to administrative reforms in central India, even-larger armies, efforts to raise more cavalry and the maintainance of permanent forces. In the deep south, large areas of the kingdom were also formed into *palaiyam* 'military camps' in what appears to have been a militarisation of the country. Here the warlike Hindu state of Vijayanaga would rise to regional domination after the Middle Ages, but even in the fourteenth century its army was notably large and effective, consisting of regular or professional infantry archers, armoured cavalry (some riding armoured horses), huge numbers of irregulars and plenty of war elephants.

Indian infantry proved highly effective in forested or mountainous terrain throughout the medieval period, archery being so important that the most complete surviving Indian military manual was called the *Dhanurveda* or 'science of archery'. Once again there was a clear and strong similarity between this and the infantry archery of pre-Islamic Sassanian Iran. Nevertheless Hindu Indian armies remained less mobile than their northern and more particularly Turco-Islamic foes, reportedly clinging to outmoded strategy, an inferior cavalry arm and an unwarranted reliance upon the moral impact of elephants. Only in the fourteenth century did the surviving Hindu states of central and southern India attempt to give cavalry a greater role. Meanwhile their reliance on fortifications increased while the importance of elephants resulted in a strategic need to control those jungle areas where the animals bred.

The old-fashioned character of Indian warfare was similarly seen at the tactical level. According to the *Atharvaveda*, archers shot from a kneeling position, supported by infantry armed with spears and javelins, the aristocracy supposedly still fought in chariots, while some elephants were armoured and carried three or more soldiers. Meanwhile Hindu military treatises seem to have been remarkably theoretical, though varied, offering ways of fighting in open country, 'hollow' or enclosed areas, in trenches, by night and by day; ruses and stratagems were declared superior to brute force. According to the Arab scholar al-Biruni, Indian tactics were already considered old-fashioned by the tenth century. In fact this Muslim observer maintained that the Hindus were too proud to be interested in, let alone to learn from, foreigners. As a result, he claimed, their infantry was undisciplined and they relied overmuch on unpredictable elephants.

An Indo-Islamic military treatise written in the mid-thirteenth century still presented Hindu tactics as highly traditional. Here the bulk of an army was drawn up behind unspecified forms of left and right advance guards, perhaps of light cavalry, and consisting of four ranks possibly divided into flanking and central divisions. The front rank consisted of infantry archers with large shields, then 'attack' warriors apparently on foot, armoured elephants protected by sword-armed infantry, and finally spear-armed cavalry with some horse armour. Behind these combat ranks were the armoury, treasury, the ruler's harem, spare horses and other animal herds, a hospital, prisoners and religious figures, plus an army bazaar and artisans. The similarity between these traditional Hindu Indian tactics and those used in pre-Islamic southern Arabia and by the earliest Islamic Arab armies could indicate that Indian military influence spread to the western shores of the Indian Ocean, as it undoubtedly did to the east.

In twelfth-century Karnataka, Indian horsemen played polo, but medieval India was better known for another contribution to the science of military training – namely the game of chess which, in its earliest form was played by two pairs of allied teams. Some Indian cavalry horses were trained for combat against elephants in which they stood on their hind legs so that their rider's could reach those on elephantback. Perhaps as a result, Indian horsemen valued strength rather than speed in their animals. Carvings made during the period of Hoysala rule in twelfth- and thirteenth-century central India also show that some horse-armour was of a distinctive, but perhaps archaic, type that might have been similar to the unillustrated horse-armour used in early medieval Middle Eastern Islamic armies.

If Indian armies, strategy and tactics were old-fashioned, this certainly could not be said of Indian metallurgical skills. The sub-continent was at the centre of a triangular trade network in which East Africa provided raw materials and smelted iron ingots. Indian smiths converted the iron into steel ingots and finished blades which were then exported to Arabia and perhaps also to southeast Asia. Steel was, of course, also manu-factured in the Middle East, almost certainly as a result of adopting Indian techniques, and recent archaeological evidence suggests that steel had similarly been made in East Africa as early as the sixth century A.D.

Relatively little is known about military recruitment in the various Hindu, Buddhist and pagan states of southeast Asia. This was almost entirely internal, though the army of the thirteenth-century Champa state in Indochina did include Islamic artillerymen. In 1282 Muslims also helped defend the Champa capital against a Mongol attack. Meanwhile, in what is now largely-Islamic Indonesia, society was organized along Hindu caste lines, members of the indigenous military élite undergoing a *Brahmin* religious rite to change them into *kshatriya*, or members of the supposedly 'Aryan'warrior caste. This Indonesian aristocracy also cemented its status by intermarrying with Indian settlers.

The elite *ahmudan* 'guards' units of the twelfth- and thirteenth-century Buddhist states in Burma were recruited from an established aristocracy on the basis of their perceived trustworthiness. The most loyal were of ethnic Burmese origin from the central regions of what is now Myanmar (Burma), rather than partially-Indian Talaigns from the southern coast or Arakanese from the west. Nevertheless, large numbers of local levies played a major role in Burmese warfare, and these included ethnically non-Burmese troops such as militarily sophisticated Talaigns who were resettled as military colonies around the country. King Anawrahta, founder of the Burmese kingdom in the mid-eleventh century, is also credited with recruiting foreign specialists including Muslim sailors from the coast. By the fourteenth century, Burmese military commanders were often selected from rebels and *dakait* bandits, but references to *feringhi* or 'Frankish' fire troops in late thirteenth- and fourteenth-century Burma were probably later anachronistic insertions in the written sources.

The invading Mongols seem to have had little difficulty dealing with Burmese war elephants in the later thirteenth century, nor in taking Burmese fortified stockades. When the Burmese clashed with the Mongols in the thirteenth century their simple bows proved far inferior to the composite bows of their foes. Nevertheless, the Burmese soon learned from the Mongols, copying their stone-throwing siege machines by the early fourteenth century and perhaps learning also from the Islamic fire-specialists, ceramic incendiary grenades identical to those from the Middle East having been found in Burma.

Seafaring was particularly important amongst the peoples of southern India and Sri Lanka. Here the Chola state was a major naval power in the ninth to eleventh centuries, sending expeditions to conquer parts of Sri Lanka, Burma, Malaya and Sumatra. The Chola's occupation of coastal enclaves in southeast Asia was, however, brief and even northern Sri Lanka was lost around 1071. The Indian Ocean and western part of the Pacific might have been peaceful when compared to the war-torn Mediterranean, but this did not stifle technological development. Many of the most important improvements in ship design were first seen in the Far East, then spread westward along the maritime trade routes. A middle-sized thirteenth-century ship, excavated near the major medieval port of Zaitun (now Quanzhou) in southern China, even had its hull divided into thirteen watertight compartments, which was an astonishingly advanced concept. It appears to have had the deck-house characteristic of Chinese vessels but much of its cargo came from what is now Indonesia, so the precise origins of this ship remain uncertain.

There was a clear Chinese influence upon ship design in Indonesia which, however, also had close maritime relations with India and the Arab Middle East. In the early centuries rectangular sails were used, but from the eighth century onwards triangular lateen sails were either introduced by Arab traders from the west or arrived from Polynesia in the east. Less is known about the hulls of southeast Asian ships, though twelfth-century Chinese records state that Khmer *junk*-type vessels had the same cargo capacity as those from China. On the other hand, Khmer carvings from Indo-China illustrate two very distinct sorts of ship; one being an ocean-going *junk*, while the other looks more like a large war-canoe for use in river warfare. The limited written evidence indicates that their crews largely fought with archery.

River warfare similarly played a major role in medieval Burma where it was again dominated by archery, often from ship to shore. By the late fourteenth century some fleets on the Irrawaddy River consisted of hundreds of war-canoes capable of bringing enough troops to assault a major enemy stockade in a sudden dawn attack. In the twelfth century the Arakanese people of the western coast of Burma were regarded as superior mariners while sources from both east and west described Malay sailors as far-ranging and courageous. Malaya would, in fact, become a centre of piracy in the thirteenth and fourteenth centuries and remained so for many years.

Although so much of India was under Islamic rule by the end of the medieval period, the Islamic population was as yet small. In northern and central India most of the local Islamic military aristocracy claimed Persian, Afghan, Turkish or Mongol ancestry, the pre-Mughul Indo-Islamic states maintaining close links with Afghanistan, Transoxania, Iran and the Middle East. Their armies were similar to those of other eastern Islamic states but were nevertheless under increasing influence from indigenous Indian military traditions. By the fifteenth century the armies of the Turco-Islamic military élites lived off land granted by the ruling Sultan. In contrast to other parts of the Islamic world, however, such land grants were already being bought and sold by non-military middle-men. The armies of pre-Mughul northern India were also equipped in much the same way as those of neighbouring Islamic states, Timurid influence from Transoxania and Iran being particularly strong during the fifteenth century while firearms were also being adopted.

The situation in southern India was different, for here Islamic conquest took place at a relatively-late date. The indigenous Hindu population had been strictly divided into military and non-military castes but, as already seen in northern India, conversion to Islam opened up military career opportunities to every man. Nevertheless, the Islamic states of the Deccan still had only a small Islamic military class and therefore made considerable use of their Hindu subjects' martial skills.

The fact that Hindu mercenaries, horsemen as well as foot soldiers, had been employed in professional armies such as that of the tenth- and eleventh-century Islamic Ghaznawid rulers suggests they were respected warriors. Furthermore, recent converts to Islam who served in the armies of Delhi almost certainly continued to use traditional Indian tactics and weaponry, as would the unconverted Hindu troops who fought for their Islamic rulers. Despite the role played by local troops, non-Indians or peoples who had only recently settled in India clearly dominated the armies of Islamic northern India from the eleventh to fourteenth centuries. Amongst them Turks were the most prominent, along with Khitai who may in reality have been Qara Khitai or Mongol refugees. The *Rum* who are mentioned in similar sources might have been Turks from

Anatolia though they could have included a few European renegades. After the fall of the Ghurid dynasty, Ghurid mercenaries who fought for subsequent Indo-Islamic rulers presumably came from Afghanistan, the Khurasanis and Tajiks from Iran or Transoxania and the supposed 'Chinese' either from China or as assorted refugees from the eastern parts of the sprawling Mongol Empire.

By the later fourteenth century the ordinary soldiers in the Sultanate of Delhi included a bodyguard formation of men from Sistan in south-eastern Afghanistan, the professional *jandar* or *mamluk* elite, plus Turks, Ghurids, Khurasanis, Khalji Turks, Persian-speaking Tajiks, *Rawats* who are believed to have been Indians, local Hindus, Khitai of presumed Central Asian descent, and possibly even some Chinese. In time of need, the entire Islamic male population could also be called to arms. Muslims serving as infantry auxiliaries were known as *paidah* whereas Hindu infantry auxiliaries were called *payaks*, the best of the latter being Bengali archers.

Not having been conquered by the Mongols in the thirteenth century, the Sultanate of Delhi was less influenced by them. Instead Persian, Turkish and local Indian traditions predominated. The main structural difference between north Indian Islamic forces and those of the Hindu kingdoms further south was the greater importance of cavalry in the former. Instead, the Sultanate of Delhi gradually adopted traditional Indian attutudes to warfare with considerable emphasis placed upon the psychological impact of display, military music and an impressive baggage train. The war-elephants used by the Delhi Sultanate were clearly for more than mere show and were probably more effective than most European historians believe, at least before the widespread intro-duction of firearms. Some are said to have carried up to ten archers and *naft* fire throwers while the animals themselves wore armour, sometimes of iron lamellae but more commonly of leather.

The tactical role of war elephants in the Sultanate of Delhi normally seems to have been as a living wall behind the cavalry and infantry. Fakhr al-Din Mubarakshah, an Indo-Persian military theoretician writing in the thirteenth century, described an ideal battle array which was similar to that of traditional Hindu Indian armies. The front rank consisted of infantry with spears, large shields and javelins; the second of armoured infantry with swords, spears and smaller shields; the third of infantry archers with swords, maces and daggers; the fourth of junior officers with leather shields, swords and maces. Plenty of spaces would be left between various units so that the cavalry could launch their charges.

Elephants normally now remained in one position, surrounded by a protective wall of infantry, and forming vantage points for archers or javelin-throwers. However, other evidence suggests that war-elephants could charge at around twenty-five kilometres an hour while one of the few defences against such a charge was buffaloes firmly tethered together as a living field-fortification.

The Indian Ocean continued to provide a vital link between China and the Middle East, supplementing the Silk Roads across Central Asia and remaining a largely peaceful arena of commerce until the Portugese arrived at the end of the Middle Ages. Large numbers of horses were also shipped great distances in specialized horse-transports including the *tarida* type. The Mediterranean *tarida* horse-transport and its European derivations are believed to have developed from the simple Red Sea *tarada* cargo raft but it is possible that the true *tarida* horse-transport actually appeared in the Red Sea before doing so in the Mediterranean. Although most such developments in medieval maritime technology travelled from east to west, the nailed hull construction may be an exception, having come from the Mediterranean to the Red Sea where most earlier vessels had been of sawn timbers.

The hinged stern rudder definitely appears on Islamic ceramics and in manuscript illustrations from the Arabian Gulf or Red Sea areas in the eleventh century, but may be illustrated less clearly as early as the ninth century. By 942/3 *naft*, or 'Greek Fire', was also being used in the relatively infrequent naval wars of these eastern seas, Omani ships manned by 'operators with fire tubes' destroying several vessels from Basra, though the Basrans later used fire-ships to sink the Omanis. Here it is important to note that Egypt's decline as a Mediterranean naval power was not mirrored in the Red Sea, where Salah al-Din's fleet not only defeated Crusader attempts to push southwards but maintained a vital strategic link with Yemen and the Indian Ocean.

The importance of trade links across the Indian Ocean can hardly be exaggerated, and Egypt may have imported shipbuilding timber from as far away as India after the Fatimids lost control of Crete in the tenth century. The canal which linked the Nile to the Red Sea, and thus by extension linked the Mediterranean with the Indian Ocean, had silted up by 723 but it was back in service by the time the Fatimids conquered Egypt in the tenth century. During the early years of Islamic history it had been used to ship Egyptian grain to the Hijaz and the Islamic Holy Cities in Arabia, just as Egyptian grain had previously been shipped to Rome or Constantinople. Its purpose later in the medieval period is less obvious and there was little need for merchant ships to sail from the Red Sea to the Nile. So perhaps this medieval version of the Suez Canal may have been primarily military, enabling squadrons based on the Nile to defend both the Mediterranean and Red Sea coasts of Egypt.

Chapter 5
Arms & Armour

European arms and armour of the early medieval period are widely assumed to have been simple, not particularly varied and far from abundant. Although this is an oversimplification, armour was, in relative terms, very expensive even in prosperous states and elsewhere it could be beyond the reach even of some members of the ruling aristocracy. Certain regulations issued by early medieval rulers may, in reality, have projected an ideal based upon Byzantine practice rather than reflecting what could be achieved within an economically stagnant Western Europe. Meanwhile, more than mere military 'ideals' came from the Byzantine world. Byzantine styles of arms and armour, plus a fair amount of actual weaponry had probably come westward, some of it reaching as far afield as Scandinavia and even Iceland. The early medieval period had similarly witnessed strong military influence from steppe peoples in and beyond Eastern Europe. Islamic military influences were probably more localised, some reaching Western Europe via these same steppe nomads while other influences stemmed directly from the Middle East, North Africa, the Islamic regions of the Iberian Peninsula and Islamic-ruled Sicily.

In fact, the centuries immediately preceding the Crusades saw greater changes in tactics than in military technology, with the possible exception of horse harness. The down-to-earth attitude of professional armies within Byzantine and Islamic civilisations during this period was also evident in military treatises which criticised extravagently decorated arms and harness while recommending good quality equipment of plain iron. Nevertheless the warrior's characteristic love of display could not be suppressed, as shown in several magnificently decorated surviving artifacts, while rulers displayed their own power and wealth by issuing guard units with eye-catching arms and armour. It is also worth noting that, as men of Turkish origin came to dominate the armies of the eastern and central Islamic regions, pre-Islamic Central Asian decorative motifs for weaponry and harness spread westward despite the fact that such troops were now Muslim.

The pace of change in Western European arms and armour quickened during the twelfth and thirteenth centuries. Archery was probably the main stimulus, above all the development and wider use of crossbows which were as yet the only infantry weapon realistically capable of challenging the fully-armoured cavalryman's domination of the battle-field. The crossbow may, in fact, have been largely responsible for the adoption of face-covering helmets, rigid body armour and horse armour. Partly as a result of such developments, there was an increasingly clear separation between the equipment of cavalry and that of foot soldiers within Western Europe. Climate also played a part, though largely in the way in which such new challenges were met and in the materials used by armourers. Here it is worth noting that many new features in the design or construction of European armour were first seen in the south, including the Iberian Peninsula and Italy, which were areas under Islamic or Byzantine military influence. Furthermore, these were countries where archery had long played a significant role in warfare.

The fourteenth century witnessed a continuation of this 'arms race' between the power of crossbows, and subsequently also of small hand-held guns, and the effectiveness of increasingly sophisticated body armour. On one hand special armour-piercing steel-tipped crossbow bolts were developed, and on the other the heavily armoured men-at-arms of Western Europe adopted increasing amounts of plate armour, covering not only their vital organs but also their limbs. At the same time it is important to emphasise that the fully developed plate armour of the late fourteenth and fifteenth centuries was not necessarily heavier than older forms of mail protection. Further more, its weight was so skilfully dispersed that a fully armoured man was entirely capable of running, fighting on foot, mounting and dismounting his horse without difficulty. The widespread idea that such men-at-arms were rendered virtually immobile by such armour, particularly if they had fallen from their horses, is a myth. Nevertheless, fully armoured men would tire more quickly and were vulnerable to heat-exhaustion.

The fourteenth and fifteenth centuries similarly saw an increase in regional variations in armour, compared to the remarkable uniformity which characterised the twelfth and thirteenth centuries. One such divergence was between the armours of Germany and Italy. This partially resulted from climatic differences but also reflected differing degrees of external influence from the south and east. For example, it was not until the end of the fourteenth century that Islamic and Turco-Mongol or Central Asian fashions in arms and armour ceased to have more than a localised influence. Those regions which remained under noticeable external influences were the Iberian Peninsula, eastern and southeastern Europe. Among the most visible examples of regional variation was the widespread use of hardened and often highly-decorated leather armour in Italy, which may have resulted from the experience of Italo-Angevin armies in the Balkans.

A greater amount of armour had been worn by horsemen than infantry for several centuries, though this was in direct contradicition of the previous ancient Graeco-Roman period. This distinction became even more pronounced with the increasing importance of virtually un-armoured light infantry forces from the later thirteenth century onwards. Documentary sources containing remarkably detailed information also became more readily available. These included late thirteenth-century mercenary contracts from Italy which stipulated precisely what a hired cavalryman must wear.

From only a few years later there are documents such as the inventory of possessions of a senior French nobleman killed at the battle of Courtrai in 1302 AD. There is no reason to believe that he was untypical of the aristocratic military élites of several Western European states. The mili-tary equipment in this inventory consisted of windlass-spanned crossbows plus other ordinary types of crossbow; quilted as well as iron and perhaps leather forms of horse-armour; armour for a horse's head; and mail hauberks of various kinds for the man himself, including one *gazerant*, which may have incorporated a padded lining. There was also armour for use in tournaments rather than in war; plated and perhaps quilted armour for the neck and throat; a 'coat-of-plates' which was essentially a cloth-covered, scale-lined armour; leg protections to which rigid shin-covering greaves were attached; arm defences and a 'whale-bone' shoulder protection.

Furthermore, the fourteenth and fifteenth centuries were a period of fundamental change in Western European male costume. The earlier loose clothes which had much in common with Byzantine, eastern European and Middle Eastern dress were rapidly replaced by a distinc-tively Western fashion for almost body-hugging male garments. Even the Crusading Military Orders, whose traditional robe-like garments reflected their religious origins, were not immune from these changes and it is clear that the brethren, when not actually involved in their religious duties, often wore clothes that differed little from those of the secular knightly class.

Distinctive Western European fashions also enabled Latin or Catholic Christians to make a visual distinction between themselves and the Orthodox Christians within those eastern Mediterranean, Aegean and other ex-Byzantine territories which they now ruled as 'Crusader States'. Meanwhile the prohibition against decorated weapons within the Crusading Military Orders was virtually abandoned. Within secular aristocratic and senior military groups, the abundance of decoration on arms, armour and clothing could be astonishing during this period.

This was the period which saw greater changes in Western European arms and, above all, armour than any other. Plate body and limb protections of iron and hardened leather had been known for some time, but their further adoption was not a regular process. In fact, traditional and supposedly more advanced forms of armour coexisted at the same time, sometimes within the same regions, while climatic factors played a part by apparently slowing the adoption of metallic plate armour in hot areas such as Italy, Spain, Greece and the Balkans.

It would, however, be wrong to assume that all such armour was of the finest quality. A great deal of that worn by lower status soldiers was what might today be called 'munitions quality' – neither being of the best steel, nor well finished, and often entirely undecorated. Though such items survive more rarely than does 'splendid' armour associated with leading personalities, archaeological finds of later medieval Western European military equipment tend to demolish some romantic images of the 'gleaming' medieval knight. More importantly, the degree of variation in such objects contrasts with the rather uniform appearance of fighting men in much medieval European art.

Whereas the arms and armour of the Crusader States, Christian Iberia, even to some extent the Byzantine Empire and other Orthodox Christian states in the Balkans, had a great deal in common, those of the Islamic world varied considerably from the Indian frontier to Andalusia. At each of these extremes there was, however, similarity between the weaponry of Muslim frontier troops and those of their opponents, be they Hindu Indians in the east or Christian Spaniards in the west. Meanwhile, these centuries witnessed a seemingly sudden spread in the use of larger quantities of iron weaponry south of the Sahara, despite the fact that iron and even to a small degree steel-working had been known in sub-Saharan Africa for centuries.

Generally speaking, influences in the design and construction of arms and armour flowed from east to west during the medieval period. Yet there was also a clear Iranian influence upon several aspects of Central Asian and Indian weaponry. Far to the north the Turco-Islamic Volga Bulgars were similarly under strong Russian military influence during the twelfth and thirteenth centuries, Russia itself having been under strong Scandinavian military influence until at least the eleventh century. Yet even in Russia, eastern influences soon predominated with high quality Asian arms and armour supposedly being introduced by Turkish 'Black Cap' auxiliaries even before the coming of the Mongols.

Mongol influence then spread beyond Russia and the Middle East, with medieval Western European commentators, and even some rulers, taking a particular interest in those Mongol forms of body armour which had proved more effective against archery than had their own European forms of protection. Paradoxically, the Mongols had traditionally been short of iron, most of those sources which they did control lying within the forested rather than steppe zones. This surely accounted for the importance of hardened leather armour amongst Turco-Mongol armies. Nevertheless, the idea that Russian military technology stagnated under 'primitive' Mongol domination is nonsense. Mongol styles of equipment were adopted with enthusiasm by the army of the Russian principality of Galich as early as 1246. Thereafter Russian troops copied many aspects of Mongol arms and armour.

In technological terms, the only real rival to China as a source of advanced technology was India. Swords of Indian origin or manufactured from imported Indian steel had enjoyed the highest prestige in pre- and early-Islamic Arabia. Thereafter, however, Indian influence upon the arms and armour of other countries tended to be localised, although distinctively Indian-style weapons survived for ceremonial purposes within Malaya and what is now Indonesia, well after that part of south-east Asia had largely been converted to Islam at the end of the Middle Ages.

Chapter 6
Arms Trade and Arms Manufacture

Western Europe

Compared with many other parts of the medieval world, Europe was rich in sources of iron. Even so, the economic decline of the early medieval period meant that iron remained in short supply until a revival in the overall European economy during the eleventh and twelfth centuries. Many of the major sources lay within the major Western European states and, furthermore, were in thickly forested legions. Where iron mines were not close to abundant sources of such timber for fuel, governments tried to keep strict control over both mining and the limited available forests; the Norman Kingdom in Sicily and southern Italy being one such region.

Wood and, to a lesser extent, water were essential for medieval metal production. The resulting huge demands for timber led to deforestation in some regions by the fourteenth century, which probably contributed to a gradual turn towards coal as a source of power. This in turn led to different problems and in 1306 the governor of Arles banned its use in forges because coal caused increased phosphorus and sulphur content in iron which was thus weaker than iron smelted in the traditional way using charcoal.

There is little evidence for a decline in European metallurgical skills following the fall of the Western Roman Empire, and the idea that an abandonment of large items of iron plate armour from the fifth to thirteenth centuries reflected an inability to make them is clearly wrong. The required technology continued to be demonstrated in early medieval helmets and there may actually have been an increase in armourers' skills during these centuries. Furthermore, metallurgical advances were introduced from the Middle East and beyond, while the twelfth and thirteenth centuries saw important changes in the intellectual climate within Western Europe. Here the educated élite began to adopt a positive attitude towards science and technology, reflecting contacts with Islamic civilisation. Indeed, from the twelfth century onwards, Western Europe became what could be called a 'mechanism-minded' civilisation in which new technologies were easily assimilated. The mechanical arts were no longer seen as a hindrance to man's spiritual destiny but as a potential help. The results included some remarkably modern, if not necessarily widespread, opinions during the early twelfth century where, at a time when the Crusades seemed to dominate the attitudes of the ruling aristocracy, a scholar like Hugh of St. Victor could advocated trade as a way of bringing peoples together in peace – even including Muslims and heathens.

During the Middle Ages several methods were used to produce iron arms and armour with differing degrees of hardness or flexibility. Most had been available to late Roman armourers but had not been widely used. The technique of case-hardening was, for example, known in the classical world but was not developed further until the tenth or eleventh century. In this process, the outer surface of a blade was hardened by repeated heating and sudden cooling or 'quenching' in cold water. In contrast, pattern welding is sometimes known as 'false damascene' and resulted from strips of harder and softer iron being twisted together, then repeatedly heated and beaten flat. This was not true welding, which required much greater heat, but pattern welding had been used for effective and sturdy sword-blades during the early medieval period, though apparently only for small knives from the tenth to twelfth centuries.

By the ninth century the famous sword-blades of the Rhineland, which were exported throughout most of Europe and beyond, were no longer made by folding or twisting strips of hard and soft iron. Instead sword-smiths used a system of piling or laminating such strips in a technique which probably demanded higher temperatures. This was in turn replaced by the 'single bar' structure of eleventh to fifteenth century Western European blades made from a single strip of higher and more consistent quality steel. As sufficiently high temperatures became possible, true welding also came into use, particularly when adding narrow strips of hard steel to form the cutting edges of wrought iron knives or daggers.

It has been suggested that the widespread replacement of plate armour by mail armour during the late Roman and early medieval centuries was because mail was simpler and cheaper to make than plate armour. It would certainly be manufactured in great quantities and the mail-maker's craft became substantially mechanised after the development of water-powered wire-drawing machines in the mid-fourteenth century. The mail itself, however, remained a largely unchanging form of protection with minor variations in construction.

Not all European armour was of iron, with copper continuing to be used in some backward areas such as Finland. Many other materials were similarly used, particularly in periods of experimentation such as the thirteenth and early fourteenth centuries. These included whalebone, horn and latten, which was an alloy of copper, zinc, lead and tin. Various forms of leather were, however, more significant and widespread; the first semi-rigid pieces of medieval Western European body armour probably being of leather rather than of iron, perhaps of vegetable-tanned cattle hide, 'cuir bouilli' hardened leather, buff leather and rawhide. Cuir bouilli was not, as is often thought, 'boiled' leather since boiling simply made the material soft. Instead, leather was soaked in melted wax, then hardened and shaped by heating and drying in a mould or over a matrix. The effectiveness and lightness of cuir bouilli armour was such that it remained in use throughout most of the fourteenth century.

Wood was another vital material, most obviously for weapons shafts or handles and for shields. Some early medieval shields may have been of a layered, almost plywood, construction with an inner layer of oak and an outer of alder. One eleventh century German text indicates that a form of cheese paste was used as glue. The thicker shields of the thirteenth century were often made of willow and poplar, while fine-grained boxwood was used for dagger-handles. Yew was the finest though not the only wood for bows of simple rather than composite construction, and cornel or dogwood was used in crossbows.

The situation in certain frontier territories of Western Europe was interesting though not necessarily very different. For example, the movement of military equipment within Iberia was similar to that in France, sometimes in the form of tribute as when Catalonia sent armour and swords to Islamic Cordoba in the tenth century. Or it could be an aspect of feudal obligation, as in the twelfth-century kingdom of León where holders of some non-noble and semi-hereditary *benefices* could inherit their father's military gear only if he had died in the service of his king. Otherwise it was returned to the government. Meanwhile several regions within the Christian-ruled northern parts of the Iberian Peninsula developed into major arms-manufacturing and exporting centres, but whereas Catalonia became one of Western Europe's main armaments centres in the fourteenth century, Portugal's similarly dated but small-scale industry was located in the south of the country, in the hands of Jewish or Muslim smiths.

The Crusader States in the Middle East and around the Aegean were more dependent upon outside supplies of military equipment than almost any other part of Catholic Christendom. Even the small metal-working industry in Beirut, which relied upon iron ore from Mount Lebanon, does not seem to have produced major military items. Perhaps because of this dependence upon weaponry imported from Europe, the rulers of the Middle Eastern Crusader States were often forced to hand over such equipment to their Islamic enemies in return for peace. This clearly happened in the mid-twelfth century when the Count of Edessa bought off a threatened Turkish attack by offering tribute and a number of horse armours.

Booty was another important source of supply, despite differences between the military equipment and tactics of the Crusader States and most of their neighbours. For example, some historians have estimated that the loot from Constantinople following the Fourth Crusade included no less than 10,000 armours plus other materiel, though this was almost certainly an exaggeration. Otherwise Western European Crusaders could donate arms and armour to the Military Orders in their wills, this then being shipped to the frontline Crusader States. The Rule of the Hospitallers similarly specified that brother knights travelling east must bring a supply of arms with them, but that such equipment should not travel in the opposite direction.

The Angevin rulers of southern Italy similarly sent large quantities of money and food to the Crusader States of Greece in the 1270s to 1290s, and it seems likely that such support included arms and armour. Within these Aegean and Greek Crusader States the difficulties of reliable military supplies led to the establishment of a substantial armoury in Clarence Castle in 1281 to serve as a strategic reserve.

The Byzantine World

The Byzantine Empire was acutely short of iron resources through much of its history, most mines being located in frontier areas such as Armenia and the Caucasus. After losing most of the east to the Saljuq Turks in the late eleventh century, Byzantine armies were sometimes seriously short of arms and armour, partly because the empire now controlled no major mines and partly because of its declining wealth.

Where military technology was concerned, the early medieval Byzantines were almost as keen to copy and to learn as were their Islamic rivals. The strict government control over armourers and arms merchants that had characterised the Late Roman period had been relaxed because of the Empire's acute shortage of military equipment and there might have been a move towards the privatisation of manufacture and distribution. Nevertheless, despite its lack of iron resources, the early Byzantine Empire still had Imperial *armamenton* arms factories descended from the late Roman *fabricae*, most of which were concentrated in the capital. Evidence from the mid-tenth century indicates that the chief official of the Imperial *armamenton* passed orders for the making of equipment to the *katepan* of the *arma* while various other items were ordered from provincial sources. The Imperial *vestiarion* similarly made fire-weapons and siege engines for the army and navy. By the eleventh century, however, many Byzantine towns had their own salaried armourers in a system which continued at least into the thirteenth century. During the twelfth century there was, for example, an armour-making *zabareion* manufacturing centre in Byzantium's second city of Thessaloniki, while others may have existed elsewhere. Less is known about later years, but in the fourteenth century bows and other simple weapons were certainly being made locally in what remained of the Byzantine Empire's Balkan provinces.

Traditionally, most Byzantine soldiers had received their military equipment from the state, the élite corps being equipped from government stores, though some foreign recruits and mercenaries arrived with their own weaponry. Amongst those equipped by the state, equipment seems to have been distributed at the start of a campaign and did not remain in the men's possession, this system still being recorded in twelfth century Byzantine armies. In contrast the equipment of provincial troops apparently passed from generation to generation.

In the early centuries the bulk of Byzantine war materiel was made by Byzantine armourers, though there had probably always been a flow of such items from outside, either as government imports, booty, tribute, or diplomatic gifts. For example, a substantial volume of southern Italian weaponry was captured from invading Normans in the twelfth century and from invading Angevins in the following century. By then, however, the empire's shrinking resources meant that the government offered tax exemptions and other inducements to encourage a peaceful importation of Western European military equipment. The mid-thirteenth century Byzantine 'successor empire' of Nicea seems to have relied primarily on Genoa for both weaponry and horses, while fourteenth-century Byzantine Constantinople purchased iron and weaponry from Dubrovnik, Genoa and Venice. The substantial trade in arms and harness from northern central Europe through southern Poland and Moldavia to the Black Sea ports during the fifteenth century may also have existed at an earlier date.

Most information about arms manufacture in medieval Russia comes from outside observers. During the ninth and tenth century the Slav Polianian tribe of the Kiev area maintained a long-established weapons making tradition while specialised metal-working quarters existed within Kiev during the twelfth century, subsequently appearing in Novgorod in the thirteenth century.

The Islamic World

Most of the Islamic world's iron resources were in frontier provinces while the mines of the Middle Eastern heartlands had largely been exhausted by the time of the Crusades. As a result sources under effective Islamic control had to be supplemented by a long-distance trade which flourished in this relatively rich, urbanised civilisation with its well developed money economy. Some regions seemed more favoured than they really were. For example Iran was not only rich in iron and other metals but also controlled major trade routes; nevertheless a lack of timber for fuel with which to smelt and work iron remained a major problem.

During the early centuries of Islamic history there had been a considerable increase in the utilisation of available iron ore both within the Islamic world and in those lands which formed part of the Islamic world's extensive trading network such as the Caucasus, Ural and Altai mountains, India, East Africa and parts of southern Europe. Elsewhere, the control of even small mines could be a matter of immediate military concern, as seen in the Iberian *sierras* during the wars of the *Reconquista*, and in Lebanon and northern Jordan during the Crusades. Similarly a country like Egypt, which was now almost completely dependent upon outside sources for both metals and timber, remained vulnerable to European trade embargoes or naval blockades.

Other materials were similarly required for military equipment. Leather was particularly important for shields, helmets, lamellar armour, scabbards, straps and horse-harness. Wood was needed for weapon shafts, bows, shields, saddle frames and above all for ship-building.

A soldier's requirements could be highly specific. For example, some thirteenth-century crossbowmen preferred their weapons to be made of cornel or dogwood from the Trabzon area of northern Anatolia while Ibn Hudhayl, writing in fourteenth-century Granada, went into extraordinary detail when listing the materials needed for such a crossbow. These included five 'cultivated' forms of wood and five 'wild' timbers which had to be taken from a particular side of the tree and be cut at a particular season to obtain the finest quality. The purchasing of horn for making composite bows seems to have been similarly specific; a surviving tenth-century Arab agricultural calendar from Cordoba stating that June was the month when government officials purchased goat and wild cattle horn for this purpose. Three hundred years later an Armenian armourer working for a Crusader king of Jerusalem crossed the frontier into Islamic Damascus to buy horn and glue for crossbows. Damascus was by then the biggest centre of composite bow manufacture in the Islamic world.

The highly practical Islamic attitude towards knowledge encouraged an absorption of new technologies and a rational classification of all sorts of information. This in turn stimulated a curiosity about military or other artefacts from distant civilisations. Nevertheless, the bulk of Islamic military equipment was probably made in an almost production-line technique. According to al-Jahiz of Basra it took at least nine different Muslim craftsmen to make a sword with its associated scabbard and belt,

while properly-trained and professional Muslim soldiers were theoretically responsible for maintaining and repairing their own kit. One
thirteenth-century Egyptian source noted that the cost of raw materials,
along with military equipment and the wages of skilled craftsmen such as
swordsmiths, armourers and polishers, increased dramatically when a
major campaign was imminent.

By this time some regions had become famous for one or more items
of equipment or harness. Khwarazm in Islamic Central Asia, for example,
had been renowned for both cavalry armour and horse armour between
the eighth and tenth centuries, though the subsequent fate of this industry
is unclear. Other eastern provinces produced armour and harness,
though the most important was the iron-rich mountainous province of
Ghur in Afghanistan. Shash in Transoxiana was noted for archery equipment while Daghestan in the Caucasus had been famous as an
arms-manufacturing centre since pre-Islamic times and remained so
throughout the Middle Ages. In fact, the earliest unambiguous references
to the new style of mail-and-plate armour stemmed from this region
during the early fifteenth century.

Military equipment had been made in Syria since ancient times but
Damascus, having long been a major arms distribution centre, appears
to have emerged as a manufacturing centre by the tenth century. On the
far side of the desert, Baghdad had a similarly specialised quarter called
the Archway of the Armourers in the eleventh and twelfth centuries.
By the eleventh century there were references to Western European
armourers working in Cairo, and further west Tunisia exported leather
cuirasses during the late fourteenth century. Armourers had been
concentrated around the main mosque in what was known as the New
Quarter of tenth-century Palermo in Sicily but the arms of the Islamic
regions of the Iberian peninsula were much more famous, especially for
sword-blades. In fact Toledo, Almeria, Murcia, Cordoba and Seville
were all major manufacturing centres at various times.

Since virtually every corner of the medieval Islamic world was incorporated into the most sophisticated trading network seen in the
medieval period, weaponry from distant lands often changed hands
within and between Islamic armies. This was clearly true of sword-blades.
Money and weapons were sometimes also given to freed fellow-Muslim
prisoners as a gesture of reconciliation. Sometimes the sheer volume of
military booty led to a sharp, if temporary, fall in prices in the arms
bazaars, as happened after the Saljuq Turkish defeat of the Byzantine
army at Manzikert in 1071.

Even after the Caliphate fragmented in the tenth century, the
established patterns of trade and tribute largely persisted. Trade between
Central Asian Khwarazm and the Slav peoples of eastern Europe

probably included mail hauberks made in the Rhineland of Germany; these then being sold in Transoxania and eastern Iran. Russian merchants were reportedly selling European swords in Baghdad in the tenth and eleventh centuries while the Volga Bulgars of what is now Russia grew rich from a transit trade between eastern Europe and the Islamic world. Diplomatic exchanges of gifts similarly played an important role, though not in terms of volume. Sometimes these gifts reflected diplomatic manoeuvring, as when Saladin and the Byzantine Emperor exchanged shipments of weaponry and mutual congratulation after defeating Crusaders in Palestine and invading Italo-Normans in the Balkans.

Medieval Islamic governments took a primary role in this arms trade, particularly when it involved imports from Europe. Most came from or via Italy, some of the earliest references specifying Venice during the tenth century. In 1173, at the height of the Crusader occupation of the Holy Land, Pisa reached an agreement with Saladin to supply strategic raw materials for his army and navy despite a supposed Papal ban on such trade. The Popes tried even harder to ban these European exports after the fall of the last Crusader outposts to the Mamluk Sultanate in 1291.

The distribution of weaponry within Islamic armies was similar to that seen in the Byzantine Empire, with professional soldiers receiving their arms and armour from government arsenals at the start of a campaign. They would then have the cost of such equipment deducted from their pay if it were lost – unless the soldier had a good excuse, such as being wounded or defeated in battle. Saladin's élite troops clearly collected their kit from the *zardkhanah* state arsenal along with their pay at the start of each campaign. Even in politically tumultuous regions like twelfth-century Yemen, rulers attempted to keep all weapons, other than what might today be called 'side-arms', within a communal arsenal and under government control. Meanwhile Muslims, like their Crusader rivals, reused captured military equipment if it suited their style of warfare.

A similar situation existed in North Africa and al-Andalus. By the ninth century, North Africa was importing swords from Western Europe; Genoa probably still selling military equipment through the Moroccan port of Ceuta in the twelfth century. North Africa had imported arms, armour and harness from Islamic al-Andalus since at least the tenth century while at the same time al-Andalus imported horse harness from Iraq, armour and bows from Iran and Central Asia, helmets and other weapons from India and even farther east. In return, the Andalusians exported sword-blades to the eastern Islamic lands and to India. Further south, the Saharan nomadic tribes purchased virtually all their weaponry from settled neighbours, even including their famous *lamt* leather shields.

Whether the relatively-sudden reappearance of iron helmets wrought from a single piece of metal in early Islamic armies was an internal development, a survival of Roman technology, or reflected technological contact with China, remains unclear. Of all the metallurgical techniques associated with the medieval Middle East, however, none was more distinctive than that of the 'damascene' blade. True 'damascene' and its associated surface patterning resulted from the elongation of an ingot of high-carbon steel, resulting in an exceptionally sharp cutting edge while retaining the flexibility of the overall blade. The density of the surface pattern, known as *firind* in Arabic and 'watering' in Europe, was also an indication of quality. Meanwhile, other techniques were being used in the Islamic world and by its neighbours. The scientific scholars, al-Kindi and al-Biruni, stated that early medieval Byzantine, Russian and other Slav smiths used what they called 'soft iron' whereas Western European smiths used a mixture of 'hard' and 'soft' iron – in other words piling or pattern-welding – when making sword-blades. The Islamic Middle Eastern states then imported blades from all these areas as well as from India.

Techniques of leather-working were hardly less sophisticated and varied. The renouned *lamt* shields of the Sahara and North Africa were, for example, made of several layers of hide glued together. A highly-detailed late twelfth-century manuscript from Egypt not only stated that a *jawshan* or lamellar cuirass could be made of horn, hardened leather or iron, but went on to provide a recipe for making rawhide lamellae or lames for armour and panels for helmets.

Central Asia

Most of the major non-Islamic iron-working areas which traded with the Islamic world also produced weaponry for more local use. For example the Altai, Tien Shan and other Central Asian mountains probably made arms and armour for the Turks and Mongols as well as sending iron ingots to Islamic iron-working centres in Transoxiana and Iran. Within Central Asia some tribes or peoples had a higher reputation as armourers than others. The Turkish Uighurs were rich in iron and were said by Chinese writers to have many smiths. The Turkish Kipchaqs were also noted metalworkers while among non-Turkish peoples the Tibetans were more noted for leather, exporting leather shields as far as the Mediterranean. References to Tibetan leather shields and leather lamellar cuirasses being used in the early medieval Islamic Middle East are probably true, given the wide-ranging trading activities of this period.

However, Central Asia itself largely remained an exporter of raw materials rather than finished equipment, and as a result even its mightiest rulers could face problems in this regard. The Mongol *khans* would, for example, send officers to buy up all available arms and armour in recently-conquered territories before setting off on new conquests. When they took over a flourishing industrialised area such as Iran, these new Mongol rulers established their own arsenals rather than relying on equipment sent from the poorer and more-primitive heartlands of Mongolia. On the other hand, eastern Central Asia's relative poverty in military equipment should not be exaggerated, as the Chinese more than once captured sufficient quantities of armour or weapons from their Turkish neighbours to warrant it being repaired and overhauled for Chinese use.

India

Most advances in medieval metallurgy took place in China or India and then spread westward, first to the Islamic world and subsequently to Europe. Iron-casting was a case in point, having been known in China since the second century BC, then reaching India and the Middle East but not being widely used in Europe until the fifteenth century. During the fifth century AD steel was being made in China by heating cast and wrought iron together. By the eleventh and twelfth centuries this method was considered almost as good as decarbonised steel, having been passed to the Arabs during the eleventh century, though again it did not reach Western Europe for another five hundred years. A spread of Chinese technology might also have stimulated the development in India of machines which could blow air into shaft-furnaces. This in turn led to a considerable increase in the manufacture of cast iron which lay behind India's superiority in several aspects of early medieval metallurgy. During the first centuries AD, Indian smiths in the southern Deccan may actually have been the first to cast blades from molten steel, and in subsequent centuries ingots of Indian steel were certainly exported as far as Damascus in Syria and Toledo in the Iberian peninsula where they were shaped into sword-blades.

Africa

East Africa had imported weapons and tools from the Mediterranean at the time of the Roman Empire but thereafter close technological and trading links with medieval Islamic civilisation turned East Africa into a major iron exporting region as well as, at least by the late Middle Ages, one capable of producing steel. Much of the ore for the flourishing Indian industry actually came from East Africa in Arab merchant ships, resulting in a pattern of long-distance trade which had no real parallels until early modern times. A technological link between East Africa and south-east Asia may also have been associated with the colonisation of Madagascar by peoples from what is now Indonesia during the early medieval period. As a consequence of this and other technological influences from North Africa and the Middle East, there was a notable increase in iron-working throughout much of sub-Saharan Africa from the tenth century onwards. During the fourteenth century the rulers of the vast and newly-Islamic kingdom of Mali, south of the Sahara desert, imposed a state monopoly upon trade in iron, weapons and horses because of their military importance.

Chapter 7
Horse Harness & Horse Armour

Horse harness

The early medieval period witnessed a number of important developments in horse harness, though their immediate military significiance has
often been exaggerated by military historians. Stirrups were, for example,
known in Central and Western Europe by the later eighth century but
were not widely used except by peoples who had recently arrived from
the east such as the Avars and the Magyars. Paradoxically, the form of
stirrups which was then most widely adopted in Western Europe from
the tenth century onwards was of a different design from that used by
nomads and ex-nomads. Indeed it looked more like a metallic version of
the leather stirrups with wooden treads characteristic of several Eurasian
forest and steppe peoples as well as some Middle Eastern stirrups. This
could indicate eastern European and Byzantine inspiration with the
Norse-Vikings having played a significant role spreading this new
addition to horse harness within tenth century Europe. Other developments included a reintroduction of horseshoes probably via the Muslim
Arabs whose own cavalry technology reflected the dry and stony terrain
of their ancestral Middle Eastern homeland.

A new form of more supportive wood-framed European saddle may
similarly have reflected Middle Eastern Islamic and Byzantine inspiration, though steppe influence also played a part. This new saddle was
associated with breast and crupper straps around the front and rear of the
horse's body. Doubled girths beneath the animal's body were another
common, though not universal, feature which was again designed to stop
the saddle slipping or tipping backwards and forwards. Like the breast
and crupper straps, it helped keep a saddle in place when riding over
rough terrain and during the stresses of mounted combat.

The breast-strap may have been even more important with the
adoption of the couched lance; certainly more so than stirrups and at least
as much as the deep or peaked saddle. Nevertheless, the very raised
pommel and cantle of the latter gave a rider with a couched lance much

greater support when he, his weapon and his horse came in contact with their target. On the other hand it can be argued that a widespread adoption of a very broad and often decorated breast-strap by western European armoured cavalry during the eleventh century may have been a result of, rather than a contributary factor towards, the further development of couched lance tactics.

Few changes were apparent in European horse harness during the twelfth and thirteenth centuries, the fully-developed curb bit not being reintroduced into most of Western Europe until the final decades of this period. Once again this development was probably a result of Islamic or Byzantine influence. Meanwhile, the influence of the nomadic peoples of the Eurasian steppes continued to be felt in the horse harness of Hungary, the Balkans, the eastern Baltic regions and parts of Poland.

On the other hand the deep-seated or peaked saddle associated with the couched lance tactic had become standard equipment for the knightly warhorses of Western Europe by the early twelfth century, along with the broad breast strap. Yet even this could burst with the impact of a shock charge, especially against opposing cavalry or while jousting. As a result such wide straps were sometimes wrapped around the rear of a saddle, rather than merely being buckled to its front, by the thirteenth century.

The fourteenth century finally saw the curb bit adopted across most of Western Europe, this type of bit having been known in the Middle East, most of eastern Europe, Hungary and the Iberian peninsula for several centuries. Rowel spurs, which consisted of a revolving spiked wheel rather than a single spike as in the prick spur, were similarly adopted, perhaps having spread from eastern Europe, Russia or Byzantium. Thereafter, Western European horse harness would not substantially change for several centuries, though the ferocity of the curb bit and the length of the shafts of rowel spurs tended to increase.

While they survived, the Crusader States remained fully within Western European traditions of harness and saddlery, except where locally-recruited light cavalry were concerned. These, judging by the very limited available evidence, had much in common with their Islamic neighbours in the Middle Eastern Crusader States, and with their Byzantine neighbours in the Crusader States of Greece

Unfortunately, very little is known about medieval Byzantine horse harness and saddles, though the illustrated evidence shows that the horsemen of this and neighbouring regions were under increasingly strong Turkish influence. Much more abundant evidence survives concerning Russian horse furniture. Russian horsemen copied the styles of both their eastern and western neighbours, the abundant harness found in tenth-eleventh century grave sites showing a lively trade in horse harness from Finns in the eastern forests, nomads in the southern steppes, Hungarians and Germans in the west. There was also a gradual move away from elaborately-decorated to much more functional horse harness, which itself points to increasing numbers of cavalry by the twelfth century.

Russian bridles, saddles and stirrups now indicated a clear differentiation between the harness of light and heavy cavalry. The former largely remained within the steppe nomad style while the latter became increasingly similar to the cavalry of the rest of Europe. Spurs were, for example adopted under Western or Byzantine influence in the mid-eleventh century, whereas these were still not used by nomads who relied upon whips to urge their horses forward. Nevertheless there seem to have been different forms of spurs for light and heavy cavalry. Furthermore, the archaeological evidence suggests that the rowel spur was known in Russia up to half a century before it appeared in most of Western Europe. This would seem remarkable for a device so closely associated with the Western form of lance-armed cavalry combat. However, it may have come from the Byzantine world since the rowel spur actually appears in Byzantine art before it did so in Western art.

A surprising variety of simple and sophisticated items of horse harness could be found within the relatively small region of the eastern Mediterrean. These even included primitive leather loop stirrups which were still being used in twelfth-century Cyprus. In contrast, on the mainland the notably advanced 'Islamic School' of horsemanship reached its peak in twelfth- and thirteenth-century Syria and Egypt. Unlike the medieval European style of riding, the Islamic School emphasized a firm seat and the ability to ride long distances without fatigue rather than the Westerners' preoccupation with remaining in the saddle despite the most powerful blows. This Islamic School of riding must not, however, be confused with the *jinete* style of North Africa and the Iberian Peninsula, nor with the Turco-Mongol riding style associated with nomad horse-archery. Both of the latter were characterised by short stirrup-leathers, with the rider rising from his saddle almost like a modern racing jockey.

Furthermore, North Africa and the Iberian Peninsula were the only regions in which there were major changes to horse harness and saddlery during the High and Later Middle Ages. By the twelfth or thirteenth century a distinctive Berber or North African saddle, harness and associated light cavalry riding style had developed, subsequently becoming known as *a la jinete*. It made early use of a rather fierce form of palate bit and was seen on both sides of the Straits of Gibraltar, as well as in Christian Iberia, earlier than elsewhere in Western Europe. In complete contrast, there was a brief period during the late thirteenth century when many Muslim Andalusian cavalrymen copied the heavy cavalry styles of their northern Iberian foes; even sometimes using a strap around a rider's waist and his saddle to hold him firmly in place. Indeed, it almost seemed that these Andalusian heavy cavalrymen went further in rigidly attaching themselves to their horses than did Spanish knights, this waist strap not being recorded elsewhere until it appeared in fourteenth-century Italy.

As might be expected in regions where warfare was dominated by cavalry, the horse harness of the Turco-Mongol peoples of the Eurasian steppes was highly developed and often very decorative. Early medieval Turkish harness, for example, included the *kemeldürük* breast strap, *kos kum* crupper strap and the *içlik* thick saddle-blanket. Horsemen could ride on this blanket alone, without using a saddle, whereas the *al* was a more decorative saddle-cloth often used as badge of rank, as were *beçkem* tassles hanging from beneath the throat-lash of a bridle. One of the most notable differences between European and steppe nomad horse harness was the way in which the stirrups of the latter were set far forward, almost making the saddle into a chair. This was very comfortable for riding long distances but provided a less secure seat in hand-to-hand cavalry combat.

Stirrups of wood, or of leather with a wooden tread, appear to have been used in the northern Caucasus and in East-Central Asia, along with the plain leather loop stirrups, from the sixth century until modern times. Horseshoes, on the other hand, were not common amongst steppe horsemen, even the name given to them being of Arabic origin.

In general, early medieval Indian horse harness had been primitive when compared to that of its northern and western neighbours, the bitless *bozal* form of bridle being widely used. On the other hand there is clear evidence that some form of support for a rider's feet had been known in India since the 1st century BC, long before true metallic stirrups were developed on the frontier between settled China and nomadic Central Asia. This ancient Indian device is believed to have been in the form of leather loop "toe-stirrups". The appearance of the same sort of looped "toe-stirrup" in eighth century south-east Asian art must similarly have reflected Indian rather than Chinese influence, at least in terms of artistic style if not in the reality of south-east Asian horse harness. It was also known in Arabia by the 7th century and may again have reflected an otherwise little-understoon Indian influence in this part of the world. Perhaps such simple devices remained in use within India until the metallic stirrup was adopted between the tenth and twelfth centuries, though this remains unclear.

Horse Armour

Horse armour, though known in Late Roman times and still used by both Byzantine, Islamic and Central Asian cavalry, had almost certainly dropped out of use throughout Western Europe in the early medieval period. It then re-appeared during the twelfth century, though remaining rare for several generations, by which time rich states such as Milan could field a large number of such 'iron-clad horses'.

Elsewhere, the textile *caparisons* shown in many pictorial sources may have covered mail or quilted *trappers* and *bards* of soft armour. Some Arab sources mentioned with astonishment the extensive style of mail horse armour used by a few late twelfth-century Crusaders, this reaching almost down to the animal's feet. These horse armours continued to be used in the thirteenth-century Crusader States but always remained rare and extremely expensive. Within the Iberian peninsula, horse armour was generally referred to as a *peytral*, meaning the front part of a complete *bard*. It had been mentioned since the late twelfth century and this sort of front-only *barding* became common in the art of thirteenth-fourteenth century Spain, being characteristic of that part of Europe.

Protection for the animal's head may not have reappeared until the thirteenth century, with the possible exception of earlier references in the Iberian peninsula. Written sources then began to mention *testières de cheval* and hardened leather *coopertus* or *copita*, sometimes with a neck-protecting extension or *poll*. Full horse armour was still very expensive in the late thirteenth century when it usually consisted of mail over a quilted padding and was sometimes also covered by a heraldic cloth *caparison*. The first piece of metallic plate horse armour was for the animal's head and it initially protected only the front of the head and face, larger forms of *chamfron* to cover the sides of the head coming into use during the fourteenth century.

In Western Europe the heaviest armour to protect the horse's body originally consisted of two large pieces of mail. This system continued well into the fourteenth century and could include some *jazeran* construction with an integral lining plus a fabric cover. A few references to European horse armour made of hardened leather date from the late thirteenth century but probably referred to pieces for the head. The first clear reference to *couvertures de plates* comes from 1338, probably consisting of a *peytral* for the front of the animal plus a *crupper* for the hindquarters. This system would become quite common by the late fourteenth century, remaining in use throughout the fifteenth and beyond.

In several other parts of the world horse armour became more rather than less widespread during the early medieval period; notably in the Byzantine Empire and several parts of the Islamic world. Back in the eighth century Byzantine horse armour may have been in Avar style, covering only the front of the animal, but by the tenth century horse armours were made of layers of glued felt, or iron or hardened leather lamellae, sometimes covering the animal from head to tail and hanging down almost to its feet. There are even references to mail horse armour being used by Byzantine heavy cavalry in the eleventh century, but according to a thirteenth or fourteenth century Turkish literary source, some Byzantine heavy cavalry were again using horse armour which covered only the front of the animal. This is likely to have reflected Iberian influence via the large numbers of Catalan mercenaries within the Aegean area.

Byzantine sources of the ninth and early tenth centuries claimed that their Islamic foes used no horse armour, but in reality this applied only to the early Fatimids of North Africa and Egypt. Khurasani cavalry from eastern Iran certainly used felt or quilted horse armours called *bargustuwan*, and had probably done so since the fall of the Sassanian Empire in the seventh century, Sassanian heavily-armoured close-combat cavalry having been renowned for their horse-armour. The Persian *Shahnamah* epic, written around 1000, described fleeing cavalry gaining greater speed by cutting off their horses' armour as they rode. Such defences seem to have declined in popularity in eastern Islamic armies in the eleventh century but would enjoy a notable revival in subsequent centuries.

Further west, felt or quilted horse armour was known by the Arabic term *tijfaf* and was used by the élite of several Islamic armies since at least the ninth century. It then became increasingly common amongst slave-recruited *ghulam* or *mamluk* professional cavalry and by 952/3 the best horsemen of the Hamdanid army in northern Syria rode horses with mail or metallic lamellar bards. A detailed eye-witness description of a military parade in Cairo a century later similarly noted Fatimid heavy cavalry mounts with iron horse armour, and one of the oldest surviving examples of a medieval, rather than Roman, iron *chamfron* for a horse's head was excavated near Khartoum in the Sudan. It came from a Nubian Christian site dating between the eighth and fourteenth centuries, but whatever its age the object was almost certainly imported from Egypt.

The use of horse armour and decorated harness as an indication of high status was similarly seen in twelfth-century Yemen where the *ghashi*, a form of horse-covering *caparison* or elaborate saddle blanket had the same purpose. Meanwhile lamellar horse-armour was used by élite *ghulam* horsemen in the eleventh and twelfth century Saljuq Turkish army in Iran, the Fertile Crescent and Anatolia. Subsequently it was used in particularly large numbers by Khwarazmian troops fighting the Qara-Khitai forerunners of the Mongols in early thirteenth-century Transoxania.

More surprisingly, perhaps, *tijfaf* felt or quilted horse-armour was used in late tenth century al-Andalus – within the geograpical if not cultural confines of Western Europe where horse armour was supposedly unknown until the late twelfth century. More remarkable still were several references to items of tenth and eleventh century Andalusian and

Christian Iberian armour known variously as *tashtina*, *testinia* and *tishtani* which could be 'plated' or gilded. They are highly likely to have been early versions of the *chamfron* rigid headpiece for a horse generally known in thirteenth and fourteenth century Europe by the French term *testière*. By the late thirteenth century, however, the most heavily-armoured Islamic Andalusian cavalry appear to have adopted Western European forms of mail or mail-lined horse armours.

Despite the considerable cost of horse armour, it was used by the armies of many Central Asian steppe peoples and states. The Turks, for example, knew it as *kedimli*, while Chinese illustrations show that in the notably rich Turkish Uighur state some cavalry horses had rigid *chamfrons* to protect their heads as well as full horse armour for their bodies. By the mid-thirteenth century the full horse armour of the Mongol heavy cavalry élite similarly included *chamfrons*, neck pieces, *peytrals*, two *flanchards* and a *crupper*, usually of lamellar construction. Some of this lamellar was even made of iron, though it was more normally of hardened leather.

The evidence for horse armour in India is rather localised. Having possibly been known in the early medieval Gupta period, it then virtually disappeared from the pictorial and written sources with the notable exception of Hoysala temple carvings. The Hoysala states or confederation of states formed the frontline of Hindu India defence against Islamic encroachment throughout much of the medieval period. Its use of horse armour, and of elephant armour apparently constructed in essentially the same way, perhaps reflected military requirements when facing the Islamic forces of what are now Pakistan and Afghanistan. These carvings indicate a variety of methods of construction, though most would seem to have been quilted. One feature does, however, set Hoysala horse armour apart from any other. That was the fact that the rider's legs sometimes reached, and thus helped control, the horse's body by being thrust through holes in the sides of the armour itself. In other cultures a rider's feet touched his horse's flanks through cut-outs in the hem of the armour or by making the armour in two separate pieces. Perhaps this Hoysala fashion was associated with an Arab-Islamic style of horse-armour that is mentioned in written sources but does not seem to appear in any pictorial evidence.

The non-appearance of horse armour elsewhere in India can hardly be attributed to climatic factors because it subsequently became even more common in the Mughal Sultanate of post-medieval India. It is also worth noting that gilded iron elephant armours were recorded in the late fourteenth-century Delhi Sultanate, probably being of the same lamellar construction as the horse armours of post-Mongol Iran and neighbouring regions north of India.

Chapter 8
Fortification

Western and Central Europe

The great majority of Western European fortifications were built as a result of power struggles between those who held some degree of power within Catholic Christian Western Europe. Only a few faced opponents who held different regious beliefs and these were, naturally enough, within frontier regions or states. During the early medieval period one such region was Italy and the south of the country continued to be more or less in the Crusading frontline throughout the Middle Ages. Italy had, of course, numerous massive, if crumbling, Roman structures which had either been built as fortifications or could be converted into fortresses. In contrast, some of the new, rather than restored, fortifications appear to have been remarkably-simple structures during the early medieval centuries.

In the tenth century, Magyar raids by land and Islamic raids by sea had prompted a period of intensive military building and the concentration of rural populations into a smaller number of defended locations. This *incastellamento* similarly reflected a widespread collapse of central authority. The Church now played a leading role in providing security, and the resulting military architecture appeared more advanced than that seen north of the Alps, probably because Italian builders had access to Byzantine and Islamic architectural forms. Notable differences also developed between the military architecture of southern Italy and that of the rest of the country; Byzantine, Islamic and revived classical Roman influence clearly being apparent in the south by the thirteenth century.

If the Norman conquerors of the southern mainland and Sicily brought northern ideas with them, these seem to have been rapidly abandoned. Instead, Arab-Islamic architectural influence grew particularly strong, not least because the new Norman rulers employed Sicilian Muslim military engineers and designers. The Norman rulers of Sicily also modelled many aspects of their court and kingdom upon the Fatimid Caliphate of Egypt, which thus had a profound influence upon both the shape and the decoration of their most famous buildings, military or civilian. This fascination with the sophisticated civilisation of Middle Eastern Islam continued after the fall of the Norman kingdom, especially under the Emperor Frederick II during the early thirteenth century. Though largely disowned by a subsequent Italo-Angevin dynasty of French origin, some degree of Middle Eastern influence remained where fortifications were concerned, most obviously in massive and strongly-garrisoned citadels which characterised the centralised state-structure of Angevin southern Italy.

Eastern Europe was another frontier zone. Here, however, the fortifications of Poland remained old fashioned for several centuries, relying upon timber and earth. Further south, German, Italian and French styles of military architecture would soon appear in medieval Hungary. Nevertheless, most eastern European fortification remained almost archaic compared with the remarkably complex structures built in Western Europe during the twelfth and thirteenth centuries.

In some areas this difference became even more pronounced in the fourteenth century. Whereas Poland had few stone fortifications even at the end of the fourteenth century, such defences had increased in number within the Hungarian kingdom from the mid-thirteenth century onwards. More were built in the later thirteenth and fourteenth centuries, largely in German styles and mostly in the Carpathian mountain passes of what are now Slovakia and Romania as a line of defence against feared Mongol, Russian or Polish threats. As yet there was no Ottoman Turkish menace from the south where Serbia's ambitions were directed against its southern, eastern and, to a lesser extent, western rather than northern neighbours.

Nevertheless, the increasingly important military role of the higher Hungarian aristocracy did lead to a wave of baronial castle-building across Hungary during the early fourteenth century. The catastrophic defeat of a full-scale, largely Burgundian and Hungarian Crusade by the Ottoman Turks at the Battle of Nicopolis in 1396 then had a profound, though not necessarily immediate, military impact upon Hungary. One of the earliest results was a serious attempt to modernise fortifications along the southern frontier, much of this being done with technical advice from professional Italian *condottieri* mercenary commanders.

The Baltic regions and parts of Scandinavia in the far northeast and north of Europe were another separate and distinct frontier zone. The huge late Viking Age fortresses of Denmark seem to have been largely abandoned during the first half of the twelfth century. Instead, these remarkable bases for overseas aggression were replaced by smaller towers sited to defend Denmark's long and vulnerable coastline against Slav naval raiders from the southern Baltic. Many appear to have been wooden motte and bailey constructions, a fashion which also spread to Sweden. A new form of brick and stone fortification then began to be erected in mid-twelfth century Denmark under King Valdemar the Great. However, Sweden and Norway were slow to adopt such styles although turreted fortresses did spring up along the Swedish coast.

The massive castles which the invading German Crusaders built as they consolidated their hold on the southern and eastern shores of the Baltic Sea were mostly erected in the late thirteenth century and naturally mirrored many aspects of northern German military architecture. This was even more true of urban defences, whereas the massive citadels of the German Crusading Orders were as much a reflection of their wealth and power as anything else. Once again the vital symbolic aspect of castle-building had come to the fore.

Small-scale, utilitarian and rather conservative fortifications were characteristic of later medieval Scandinavia, especially Norway and Denmark, and the strongest external influence still stemmed from Germany. In contrast, some of the fortresses erected by the Crusading Teutonic Knights in the Baltic States and what is now northern Poland were massive. They made use of many of the latest ideas, while their frequent reliance upon water-filled moats was distinctive feature of such low-lying and often swampy regions. At the same time the German and Scandinavian Crusader conquerors, like their Lithuanian opponents, continued to make use of small fortifications that could almost be described as blockhouses. There was little to distinguish them, although the indigenous Baltic forts were generally more primitive.

Fortification was not highly developed within the Christian Iberian states until relatively late in the Middle Ages. Instead the Christians largely relied upon urban fortifications, plus watchtowers and small forts linking relatively few larger castles. This was much the same system of mixed fortifications as seen on the Islamic side of the frontier and, indeed, such structures were known by the originally-Arabic terms *almenara* and *atalaya*.

By the close of the medieval period, however, the Iberian peninsula probably had a greater number of more varied medieval fortifications than any other part of Europe. The Iberian Peninsula was, of course, a melting pot of external influences in military architecture as it was in so many aspects of warfare. The remarkable walls and towers of the city of Avila, for example, are sometimes said to have been designed by a Burgundian, though their overall appearance looks more Italo-French with a strong Islamic element. A large number of Muslim Andalusian military architects are likely to have been captured during the *Reconquista* campaigns of the twelfth and thirteenth centuries, accounting for a notable Andalusian, North African or Egyptian Fatimid influence in the design of Spanish fortified gates. During the fourteenth century a stronger French architectural influence resulted in more regular plans and less obvious use of defensive topographical features while a continuing Islamic influence was seen in a preference for tall keeps, elaborate curtain walls, various decorative features and an abundant use of brick.

The Crusader States

Few castles have been studied in greater detail than those of the Crusader States in the Middle East. Yet the basic question of why many of them were built remains a matter of debate. Some may primarily have been affirmations of royal power. Others were sited at vulnerable spots as defensive strongpoints, refuges, bases for aggression or to overawe the indigenous population. In the early years, Crusader castles tended to make use of existing 'second-hand' masonry, built crudely, quickly and making full use of topographical features. A Crusader proverb actually states that 'a castle destroyed is also a castle half built', because blocks of masonry were normally left scattered around and ready for re-use.

The impact of local architectural and masonry traditions remained for as long as these Crusader States survived. Armenian traditions were, for example, particularly noticeable in the northern Crusader States. In general terms, however, Crusader castles tended to combine the Islamic 'tower' tradition with the Byzantine 'curtain-wall' tradition. Of course they also paid close attention to the provision of water supplies in this arid part of the world, usually in the form of underground cisterns. Crusader architects similarly copied the *machicolation* from either the Muslims or the Byzantines to replace the wooden *hoardings* used for a similar purpose in Western Europe. The latter proved unsuitable in Syria not only because of a shortage of timber but also because of the Middle East's advanced incendiary weapons. In addition the Crusaders soon adopted the Muslims' sloping *talus* or anti-mining revetment at the base of a fortified wall.

The concentric castle plan, consisting of at least two walls one within the other, may have originated in the Crusader East, the earliest Crusader example being at Belvoir in Palestine, but this was built by the Hospitallers and its design is as likely to have been religiously symbolic as militarily functional. In fact the Crusader conquerors really only accepted the need for fortified frontiers in the 1120s. This resulted in a series of small castles to blockade fortified ports that were still held by the Fatimid rulers of Egypt. Meanwhile, large stretches of frontier remained virtually unfortified, often because the area in question was shared with a neighbouring Islamic state or because the border was undefined.

Although some of the castles erected in what is now southern Jordan were small and rudimentary, they could include churches as architectural statements that the land now belonged to Christendom. Further north, the Crusaders adopted the Byzantine-Islamic idea of excavating a massive ditch or 'fosse' through virgin rock. This they took to extraordinary lengths at Saone (Sahyun) in Syria, cutting away no less than 170,000 tonnes of rock. However, military engineering on this scale was more characteristic of the thirteenth than the twelfth century, resulting in such impressive structures as Krak des Chevaliers, Margat (Marqab) and Montfort. Whereas the former two Hospitaller fortresses were essentially French in style, with round and half-round towers, the latter was a Teutonic Knights castle incorporating many German Rhineland features.

The garrisons of Crusader castles varied considerably and were not solely military. The night patrol of Margat, for example, consisted of only four Hospitaller brother-knights and twenty-eight ordinary soldiers while the total inhabitants of Margat numbered around one thousand. Although there was not one overall type or style of Crusader castle, Crusader fortifications evolved further during the thirteenth century with smoother masonry, bigger or more numerous water cisterns, often more complex gates, arrowslits and other defensive features. As a result the cost of maintaining and garrisoning them grew beyond the capability of local rulers, let alone the local aristocracy, and the major castles were handed over to the wealthier Military Orders.

Rulers did retain control of the major towns, the bulk of whose original inhabitants had been slaughtered or expelled during the Crusader conquests. Until well into the thirteenth century the Crusader occupiers merely restored or strengthened existing Arab-Islamic urban fortifications. In some places like Jerusalem additional fortified walls had to be built because the existing Islamic walls were too extensive. In fact, there was usually plenty of open space within the walls for gardens or orchards and sometimes enough to permit the doubling of walls to provide an unobstructed means of communication for the garrison.

During the second half of the thirteenth century, however, the Crusader States' continuing loss of territory caused their remaining coastal cities to fill with refugees. This was particularly true of Acre where rival Italian merchant communes also erected urban towers, not as defences against Islamic attack but in mutual rivalry. Acre also had a small tower and garrison on a rock at the harbour mouth, controlling one end of a floating chain which could close off the harbour. Its little garrison identified approaching ships and probably provided then with pilots.

More unusual forms of Crusader fortifications included caves, these often being abandoned Byzantine *lavra* (monastic retreats) such as Ain Habis, overlooking the Yarmuk river in northern Jordan. Others in the mountains southeast of Tripoli in Lebanon appear to have been associated with indigenous pro-Crusader Maronite Christian communities. There was relatively little fortification in the Crusader Kingdom of Cyprus during the thirteenth century; an exception being the Hospitallers' Castle of Forty Columns at Paphos which was destroyed by earthquake in 1222. Archaeologists have found that, at that time of the earthquake, the castle contained 1,500 carefully carved stone mangonel catapult balls, perhaps ready for shipment to Hospitaller castles in Syria. In contrast to the increasingly-impressive castles of the Crusader States in the Holy Land, those of the Crusader States in Greece were of cheap, even shoddy construction, old-fashioned and essentially Byzantine in design and craftsmanship. A notable feature of thirteenth-century Crusader Greece was, on the other hand, a large number of isolated towers. They were simply constructed, entered by a ladder at first-floor level, lacked loop-holes and were almost entirely passive in defence. Like similar towers on both Crusader and Byzantine-ruled Aegean islands, they may have been rural refuges for people and livestock in case of sporadic local warfare or pirate raiding.

The Byzantine Empire

Early medieval Byzantine and Islamic military architects had both tended to reuse and rebuild earlier fortifications, especially those dating from the Roman Empire in the Middle East. In addition the Byzantines converted several massive but originally non-military structures into fortresses. Meanwhile the major cities of the Byzantine Empire were strongly forti-fied, though the huge land walls of Constantinople (Istanbul) remained atypical. Most Byzantine cities had citadels at their highest point, with numerous towers, in several cases double gates enclosing a so-called 'killing zone', and multiple walls around the most important cities. By the ninth century, Ankara, as a vital military centre close to the eastern frontier, possessed the first Byzantine example of a 'bent entrance' gate. The inhabited area of ancient Ephesus had been reduced by half but the city had been given a new wall as well as water cisterns to replace old and vulnerable aqueducts. During the same period the ancient Roman theatres of Sardis and Aphrodisias were converted into massive fortresses.

As the cities of Anatolia declined, the rural landscape was dotted with smaller fortified towns and castles. The former tended to have long walls but few towers which suggested passive defence, while the design of the latter evolved from Roman *castrae* and were more varied in design. Isolated Byzantine castles tended to be square in plan with crenelated walls and corner towers reached by wooden stairs. Those in frontier regions were smaller, made greater use of topographical features and often had covered galleries within their walls. Yet the larger frontier fortresses still seemed more like refuges than major military bases. In some areas, such as the the Byzantine Empire's European border along the Danube, the frontier itself was hardly fortified, the main castles being within the mountains to the south. When the Byzantine Empire expanded during the tenth century, the Byzantine authorities refortified new areas including northern and coastal Syria.

Following the disasters of the later eleventh century, the Comnenid Emperors of Byzantium put great effort into fortifying their new frontier and coastline after regaining part of western Anatolia. Some Comnenid fortifications were large and served as bases or assembly points while others attempted to block the valleys which led from the now Turkish-ruled interior to the Aegean coast. Their designs also reflected the growing importance of crossbows while a few incorporated larger towers on which stone-throwing counterweight *trebuchets* could be mounted. Big towers became much more common in the thirteenth century 'Nicean Empire', while the policy of trying to block valleys from the interior to the more fertile Byzantine-ruled coasts was continued well into the four-teenth century, both in the Empire of Constantinople and the separate Empire of Trebizond. The Emperor Michael VIII Palaeologus was even credited with planting new forests in an attempt to impede Turkish raiders.

The famous fortifications of the imperial capital of Constantinople were strengthened in the late fourteenth century when the Byzantine Empire was nearing a state of complete collapse, with additional towers between the Golden Gate and the sea walls providing a final refuge. Less study has been made of the numerous smaller Byzantine *kastra* of these later centuries, or of the small isolated towers which are thought to have been built by monasteries and local landowners as refuges against bandits or pirates. Nevertheless it is clear that almost all Byzantine towns and cities were fortified with such *kastra*. One interesting piece of thirteenth-or fourteenth-century Turkish literature also stated that fortified monasteries were defended by large, probably frame-mounted crossbows and moveable wooden mantlets or palisades.

Timber fortifications remained the norm in the Balkans throughout the early Middle Ages, although a small number of stone, brick and essentially Romano-Byzantine design reappeared in the newly inde-pendent kingom of Serbia in the second half of the twelfth century. Byzantine military architecture similarly predominated in Bulgaria. In general, however, most early Byzantine stone fortifications in the southern Balkans seem to have been destroyed and were not rebuilt by the expanding Serbian state. Even in the mid-fourteenth century the most significant Serbian stone defences were in the far west, close to the Dalmatian coast. The rest largely remained simple structures of earth with a single wooden wall. Subsequently, as the Ottoman Turks advanced deep into the Balkans in the later fourteenth century, rather old-fashioned fortresses and fortified monasteries began to appear in direct imitation of traditional Byzantine styles. The few stone fortifications of Bulgaria, before it fell to the Ottomans, were again in an old-fashioned Byzantine style, largely relying on the height of their not-particularly-substantial walls and towers.

The local Vlach-Romanian tribes of the southern Carpathians were erecting large fortified earth and timber camps by the twelfth century, as a protection against the Kipchaq Turks. More surprisingly, perhaps, was an Arabic and Turkish influence upon later medieval fortifications in these regions of Wallachia and Moldavia, and upon its terminology. In general, however, later medieval Wallachian and Moldavian military architecture was in late Byzantine style, although the fortifications of some Carpathian valley towns also showed Hungarian influence.

The early medieval Christian Armenian provinces of eastern Anatolia were even more strongly fortified than the rest of the Byzantine world, with seventy castles reportedly existing in the province of Vaspourakan alone, plus fortified villages, churches and monasteries. So it is hardly surprisingly that, by the eleventh century, the Armenians were widely regarded as the best military architects of the Middle East. Further south, during the twelfth to fourteenth centuries, three distinct types of fortification emerged in the newly-established kingdom of Cilician or 'Lesser' Armenia. These were small watch-posts, fortified baronial manors or large garrison bases. The watch-posts could probably be manned by about five soldiers and may have communicated with garrison bases via beacons. Cilician baronial manors were like smaller versions of the Western European *donjon* castle, normally being sited in agricultural areas. The major garrison bases apparently housed ten to thirty men and sometimes included elaborate defensive architecture. Meanwhile, bigger castles on the coast were in a separate category and some are known to have been built by the Crusading Military Orders.

Russia

The majority of early Russian fortifications had been in the southeast, mostly along the Dnepr river facing the steppes. Having failed to conquer the western steppes during the tenth century, the rulers of Kievan Russia then erected a large number of simple earth and timber forts along the edge of the forest zone, plus others deeper within the steppes, to protect their trade. From these the Russians could also attack the nomadic Turkic peoples whose states dominated the western steppes. Almost all of these Russian fortifications were built next to rivers which, unlike the open steppes, Russian forces could dominate. However, this castle-based offensive provoked a counter-attack and most of these small Russian forts were destroyed by the Pechenegs and their Kipchaq Turkish successors.

During the eleventh and twelfth centuries another series of larger and stronger fortresses was constructed within the Russian frontier, many having fields inside their walls so that their garrisons could withstand a blockade. Deeper within Russia traditional Slav-type forts of earth, rubble and timber forts had existed since at least the tenth century. This form of construction continued, often on a massive scale but with little variation until the thirteenth century. Though seemingly old-fashioned, they were successful and contributed towards the steady expansion of Slav Russian territory eastwards at the expense of indigenous Finn peoples such as the Mordva.

The architecture of northern Russia was similar but less elaborate and was characterised by more steeply pitched roofs to shed huge quantities of winter snow. Here a rich trading city like Novgorod possessed a defensive wall since at least the eleventh century, though it appears to have been made in several different ways depending upon the whim and wealth of the city quarter which it protected. Parts appear to have been made of stone while others remained a timber palisade on an earth rampart. The sometimes-rival city of Pskov may have had some stone fortification as early as the tenth century, and Old Ladoga to the north certainly had a high stone wall during the twelfth century.

The idea of fortifying an ill-defined frontier with a series of small forts as a defence against Lithuanian raiders was attempted in the northwest by Alexandre Nevskii, the ruler of Novgorod in the mid-thirteenth century. However, Russias's first significant stone or brick castles, comparable to the *donjons* of Western Europe, were constructed in response to western rather than Mongol pressure in the later thirteenth and fourteenth centuries. Most of these 'single-sided' stone fortresses still relied upon naturally-defensible positions and generally consisted of a simple wall with a single tower placed against their most vulnerable side. The details of their construction often indicate Hungarian and Polish influence. Meanwhile the great majority of Russian cities continued to rely on traditional earth and timber, the oak walls of the Moscow *kremlin* or citadel only being replaced by stone in 1367-8.

The Islamic World

There was greater variation in Islamic fortifications which drew upon several separate pre-Islamic traditions than there were, for example, in Byzantine military architecture. The tower remained fundamental, both in larger urban and smaller rural fortifications. In early days of Islamic civilisation these were usually solid, merely giving a height advantage to the defenders, and were incoporated into even the most elaborate urban defences. In contrast the concept of a huge imperial palace, set within gardens and surrounded by administrative offices and barracks, had more to do with Iranian traditions of a supreme ruler set above ordinary men than it did with Islamic concepts of equality before God. In contrast, the fully-developed *bashura*, or 'bent gate', as a defence against surprise attack by cavalry was a new feature for the Middle East.

There were always fewer small-scale rural fortifications in most parts of the Islamic world than in the Byzantine Empire and its Orthodox Christian neighbours. Those which did exist tended to be close to strategic frontiers or barely-governed tribal, desert or mountainous regions. They could nevertheless include very advanced features such as a doubled gate with a portcullis and an elongated machicolation incorporated into the circuit wall.

Following the fragmentation of the Abbasid Caliphate, some Islamic successor states built remarkably strong fortifications, often being more advanced than those of the Abbasids themselves, though rarely on the same scale. The main garrison towns of the tenth-century frontier province of Cilicia remained Massissa, Adana and Tarsus, the latter having a doubled wall and five iron gates. Those in the outer wall were covered in iron while those of the inner wall were entirely of iron, probably in the form of a portcullis. The inner wall of Tarsus had no less than 18,000 crenellations and 100 towers, twenty-three having various forms of beam-sling stone-throwing mangonels on top while the remainder were manned by crossbowmen.

In contrast, the now-famous and huge citadel of Aleppo did not exist in the tenth and eleventh centuries. Instead the *tel* or hill on the eastern side of the city was used as a refuge, barricaded with whatever timber was available while enemies plundered the city below. During the eleventh century, Aleppo itself was surrounded by a wall almost fifteen metres high. It is hardly surprising that most towns of war-torn northern Syria and the Jazira (northern Mesopotamia) were strongly fortified by the late eleventh century, the major cities of these regions having the strongest fortifications anywhere in the Middle East. Diyarbakir was the most impressive with particularly massive towers and four 'iron gates'. Its main wall incorporated a passage large enough for armed men to fight inside while ahead of this stood a smaller wall of similar design whose watch-towers were approximately five metres high.

The smaller castles of pre-Crusader northern Syria mostly dated from the Arab-Byzantine wars of the ninth and tenth centuries. Damascus had also been refortified in the late tenth century when the now-collapsed ancient Romano-Byzantine defences were replaced by new mud-brick walls. Within the semi-desert fringes, rough fortifications remained adequate in the *razzia* or raiding warfare typical of such areas, serving as shelters to protect harvests and deny water sources to an enemy. Many such tribal fortifications existed in mountainous southern Jordan when the Crusaders arrived in the early twelfth century.

The architects who designed fortified towers for the Fatimid rulers of Syria and Egypt displayed particular originality. Nevertheless, Jerusalem still relied upon its old Byzantine defences in the tenth century, perhaps with an additional doubled wall in some places. Within Egypt the Fatimid Caliphs erected a fortified palace enclosure similar in concept to the famous Abbasid 'Round City' of Baghdad. With eight gates and a notably high brick wall, it was named *al-Qahira*, 'The Victorious' – namely Cairo – and included the ruler's palace plus administrative offices and barracks for guard regiments. Unlike Abbasid Baghdad, however, Fatimid Cairo was rectangular.

The existing stone gateways of Fatimid Cairo were built later in the eleventh century when the palace enclosure was extended. Though they are sometimes attributed to Armenian architects, their design actually looks more Syrian. The lower parts are again solid and only the upper portions could be used for active defence. In reality the main function of these magnificent structures may have been symbolic rather than military. Whereas the southern *Bab Zuwayla* was used by ordinary citizens the twin northern Gates, the *Bab al-Nasr* and *Bab al-Futuh*, were used by official embassies. Furthermore the *Bab al-Nasr* originally had a small *musalla* 'prayer hall' just outside, serving as a religious talisman to protect both the gate and the caliphal city within. The number of shrines and religious buildings concentrated around Aswan on Egypt's southern frontier during the Fatimid period suggests that this fortified outpost against Nubian raiders was similarly protected by religious 'talismans'.

With these few exceptions, the fortifications of most early medieval Middle Eastern Islamic cities had not been particularly impressive. Many were then greatly strengthened in the face of Crusader and Mongol threats from the twelfth century onwards. For example, originally-undefended Mosul in northern Iraq had a plain wall built in the late eleventh century, this being given stronger ramparts and a ditch in the early twelfth century, followed by a new gate, a doubled wall and many towers. By the end of the twelfth century Mosul's walls incorporated an enclosed passageway and at least eleven gates.

Nor were the Crusaders the only local power to erect isolated castles, Subayba on the Golan Heights being built to defend Damascus in the early thirteenth century and incorporating the latest form of bent entrance. In contrast, the ancient Roman Temple of Artemis in Jerash was converted into a small but sturdy fort by a garrison from Damascus, using the stone drums of fallen Roman columns as a form of outwork.

The Ayyubid dynasty, founded by Saladin, which ruled Egypt and

Syria from the late twelfth to mid-thirteenth century, inherited a variety of military architectural traditions. The simplest was represented by the plain mud-brick wall without a ditch that defended the Nile Delta town of Bilbais, while the most sophisticated is represented by the massive Citadel of Cairo. The latter was based upon Syrian rather than Egyptian traditions and may have originated as a base from which Saladin, as a new and foreign ruler, could overawe the huge population of Cairo which by then inhabited an area much larger than the original Fatimid palace-complex of *al-Qahira*. Saladin then decided to concentrate the scattered city and its surburbs into a smaller area southwest of his Citadel. Next he began extending the fortifications from the Citadel to the Nile, to protect the entire city of Cairo from Crusader attack. This ambitious project, which included a fortified aqueduct from the river to the Citadel, was eventually completed by Saladin's successors.

The biggest architectural change during this period reflected the widespread adoption of counterweight *trebuchets* in the late twelfth and early thirteenth centuries. As a result several Ayyubid rulers built new, or strengthened existing, fortifications with additional larger towers. Being more closely spaced and projecting further from the curtain wall, these served as firing platforms for new *trebuchets* while chambers inside the now more massive walls may also have permitted the use of powerful weapons which shot along a horizontal rather than parabolic trajectory. The best example of this new style of fortification is the Citadel of Damascus. At the other end of the scale, the thirteenth century saw smaller castles and isolated towers being erected in southern Syria and Jordan to watch for Crusader raids. Meanwhile several ancient Roman theatres in Syria, as well as abandoned Roman legionary forts deeper in the desert, were converted into respectable fortresses.

Ayyubid ideas were taken further by the subsequent Mamluk dynasty which continued the strategy of demolishing coastal fortifications which could be captured and used by invading Crusaders. Larger coastal defences were normally replaced by smaller isolated towers which only served as observation points against the increasing threat of piracy. In Lebanon the ancient coastal city of Tripoli was gradually replaced by a new urban area next to the ex-Crusader castle which was itself strengthened by the Mamluks. Fortifications along the Nile Delta coast in Egypt were not, however, razed because this area was close enough to Cairo to be rapidly reinforced if danger threatened.

Although the Syro-Palestine coast was to some extent 'demilitarised', several inland fortificiations were strengthened by the Mamluks, particularly in mountainous areas. The only major exception was Jerusalem, the presumed target of future Christian aggression, where the walls were demolished. In contrast the great cities of Damascus and Aleppo were given immensely strong citadels, not against the Crusader menace but against the great danger posed by the Mongols. Each had its own arsenal, water cisterns, baths, stores rooms, barracks, gardens, offices and mosque. There was also a flour mill at Damascus.

The wealthy Saljuq Turkish rulers of twelfth- and early thirteenth-century Anatolia seem to have felt little need for fortifications. Instead the most notable defensive architecture of this area was the walled *caravanserai* 'hostels' along the main trade routes. Here merchants and their wares could find safety from bandits and wild animals, though, after the Mongol invasion, Turkish Anatolia went through a period of fragmentation and confusion during which *caravanserais* were sometimes used as military outposts. The Ottomans would bring back order and stability, but they too had little interest in fixed fortifications for several centuries. The few military buildings which can be attributed to the Ottomans or other fourteenth century Turkish *beyliks* were almost entirely within an already old-fashioned Byzantine style.

The twelfth to fourteenth centuries were a period of consolidation rather than innovation in the military architecture of the eastern Islamic lands. For example the huge mud-brick walls of Herat in Afghanistan surrounded a mile-square area and stood on top of a tall embankment. The walls themselves were rebuilt several times, being almost five metres thick at the base, three at the top, plus a parapet over two metres high. A ditch outside the ramparts was from eight to fifteen metres wide, over three to five deep with a partial counterscarp beyond. Herat also had five gates, each of which projected almost seventy metres from the wall to enclose a substantial area like that enclosed by the outer walls of Chinese city gates. Like several other major Islamic cities in this region, including eastern Iran and Islamic Central Asia, Herat became a symbol of the power of settled and urban populations in their rivalry with surrounding nomadic peoples.

Another chacteristic of Transoxania, Afghanistan and Islamic northern India was the use of very tall minarets as observation posts; some free standing water-towers being used for the same purpose. It is also important to realize that earth or mud-brick walls were not necessarily inferior to those of stone. In fact they offered several advantages, being easily demolished if an area was about to be lost to an enemy, as well as being quick, cheap and easy to rebuild. Furthermore, they absorbed the shock of battering and even of earthquakes better than most stone structures. For precisely these reasons the Islamic conquerors of northern and central India tended to reuse, repair and update Hindu fortresses which were themselves often remarkable examples of the strength and sophistication possible with mud bricks.

The early Islamic period had seen a considerable increase of urban fortification across North Africa. Subsequently a series of coastal *ribats* were built from Tunisia or Morocco, as well as in Sicily and Andalusia; these being a defence against Christian piracy. The religiously-motivated garrisons of such *ribats* may have influenced the development of Christian Military Orders in the Iberian peninsula. Meanwhile, the design of these early fortifications continued in an old Romano-Byzantine style until the Aghlabid and Fatimid dynasties introduced new ideas from the east in the ninth and tenth centuries. Around the same time, an independent style of fortification began to develop in Morocco and al-Andalus using good quality masonry. Here towers, though still closely spaced, began to project further from the curtain wall during the tenth century, suggesting greater use of them as artillery bastions.

The rammed earth used for rapidly erected fortifications in North Africa and al-Andalus was later combined with some brick in an amalgamation of local and eastern traditions. However, the most distinctive form of construction in the far west of the medieval Islamic World was a form of concrete which had developed by the tenth century in Andalusia and spread to Morocco somewhat later. Its closest technological predecessor seems to have been the traditional mud and straw architecture of southern Arabia which was, and remains, capable of supporting structures many stories high. Both systems laid the wet mixture within wooden shuttering, additional layers being added as the preceding ones dried. In al-Andalus and Morocco a concrete mixture of gravel, earth, lime, straw and bones called *tabia*, or 'tabby' in its European derivation, soon replaced the south Arabian mud and straw. This was not only very fast but was useful when repairing damaged stone fortification. On its own, *tabia* concrete resulted in structures almost as strong as twentieth-century 'pill-boxes' – and almost as ugly.

Al-Andalus had been strongly fortified from the start of the Islamic period because Islamic manpower remained dangerously low. The palace-city of Madinat al-Zahra, near Cordoba, was unusual in having a double wall which enclosed a passage in what might have been a smaller-scale imitation of the great Abbasid palace-city of Baghdad. A remarkably-large number of Andalusian fortifications also seem to have incorporated 'magical' or totemic number combinations in their plans and design. Most of the large frontier fortification in the north dated from the ninth century, but Viking naval raids also led to the fortification of Seville in the deep south of the Iberian Peninsula.

Iberian-Islamic urban fortification initially used the foundations of existing Roman walls before a rapid growth of population necessitated expansion. As a result cities in the plains of what are now Spain and Portugal continued to have regular plans while those in the highlands followed the line of terrain and, if possible, enclosed the highest point of a hill where a citadel would be constructed. Such a *qasr* or *qasaba* usually served as a governor's residence and barracks. Other more distinctive features of Andalusian urban fortification were a widespread use of barbicans ahead of city gates, gate towers with overhanging *buherada* defensive balconies, and separate external towers linked to the main wall by bridges. The latter concept seems to have been invented in al-Andalus during the eleventh century. Double-bent entrances also appeared under North African Almoravid rule in the late eleventh or twelfth centuries.

As in the Middle East, the provision of reliable water supplies remained basic to the design of Andalusian fortifications. Caves were sometimes used for this purpose, most famously St. Michael's Cave beneath the Rock of Gibraltar. Elsewhere large underground or basement cisterns had appeared in the mid-ninth century; these being waterproofed with lime-plaster. In other cases walls were extended to enclose or at least reach a reliable source of water, sometimes by having an outlying bastion at the water's edge and up to one hundred or so metres from the main defences.

Small rural or isolated fortifications similarly became characteristic of both the Islamic and Christian parts of the Iberian Peninsula, including small outposts along the main military roads and more substantial fortified *caravanserais*. Isolated circular towers, some probably used as beacons, were called *taliya* in Arabic, which entered Spanish as *atalayas*. Small castles appeared in the tenth century, usually on hilltops with a wall, cistern and small settlement outside. Most seem to have been sited to observe the mountain passes and perhaps cut off returning raiders. Similarly-small towers with remarkably-large storage facilities and perhaps-permanent garrisons tended be sited high in the hills, and in al-Andalus many later *ribats* probably developed out of such towers.

These patterns of fortification and defence lasted many centuries and remained characteristic of the tiny *taifa* states of fragmented eleventh-century al-Andalus. Meanwhile, the first Islamic response to a Christian thrust southwards had been to build a series of large fortresses within the mountainous *thughur* border provinces. These included Medinaceli and Gormaz which served as regional defence centres and major garrison bases. The strongest Andalusian castles were, in fact, located in the mountains which ran east-west across the Iberian Peninsula. These castles were also linked to the main southern cities by a network of north-south roads.

Many subsequent Andalusian fortifications continued to be made or repaired using *tabia* concrete. The gradual replacement of solid towers with hollow ones also permitted more active defence. In other respects the pressure of the Spanish *Reconquista* spurred innovations, some of which remained specifically Andalusian or Maghribi (Islamic North

African). One was the external *albarrana* tower, from the Arabic word *barrani*, meaning 'exterior'. They were seen in several late twelfth- and thirteenth-century towns close to a constantly threatened northern frontier, usually being credited to the Muwahhidin rulers who, originating in Morocco, had taken over what remained of Islamic al-Andalus.

Once a reasonably stable frontier was re-established between the surviving Islamic state of Granada and its Christian neighbours in the later thirteenth century, this was again fortified along traditional Andalusian lines. Most of the walled towns and castles were, however, seen along the densely-populated western part of the Granadan frontier whereas the eastern part ran through sparcely-populated mountains and near-steppe terrain behind Almeria. In all these areas, Granada's fortifications reflected a certain amount of Christian Spanish or more general Western European influence, including *donjon* keeps and some styles of masonry. In contrast there was noticably less Spanish influence upon fortifications in the interior of the *amirate* of Granada.

The eleventh and twelfth centuries saw a further spread of Andalusian military architectural forms to Morocco and other parts of North Africa. The result was a gradual move away from simple rubble walls to ones of *tabia* concrete and, rather later, to the erection of *albarrana* towers. The true bent entrance only reached al-Andalus in the twelfth century and was not recorded in Tunisia until the thirteenth century. Prior to the start of Christian piracy in the Atlantic during the twelfth and thirteenth centuries, the Atlantic coast of Morocco had been largely unfortified. Many of the ports were completely undefended or consisted simply of roadsteads associated with towns several kilometres inland. Any existing fortification faced a threat from inland rather than the sea.

Tit, dating from the mid-twelfth century, was the oldest major Atlantic coastal fortress and was built with concrete walls over a traditional stone foundation. Christian piracy and the need to maintain a maritime link between Morocco and Granada also lay behind the Marinid dynasty's decision to strengthen the defences of Sabta (Ceuta) on the southern side of the Straits of Gibraltar in the fourteenth century. These formidable fortifications eventually included a ditch right across the isthmus linking the Rock of Sabta with the mainland, plus new walls, towers, gates and an isolated tower on tidal rocks to defend the southern harbour; this being linked to the mainland by a bridge.

Central Asia and The Mongols
The Turkish and Mongol rulers of the steppe empires of Central Asia and south-eastern Europe built palaces and fortifications, though their way of life and that of their followers remained largely nomadic. The

palaces were often based upon an ancient concept of having separate residences for summer and winter. The *ordu* for summer needed to be close to summer pasture which was normally in the mountains, often close to villages where metalworkers and bow-makers lived; preferably also close to trade routes where the ruler could levy taxes and thus reward his followers. Some of the more elaborate royal *ordus* consisted of two concentric walls with fortified towers. Winter residences were sometimes fortified and could be more extensive because the ruler's own herds had to be kept safely within their walls.

The Western Turks had also built fortified towers within the mountains. Their construction techniques, like those of the *ordu*, were largely learned from Chinese frontier defences. However, unlike the linear Chinese walls and towers, Turkish fortifications consisted of isolated outposts. The Turks' small fortified towns or enclosures known as *baliqs* similarly incorporated Chinese defensive ideas and by the early eleventh century some Central Asian fortifications were quite imposing. One such was Semiran, capital of the Tarim Basin area, which had a triple wall and a secure underground channel linking its water supply to the river. Other Turkish fortifications incorporated flanking towers called *ükeks*.

Extensive fortifications had been built by some rulers of the western steppes. Significantly, those of the Khazars on the lower Don river at Sarkel faced westward in apparent anticipation of Magyar or Varangian-Russian threats. Within the forest zone north of the steppes, several medieval Turkic and Finnic peoples erected elaborate fortifications of wood and earth, the largest perhaps being those of the Volga Bulgars. In addition to their fortified capital city and trading centre, the Volga Bulgars had many smaller, local, timber castles which generally made full use of any natural defensive features such as escarpments, river junctions, hill-tops and river islands. There were even cases of artificial islands being constructed for such a fortress.

Given the fact that the art of fortification was known amongst the largely-nomadic peoples of Central Asia, the Mongols' success in siege warfare should come as no surprise. Nevertheless, the staggering success of their initial conquests meant that, for many years, they themselves felt no great need for fortifications. On the other hand, the ability, as well as the ruthless willingness, of Mongol rulers to dismantle, move and rebuild fortresses and even entire towns in the later thirteenth and fourteenth centuries indicates a thorough understanding of their importance. This practice seems to have been particularly prevelant in Transoxania, eastern Iran and Afghanistan where fortifications had traditionally been made of mud-brick, which lent itself to such strategies.

Timur-i Lenk was a product of a mixed Turkish and Mongol military heritage, but his attitude towards fortification seems to have been thoroughly Iranian. Timur was, in fact, particularly concerned to defend his empire's northeastern frontier against attack from the Turco-Mongol steppes. Consequently he built or repaired many fortifications in this area. Timur-i Lenk then went further, erecting a series of forts beyond the Syr Darya River almost far as Mongolia, most being sited in low-lying areas or river valleys.

India

The military, cultural and ecological heritage of India was very different from that of Central Asia. Pre-Islamic India had, in fact, been notably well fortified. Nor did India's established traditions of military architecture change much during the early centuries of Islamic conquest. This tradition was characterised by towers which only projected a short distance from the wall, a distinct slope, or 'batter', on both walls and bastions, plus long galleries within the main wall. Other galleries were sometimes added to the outer face of the main walls while barbicans comparable to those of China were often built outside the main gates.

The most impressive such fortresses were made of dressed stone over a rubble core. However, much of the Indian sub-continent lacked good stone and so brick was used in Sind, Punjab and Bengal, whereas in Kashmir wood was the most abundant building material. Mud-brick walls were, of course, particularly capable of absorbing the shock of missiles and battering rams, as well as subsidence caused by enemy mining. According to the Chinese traveller Hiuen Tsang back in the seventh century, most Indian towns and even villages had inner gates, high wide walls of both unfired and fired bricks, plus towers of wood or bamboo. In the broad river plains of northern India considerable use was made of water-filled ditches and moats, while smaller fortifications were often built upon artificial mounds surrounded by marshes. In the hilly and mountainous parts of central and southern India greater use was made of high or naturally-inaccessible positions. As in the Middle East, however, the provision of reliable water supplies was fundamental to the design and location of most Indian fortifications.

Differences started to appear in Hindu and Islamic military architecture within India during the eleventh century. During the late fourteenth century, however, both started using that most distinctive feature of later medieval and early modern Indian defensive architecture: the ceremonial *chatris* or kiosk erected above the main gate. Here a ruler could both see and be seen by his subjects.

Much less fortification survives in southeast Asia where most such defences were made of wood. On the other hand, a Chinese traveller stated that the as-yet unidentified capital of the Malayan Hindu kingdom of Langkasuka had brick walls which were already 'ancient' when he saw them in the sixth century. Nor was military architecture a major feature of medieval sub-Saharan Africa, with the major exception of the Christian kingdoms of Nubia. Yet even here the situation is not particularly clear. In fact, Nubian fortifications dating from the twelfth century are few and of crude construction. In contrast the final, later centuries of Christian Nubian independence seem to have been characterised by the erection of much more substantial castles, only a few of which have, however, been studied to any great extent.

Chapter 9
Field & Camp Fortifications

Although there is evidence for the use of field fortifications and fortified encampments in early medieval Western Europe, little is known
about them and they probably remained relatively unusual until the
eleventh century. Despite the fact that Carolingian military regulations
indicated that large armies were expected to erect temporary wooden
defences, it seems that invaders such as the Magyars, Saracens and
Vikings made more effective use of them during the ninth and tenth
centuries.

Thereafter the little detailed surviving information concerning field
fortifications suggests that there were no great changes. They continued
to consist of ditches, earth banks or ramparts, wooden palisades and
occasionally iron-tipped wooden stakes. However, the existence of the
latter clearly indicates forethought, planning and the preparation of
perhaps-reusable field fortifications before the start of a campaign.

During the period of the Crusades there may actually have been a
relative decline in the importance of field fortifications from the twelfth
to fourteenth centuries and they feature less prominently in the written
sources. On the other hand, the Rule of the Templars included specific
instructions concerning what brother knights and sergeants should do if
their fortified encampment was attacked. Those nearest to the threat
should join in the defence while the others should assemble around the
chapel tent to await the Master's instructions.

For reasons which are probably associated with a revival in properly-
trained, equipped and, above all, reliable infantry forces, long-established
and traditional forms of field fortifications now seem to have increased
in military significance in several parts of Western Europe during the
course of the fourteenth and fifteenth centuries. However, even in
the mid-thirteenth century the Hungarians had used their baggage
waggons as a primitive form of *wagenburg* against the Mongols at the
Battle of Mohi. A form of 'offensive field fortification' was recorded just
over a hundred years later in 1359 when the Moldavians defeated an

invading Polish army by trapping it within a dense forest, felling trees across the only road ahead of, and behind, the enemy.

The well-described field fortifications used by English infantry during the Hundred Years War probably had much in common with those used by armies of the later Crusades in the Balkans and eastern Mediterranean region. The English examples often refer to each man cutting one pointed stake in order to make a thicket of such stakes. These were driven into the ground about a metre apart, six or seven stakes deep and angled towards the expected enemy attack. Infantry could then retreat into a thicket of stakes where a man on horseback would find it difficult to manoeuvre. By placing such defences in specific parts of the anticipated battlefield, an enemy cavalry charge could be diverted away from lightly-armoured infantry archers towards an awaiting line of dismounted but heavily-armoured men-at-arms who were better able to meet the attackers in close combat.

It is possible that the pointed stakes could be obscured from the approaching cavalry by the foot soldiers themselves who were standing in front. Apparently the archers stepped back into the protection of their stakes almost at the last moment; thus causing the front rank of densely packed cavalry *conrois* formations to crash into the stakes. The often-huge casualties suffered by cavalry if they were defeated by infantry often seem to have been inflicted by daggers, swords, pole-arms and even the mallets used to drive in the stakes. Perhaps these massacres took place during the confusion resulting from heavily-armoured horsemen being brought to a sudden halt by a line of sharpened stakes. Similarly, the ability of new forms of relatively-high status Western European infantry to face and defeat cavalry charges, whose impact was in any case psychological rather than physical, says much for the foot soldiers' increasing confidence and the effectiveness of their field fortifications.

Byzantine sources provide greater detail about field fortifications than do most Western Europe sources. One tenth century military text book even mentioned a corps of 'measurers' who went ahead of an army on the march to select suitable camp sites. The Byzantine army clearly took great care to defend such encampments, including scattering spiked caltrops around their perimeter. Several of these could be attached by cords to a small stake so they could be retrieved, both for reuse and to avoid injuring friendly troops. Strings of bells around a camp could similarly provide warning if an enemy crept past the outer sentries, these bells theoretically rousing the inner watch of javelin throwers and archers.

How far these sophisticated and complex forms of field fortification survived in the later medieval Byzantine period is unclear, as is the degree to which the Russians learned from the Byzantines or from the peoples of the steppes. Nevertheless, the sources do refer to Russian armies making considerable use of prefabricated wooden palisades called *obos* to protect their military encampments, at least from the thirteenth century onwards.

During the early medieval period the main Islamic armies clearly made use of a variety of field fortifications and defended encampments drawn from several military traditions. Amongst the most distinctive were *zaribas* largely made of brush wood and other thorny or spikey shrubs which were sometimes, perhaps normally, surrounded by ditches. Within this man-made 'hedge' soldiers would erect tents while on prolonged summer campaigns, or wooden huts during winter. By the tenth and eleventh centuries *zaribas* were specifically described as being made from woven vine stems, willow osiers or brambles. They could also be used in open battle. Some seem to have been like small fortified emplacements, defended by fifteen to twenty archers – virtually medieval pillboxes.

One particularly well-described twelfth-century Middle East campaign was conducted by Nur al-Din, the most successful Islamic leader against the Crusader occupiers of Syria and Palestine before the rise of Saladin. On this occasion Nur al-Din's army erected encampments which consisted of a circle of tents surrounded by a ditch, outside which spiked caltrops were scattered. An advance guard called the *yazak* was stationed outside the perimeter, sometimes with an additional detached unit at a greater distance along the enemy's expected line of approach.

A similar encampment, this time consisting of two concentric circles of tents, was described during the subsequent Ayyubid period. Here the troops were advised not to light fires unless the weather was very cold, in which case such camp-fires should be put in holes around which the men would sleep. For sanitary reasons, the camp ought to be located near its source of water but not actually grouped around it. According to Islamic military treatises dating from this period, attacks on these fortified encampments involved skills similar to those of street fighting, as well as the use of *naft* incendiary-weapons, some of which were thrown by hand.

It sometimes happened that rival encampments were set up close enough to trade fire-weapons and rocks thrown by mangonels, or over-sized javelins shot from frame-mounted siege engines or giant crossbows. This clearly happened on at least one occasion when Crusaders invaded Egypt in the mid-thirteenth century. It resulted in a unit of fully armoured *mamluks* dismounting and sniping at Crusader positions from behind a hastily-erected barricade of stones. According to traditional, and in some respects updated, books on Islamic military theory written in Egypt in the fourteenth and fifteenth centuries, encampments that were erected along the line of march should similarly be defended by a ditch and have two or more entrances guarded by both cavalry and infantry archers. The fact that ready-made *zaqaziq* spiked hurdles were no longer used, was, however, a matter of regret for at least one later Mamluk author. These seem to have been used in earlier centuries as an outer defence and were virtually identical to the prefabricated spiked obstacles long used in China.

A perhaps-new development for Islamic Middle Eastern armies was the Ottomans' adoption of *wagenburg* field fortifications made from specially prepared carts. This may have been copied from the Hungarians during wars in the Balkans and was probably not seen until the early fifteenth century. Since ancient times many of the nomadic peoples of the Eurasian steppes had, however, made considerable use of large waggons for transport and occasionally in battle as field-fortifications. Indeed, Chinese commentators divided the early medieval Turkish tribes into those 'with waggons' and those 'without waggons'. Far to the west, the mid-eleventh century Pecheneg Turks in the Balkans used their waggons like a wall to foil a Byzantine attack, then pursued their retreating enemies with horse archers. The Kipchaqs who pulled back from Byzantine territory in the twelfth century similarly made a *wagenburg* to defend their families. On that occasion the carts were put very close together and were covered with hides to create a highly effective screen against archery. They may also have had a ditch dug in front of, or around, the laager.

Comparable field fortifications were used by the Mongols and their successors from the thirteenth century onwards and may have led to a revival in the use of such defences within the Islamic Middle East. However, in 1402 Timur-i Lenk's army defended its camp at the Battle of Ankara with a ditch, boulders and wooden palisades rather than waggons. They also poisoned the wells between their position and that of their Ottoman Turkish foes.

Some of the most specific information about the use and design of field-fortifications in India actually refers to Islamic northern India, and might not be applicable to the rest of the sub-continent. These sources indicate that army camps were fortified with a ditch and palisade, trees sometimes also being felled to form a smooth *abatis* on the near side of this ditch while buffaloes could be tethered outside as a barrier against an enemy's war-elephants. Little is otherwise known about field-fortification in India except that, amongst the Hindus, their shape and location was decided by the senior military officer in collaboration with the army's chief carpenter and chief astrologer. The resulting defences consisted of ditches, usually with four gates and a separate enclosed space for the ruler's harem.

Chapter 10
Siege Warfare

Most advances in siege engineering and siege weaponry during the early Middle Ages are believed to have originated in China, then spread to the Middle East and eventually to Western Europe. Until the later twelfth century, war machines were of limited power and were normally used to clear defenders from a wall rather than attempt to demolish the wall itself. Smaller siege machines also tended to be made on the spot, though metallic and other key pieces were brought 'from store' with the besieging force. As the medieval period progressed, however, at least one major technological advance originated in the eastern Mediterreanean region then spread both west to Europe and east to China. This was the counterweight mangonel, normally referred to in Europe as a *trebuchet*. There also seems to have been an increasing tendency to prefabricate the larger offensive siege machines, then reassemble them at the site of a siege. In contrast, defensive or protective devices may still usually have been constructed on the spot with available materials.

Throughout the Middle Ages, most armies attempted to reduce enemy strongholds by prolonged raiding of surrounding agricultural areas, though direct sieges would become more common in the later centuries. Early medieval Byzantine military treatises maintained that, if a direct assault was considered necessary, cavalry should be sent to survey the fortifications then secure the area immediately outside them. Infantry would then take up position opposite the enemy's gates, a camp would be set up at least two bowshots from the wall and units would be allocated for the defence of siege machines in case the enemy made a sortie in an effort to destroy them. Direct attacks upon the walls would be launched at what was perceived to be their weakest points or across the shallowest part of any surrounding moat. This sort of direct attack would, as far as Byzantine and other more sophisticated armies were concerned, involve battering rams; 'tortoises' or moveable, sometimes-wheeled protective sheds; assorted stone-throwing machines; scaling ropes; ladders; and wooden towers which could be moveable or stationary. An artificial hill might be also thrown up to provide a better position for the attackers' artillery and archers.

This early Byzantine tradition of siege warfare was inherited by both the later Byzantine Empire and much of the rest of Europe. The most important addition to the artillery since classical times was the beamsling mangonel, a stone-throwing machine which was powered by traction rather than torsion energy. For several centuries the source of this traction energy remained a team of men or women pulling in unison upon ropes attached to the shorter end of the pivotted beamsling.

Within the early medieval period in Western Europe the defence of fortified positions had remained largely passive, with little effort being made to engage the besiegers in a more effective manner. Only by making sorties and fighting against direct assault did defenders normally come into direct contact with their attackers. On the other hand, fortifications had played a major role in the warfare of the Carolingian period, with scaling or rope ladders, wooden roofs or sheds to protect miners, and battering rams all being mentioned. Small fortifications were clearly vulnerable to this sort of assault, but the siege of a city, even of the small ones which were all that Christian Western Europe could yet boast, might take several months. Consequently, most larger sieges relied on blockade rather than close siege.

During the ninth century, if not earlier, simple versions of the beamsling mangonel had been introduced into Western Europe. Thereafter there were numerous references to the use of stone-throwing machines, usually of the new beamsling traction form introduced from the east by the Avars and from the south by the Arabs. Their missiles were usually directed at the gates rather than the walls; this remaining the case throughout the eleventh century. Meanwhile the old torsion-powered stone or javelin-throwing siege weapons of the Roman Empire dropped out of use almost entirely, though remaining known 'in theory'.

Because the majority of western and southern European sieges that were recorded during the eleventh century had been conducted on a very small scale, increased efforts seem to have been made to get spies inside to discover their weak points. Otherwise an attacking force might have to rely on a sudden assault in the hope of seizing an unsecured gate. More often than not, however, the attackers fell back upon a prolonged blockade, operating from a fortified encampment nearby because they were rarely in a position to surround an entire town. Both sides might now use relatively-small stone-throwing weapons to bombard one another. The attackers could also excavate trenches in order to reach the enemy wall in relative safety. Once there they could erect various forms of wooden tower or sturdy shed from which to attack the structure of the wall. Essentially the same pattern of siege warfare persisted throughout the subsequent period of the Crusades and *Reconquista*, though the fortifications and weaponry involved clearly became stronger or more complex.

The Crusaders

The Crusaders arrived in the Middle East with a less-sophisticated tradition of siege engineering than that of their foes. In attack they would dig trenches to isolate a beseiged position from hope of relief, form a *testudo* of shields to protect a squad of men attempting to force a breach and might even pose as a band of lost travellers in an attempt to trick a night watchman into opening his gate. When this failed against the Arab castle of Shayzar early in the twelfth century, the would-be attackers then shot an arrow through the door's inspection slit and fled.

While besieging Damascus a generation later, a large Crusader army found itself counter-beseiged in its own camp by the defending forces and their allies. The Crusader knights waited in vain to charge an enemy who refused to come into range, instead sniping at the invaders with arrows, javelins and sling-stones. Later in the twelfth century a Crusader charge did succeed in breaking the 'square' formations of Islamic troops who emerged from Acre to challenge them. While this particularly prolonged siege was going on, the younger boys from both armies fought mock fights between the opposing lines.

In defence, it appears that Crusader castles had a minimal effect on anything approaching a full-scale invasion. On the other hand it took the Muslims a great deal of time and effort to reduce substantial fortifications which could rarely be taken by surprise assault. According to the *Rule of the Hospitallers*, the gates of castles near a frontier were closed after *compline*, the last service of the day, and should not be opened until the following morning. Other sources describe Crusader cavalry dismounting outside the gate of their own small castle in the twelfth century, then using their lances as pikes to defend its entrance.

In almost all cases the garrison would make vigorous sorties for as long as they could. On one occasion those making the sortie included men riding mules, though these troops were probably mounted infantry rather than knights who lacked proper mounts. Even at the start of the final siege of Acre in 1291 the Crusader garrison did not initially close its gates and instead frequently emerged to attack the Mamluk besiegers, either in major sorties or as individual challenges to combat. Apart from making sorties, the Crusader garrisons also shot at their enemies so vigorously that anyone coming within range of their walls had to wear armour.

Some Crusader castles had more specific functions, Darbsak near Antioch apparently serving as a regional armaments depot. Others on the Lebanese coast could expect assistance from the indigenous Christians of the mountains who ambushed the invaders' supply columns. Is it also clear that the Crusaders soon employed local Armenian siege engineers and siege-machine operators who became a highly paid élite. Even before that, however, the soldiers of the First Crusade used a wooden tower on wheels during their attack on al-Bara, this having knights on top while other armoured troops pushed it forward. The two wooden siege towers used during the Crusader attack on Tyre in the early twelfth century were between twenty and twenty-five metres high. They contained rams whose heads weighed around ten kilograms and were swung from ropes. Nevertheless both were burned by the defenders.

Similar towers were used in the later twelfth century while the wooden *chats châteaux* used against Damietta (Dumyat) in the mid-thirteenth century were described as siege-towers with additional protections for miners attacking the base of a fortified wall. The *chat* or 'cat' part of the device was a roofed structure for the miners, with two *châteaux* towers behind it. Behind the towers were two 'houses' where men could either take cover or watch for enemy counter-attacks. The troops inside wooden siege-towers were sometimes said to have had stores of water and vinegar to douse fires, this perhaps being standard practice. In turn, Crusader archers shot fire-arrows to ignite the bundles of straw which Muslim defenders hung in front of their walls as buffers against mangonel stones or rams.

The ceramic fire-grenades normally associated with Islamic armies have also been found in the collapsed storerooms of a Crusader castle on Cyprus. Although the Crusaders never used stone-throwing mangonels in the same numbers as did their Islamic foes, they clearly had the latest types, including the *boves* which seems to have had an adjustable or additional counterweight to alter its range. Those defending Acre at the end of the thirteenth century could throw a stone weighing forty-five kilograms. On other occasions Crusader and Islamic mangonels engaged in duels which ended when one machine was smashed by the others' missiles. In contrast the *espringal* was a torsion-powered anti-personnel engine which came in various sizes, the best being made of beech, elm or oak. Its power was provided by twisted skeins of horse or cattle hair rather than the animal tendons probably still used in comparable Byzantine machines.

The Iberian *Reconquista* was primarily aimed at cities, some of which were so large and well fortified that their reduction took prolonged blockades lasting several years. Occasionally the final struggle was resolved by bitter street-fighting of almost modern savagery which also involved the use of slings and stone-throwing mangonels. Siege engineering in the Christian states of northern Iberia was, of course, greatly influenced by that of the Islamic south, the Spanish *algarrada* stemming from the Arabic *al-arrada*, a simple form of man-powered mangonel. The *manganell torques* or 'Turkish mangonel', mentioned in early thirteenth century Aragon was probably a new form recently introduced from the Middle East, probably with a counterweight.

Byzantine Siege Warfare

Early Byzantine sources had sometimes used the term *manganikon* for a torsion-powered, single-armed stone-throwing device, but in general the Western term 'mangonel' and its various linguistic derivations referred to a beam-sling machine of ultimately Chinese origin. Meanwhile Byzantine *cheirotoxobolistrai* and *toxobolistrai* of the ninth and tenth centuries seem to have been large frame-mounted crossbows for use in sieges or naval warfare. The addition of the prefix *cheiro* probably meant that the device could be operated by one man rather than that it was hand-held. The few archaic torsion machines powered by twisted ropes still apparently used animal tendons as in earlier times, probably because of the Byzantine Empire's generally dry climate.

Siege technology had been the field in which Byzantine and Islamic superiority over western European Crusaders was most pronounced. By the thirteenth and fourteenth centuries, however, the Byzantines were slipping behind while the Muslims retained their dominance until the introduction of gunpowder. One reason why the Byzantines lost their preeminence may have been a tendency to rely on traditions which had served so well for so long. These included the simplest tactics, as when local defence forces drove off twelfth-century nomad raiders by erecting a barricade of farm carts around a local church near the Sea of Marmora. Elsewhere, local garrisons habitually emerged to challenge their enemies in the open before retreating inside their fortifications, a habit that persisted well into the fourteenth century.

At the other end of the technological scale the Byzantines made use of extremely advanced siege machines. The earliest illustrations of a Byzantine 'great crossbow' mounted on a frame or chassis came from the eleventh century. Such pictures are far from clear but the weapon was apparently spanned by a winch, and could be turned, aimed and shot by a single operator. In the twelfth century, Byzantine forces used small stone-throwing *ballistas* mounted on wagons, and the late thirteenth-century French scholar Egidio Colonna attributed the *biffa* or *trebuchet* with an adjustable counterweight to the 'Romans', by which he probably meant the Byzantines.

There is little evidence that the Russians learned much about siege warfare from the Byzantines, despite their close cultural and political links. Stronger influences came from central Europe and even more so from the steppes, Russian garrisons apparently adopting more active forms of defensive measures by the twelfth century. A century later most of Russia was under strong Mongol, and thus by extension Chinese, influence in techniques of siege and counter-siege. As a result large numbers of mangonels were adopted quite suddenly from the 1240s onwards. These proved particularly effective against the Russians' western foes such as Hungarians, Poles and German Baltic Crusaders. A remarkable all-iron crossbow bolt with iron fins, about two metres long and probably designed to carry some sort of fire-cartridge, was discovered in the thirteenth-fourteenth century fortified city of Vladimir in eastern Russia, though this missile might actually have been of Mongol origin. The widespread impression that Russian military engineering stagnated under Mongol domination is, in fact, a gross oversimplification. Clearly Russia did not follow the elaboration of military architecture seen in western Europe, but there were equally clearly major advances in defensive tactics and siege equipment.

The Islamic World

From the eighth to eleventh centuries Islamic armies tended to rely on surprise attack, blockade and *naqb* (mining) to reduce enemy fortifications, with less reliance on *kabsh* (battering rams) and *manjaniq* (mangonels). Several well-recorded Islamic sieges from this period show remarkable similarity with Chinese siege warfare, but of course these two most powerful world civilisations were by then in close economic and cultural contact. The vital role of cavalry in defence of a fortified place was similarly illustrated on several occasions, with horsemen launching sudden sorties which struck enemy assault squads in the flank as they attacked a breach in the fortified wall.

The main Islamic armies soon included a special corps of *manjaniqin* siege engine operators under their own officer of *amir* rank. Most such technical officers appear to have started their careers as ordinary soldiers and were numbered in the garrisons of all major citadels. Where siege weapons were concerned, the moveable wooden siege tower known as a *burj* was reatively rare, while one source specifically accused the ninth-century Arabs of not knowing about the *dabbabah*, a ram within a protective timber roof. The Arabs in question would, however, have been nomadic Bedouin rather than settled and urbanized tribes. The *arrada* was a relatively small and simple version of the basic man-powered *manjaniq*, not a torsion-powered weapon as once thought. Incendiary-soaked rags wound around rocks were hurled from *manjaniq* by the start of the ninth century, if not earlier, this tactic often being used to set an enemy-held residential area on fire.

All the successor states, including the powerful Fatimids and the Islamic dynasties of the Iberian Peninsula, used siege and counter-siege weapons which had been developed by the Abbasids from the late eighth to tenth centuries. The main variations were, in fact, seen in the east where the Ghaznavids learned much from the Hindu Indians. This included the use of elephants to haul heavy siege engines and even as living battering rams to knock down enemy gates. Some armies were, meanwhile, better equipped than others. The Fatimids, for example, lacked an adequate answer to the defenders' wall-mounted *arrada* stone-throwers when attacking Damascus in 983 AD, so countered with an indiscrimate bombardment of the city using rocks wrapped in *naft*-soaked rags.

By the eleventh century things had changed and the Fatimid Caliph's arsenal included all the latest weaponry for siege warfare. These included fire weapons known as 'Chinese arrows', long-necked glass incendiary grenades, jars of saltpetre and special screens to hide the movement of troops during siege operations. Early in the twelfth century, during the Fatimid defence of Tyre against the Crusaders, a naval officer designed special iron hooks which, when lowered from the city wall, deflected and jammed enemy rams operating from inside wooden siege towers. The same sailor was also credited with inventing a device for tipping refuse, faeces and burning substances onto the enemies' heads. This consisted of panniers on a large T-shaped beam mounted on the wall, moved by the sort of pulleys used to raise a ship's mast or yardarm. The remarkable similarity between this device and one used in China perhaps suggests that the sailor in question may have been a veteran of long-distance voyages to the Far East.

Existing siege engines, such as the beam-sling *manjaniq*, had already spread further, reaching Andalusia by the tenth century. New classes of weapon also appeared, such as the *qaws al-ziyar* which included a two-armed machine later known in Europe as the 'espringal'. It was spanned by a winch and was also known in eleventh century Byzantium. Other countersiege measures included the normal filling of water cisterns, the storage of weapons including *arrada* stone-throwers for use in counter-battery work, and the construction of flour-mills within the defences. More original were the hidden pits dug by Muslim defenders of Brindisi in southern Italy, into which counter-attacking Lombard cavalry tumbled.

Islamic armies continued to use both simple and sophisticated siege techniques against Crusaders and others in the twelfth and thirteenth centuries. During offensive operations, light troops were sent ahead of the main force to blockade the targeted castle or city, after which the surrounding orchards and groves were progressively cut down to induce surrender. As in earlier centuries, the first phase of a direct siege involved erecting palisades or *zaribas* made from available materials and the digging of entrenchments. A theoretical thirteenth-century account of siege warfare lists the sequence of events as follows. First the commander gathered his labourers and ordered them to assemble siege machines. Bombardment of the enemy began with small engines which could be assembled quickly, followed by those of increasing power and sophistication as a means of imposing psychological pressure on the foe. The besiegers must also defend themselves with trenches as they were vulnerable to sorties by the garrison, and units of cavalry should be posted at an arrow-shot from each gate to face such sorties.

A detailed description of the Islamic military encampment during Saladin's siege of Acre mentioned seven thousand 'shops', including 140 farriers and over 1,000 bath houses, mostly run by North Africans. The whole area was patrolled by special 'market police' and the merchants paid soldiers to help them move their goods when the first campsite had to be shifted for sanitary reasons. In fact Saladin's *thuql*, or siege train, included a variety of specialists such as *naqqabun* engineers, *naffatun* fire-troops, *zarraqbun* fire-throwers, assorted craftsmen and *massahis*, or surveyors.

It is similarly clear that the Muslims used much more mining than did the Crusaders, with the Mamluks using more than did their Ayyubid predecessors. Their corps of specialist miners included those expert in burning tunnel props beneath an enemy's walls, as well as those specialising in razing castles once they had been captured. The originally-Chinese tactic of erecting mounds of earth or sandbags as emplacements for stone-throwing mangonels was similarly used throughout these centuries. Such a mound used in Saladin's siege of Diyarbakir enabled the mangonels, which could be highly accurate, to steadily knock the battlements from the fortifications so that enemy archers could not find cover.

Assault parties would then be put under the best officers while the men themselves were heavily armoured, some carrying fire-weapons as well as tools to further demolish the defences. An assault party was supposed to occupy the breach while the defenders were given a final chance to surrender. Other sources mention assault archers being armoured right down to their heels while those taking the breach carried large leather mantlet-style shields. A further variation was to use any numerical advantage to make many small attacks against different parts of the wall and thus exhaust the garrison who had to rush from one place to another. On one occasion the Crusader defenders were so physically and psychologically worn down that the shouts of their own Muslim prisoners within the castle made them think all was lost, and so they surrendered.

In defence, Islamic garrisons resorted to imaginative stratagems, for example sending men with torches out of a postern gate by night, returning with their torches extinguished and then coming out again relit to make the size of the garrison appear more formidable. Psychological warfare was clearly considered important, as when the defenders of Aleppo wrapped bales of costly fabric around their strongest tower before sending a message to the besiegers stating that the enemy's mangonel stones had given the tower a headache. On this occasion the use of costly fabrics indicated how wealthy and powerful the city was.

A local militia, which was largely responsible for defeating a Crusader attack on Damascus in 1148, used local knowledge of the surrounding fields, orchards and lanes to trap and destroy small groups of invaders. This obliged the Crusaders to move their attack to the more open eastern side of the city where, however, they were soon said to be short of water. Although the small Barada River ran past this area, it had already flowed through Damascus where it served as the city's main sewer, and may therefore not have been suitable for drinking.

Sorties would often be made at night in attempts to destroy the enemy's siege machines; another method being to shoot red-hot iron crossbow bolts at them. During the Third Crusade's siege of Acre, the son of a coppersmith annoyed the garrison's professional fire-troops by designing a more effective way of shooting *naft* and thus destroying the Crusaders' siege engines. During that particular siege the defenders used a long grappling hook to ensnare one of King Richard's leading men, hauling him up the wall.

The relative abundance of written material from the Islamic side during the Crusades shows their siege trains were well organised. One early thirteenth-century technical treatise listed the items needed by a force besieging an enemy stronghold as ready-made parts for siege engines, plenty of rope, ready-cut mangonel stones, iron rings, nails and hides. The nails were also used as pegs driven into the wall to enable men to scale the defences. A comparable fourteenth-century manual added scaling ropes, ladders and grappling hooks.

The counterweight mangonel or *trebuchet* was invented in the eastern Mediterranean region by or during the mid-twelfth century, first being illustrated in detail in a manuscript written for Saladin by al-Tarsusi, an Egyptian, along with many other sophisticated and sometimes impractical devices. Although the author was writing about machines which had been used by Fatimid armies, the *trebuchet* only came into widespread use from the late twelfth century onwards. Al-Tarsusi also described several other simpler man-powered mangonels of which the Arab form was considered the most reliable. It consisted of a flat-topped wooden frame, sometimes with a roof or wall to protect its operators. The Turco-Persian type needed less work and materials, and was mounted on a sloping frame supported by another at an angle, while the 'Frankish' or European type was an improvement on this simple form.

Al-Tarsusi's counterweight *trebuchet* was described as an elaboration of the Turco-Persian type and had a counterweight consisting of rocks in a sturdy net rather than a wooden box. Meanwhile the smallest *lu'ab* type had the least range but, being mounted on a single pole with a swivel on top, could be traversed to aim in any direction. The terminology of such Islamic *manjaniqs* changed slightly during the thirteenth and fourteenth centuries, the smallest and simplest Turco-Persian form now being called the *Maghribi* or North African type. A 'black bull-like' mangonel incorporated a sling to shoot large arrows or javelins while the easiest to assemble and fastest to shoot was now known as the 'devilish' mangonel.

During the late thirteenth century substantial numbers of pre-fabricated mangonels were transported to the scene of a siege where they were re-assembled, sometimes apparently in batteries, over ninety being aimed at Acre by the Mamluks during the final siege of 1291. Elsewhere they were mounted on towers to defend a harbour entrance, perhaps having been pre-targeted on a spot where ships must pass. Apart from the 'black bull-like' mangonel which shot large bolts or arrows, the main low-trajectory bolt-shooting machines included the 'great crossbow', mounted on a rotating wooden frame and probably spanned by a winch. This had been used since at least the twelfth century. A pair of large bow-staves, one made of palm-tree wood, the other a composite of wood, horn and sinew, were found in the Citadel of Damascus and probably came from 'great crossbows', both being about two metres long.

The effectiveness of such weapons in defence of fortified places was such that the operators of *jarkh* large crossbows sometimes had their thumbs cut off when captured, so that they could not use these weapons again. The *qaws al-ziyar* was an even more devastating device, having two separate arms powered by twisted skeins of hair, silk or sinew according to al-Tarsusi. It was known in twelfth-century Egypt where the largest form was was spanned by a winch said to have the power of twenty men. A later reference from Morocco said that it took eleven mules to carry a dismantled *qaws al-ziyar*. By the fourteenth and fifteenth centuries, however, the torsion-powered siege weapon was known as a *kuskanjil* in the Middle East.

Dabbaba, wooden sheds to protect men working *kabsh* (rams), were still used by Islamic armies but, like the *burj*, or wooden siege-tower, were considered ideal targets for *naft* and other forms of incendiary-weapon. Perhaps for this reason they had largely fallen out of use by the late thirteenth century. Other more abundant devices were screens and mantlets to protect, or at least hide, sappers and miners. One particular example was used during the final siege of Crusader-held Acre in 1291. It consisted of a large piece of felt erected on a system of pulleys, raised at night to cover those building an 'assault road' towards a breach in the enemy defences. It not only hid individual men but absorbed mangonel balls and crossbow bolts. The *zahafah* is less clearly understood, but appear to have been a stationary wooden tower for archers, possibly to protect the entrance to a siege-mine.

The Mamluks were using cannon in siege warfare by the late fourteenth century, though apparently more for their moral impact than their destructive capability. Meanwhile, Mamluk armies were still noted for their massed batteries of stone-throwing mangonels. The first clear reference to an Ottoman Turkish use of firearms in siege warfare is found in a Bulgarian account of the Ottoman threat to Constantinople in 1398.

Siege technology in the westernmost parts of the medieval Islamic world was virtually identical to that in the Middle East. It became particularly sophisticated under the Muwahhidin in the later twelfth century, entire rivers being dammed and diverted to undermine an enemy's fortifications. There were also continued references to the commanders of besieging forces occasionally using a *marqaba*, or special observation post, from which they could direct operations.

Another notable feature of prolonged sieges in these western Islamic regions was the building of entire towns with their own stone fortifications next to the city under attack. The moral impact of such a commitment must have been enormous, and the walls and minaret of one such 'counter-city' survive at al-Mansurah, outside Tilimsan in Algeria. On a smaller scale a new castle was erected at Bailush near Granada in the later eleventh century, from which invaders could harry the cultivated zone of orchards and fields around the city. Otherwise the usual sequence of events was followed, with the defenders fighting outside their walls until they became convinced that the attackers could not be driven away. In fourteenth-century Granada this was followed by walling up all the city gates except those needed for sorties, while stone-throwing mangonels always played a major defensive role in counter-battery bombardment. Particularly-advanced semi-explosive pyrotechnics seem to have appeared in North Africa and Andalusia quite suddenly in the late thirteenth century, some of them possibly incorporating primitive forms of gunpowder.

The Peoples of the Steppes
The role of Central Asian peoples in the spread of various aspects of medieval siege warfare can hardly be overestimated, although they generally acted as transmitters of Chinese technology rather than originators of new ideas. In the western steppes the tenth-century Pecheneg Turks subdued Russian forts by simply blockading them, but by the twelfth and early thirteenth centuries the Kipchaq Turks not only assaulted the Russians' walls but used various forms of incendiary-weapon. A

generation or so later, and far the the east, the strongly Indian-influenced and Iranian-speaking Khotanese attempted to defend their city wall against the Mongols' stone-throwing mangonels by hanging netting made of tree bark outside the fortifications.

The fact that the Mongol armies which invaded central Europe were not fully equipped for siege warfare does not indicate that the Mongols were inferior in this technology. On the other hand, they did tend to rely on Chinese and Muslim specialist engineers, the latter now being in advance even of the Chinese in several fields. The Mongols also made use of massed batteries of mangonels of both the man-powered and counterweight types. Other Mongol siege machines included Chinese operated but Persian-named *kaman-i-gav* 'ox-bows', which shot large bolts dipped in burning pitch. They are said to have achieved a range of 2,500 paces, though this may perhaps be doubted, and may have been similar to the slightly later *qarabughawiya* 'black bull-Like' mangonels of the Mamluk Sultanate. Otherwise Mongol armies employed massed infantry archers; assorted fire-weapons; the blocking or diverting of small rivers to flood or undermine defensive walls; and, of course, prolonged blockades.

All these tactics and machines were used to devastating effect by Timur-i Lenk at the end of the fourteenth century. Minor variations may have included the blockading of an otherwise inaccessible mountain fortress in Luristan, forcing its garrison to surrender by building and garrisoning several watchtowers in surrounding territory. Here, however, the siege lasted no less than twelve years and the fortress eventually fell as a result of treachery. In Anatolia in 1400 AD, Timur's siege engineers erected a substantial man-made hill, overlooking the main gate and wall of Sivas, from which *arrada* mangonels threw blazing *naft* and *manjaniq* mangonels hurled large rocks into the city.

India

Indian armies used elephants with protective iron plates on the fronts of their heads as living battering rams, particularly against gates. Otherwise rotating drills and rams swung on iron chains were used to penetrate walls, as similarly seen in Islamic and Byzantine military engineering. Additional Indian devices included the *pashtib*, a raised platform of sand-bags, these often also being used to fill a defensive ditch or the space between concentric walls; and the *gargaj*, which was the Indian version of a moveable wooden siege-tower. Indian armies used the same mangonels and *trebuchets* as seen in neighbouring Islamic countries. They included versions of the Arab *arrada* which could be traversed to alter its aim, while others were described as faster-shooting than normal types.

The spiked objects rolled down upon an attacker sound virtually the same as Chinese 'thunder sticks' while the especially-long spears used to defend gates from elephant battering-rams were probably a local characteristic. Indian references to the use of fire and smoke to defend fortresses sometimes sound so devastating that they recall the weapons used by gods and heroes in ancient Hindu religious epics rather than the reality of medieval warfare. Behind such exaggeration, however, were genuinely sophisticated forms of fire, smoke and apparently even heated iron grills or doors which even the most determined enemy could not open – at least until they cooled down.

Although Indian siege and counter-siege warfare and its associated engineering skills were highly developed, defence continued to pre-dominate over offense. Hence attackers tended to fall back upon ruses and strategems, attempting to lure garrisons into the open and trying to subvert the population. Scaling ladders were, however, the normal means of direct assault, these being secured to the characteristic mud-brick walls of northern Indian fortresses with iron pegs. Meanwhile siege warfare in southeastern Asia was rather primitive when compared with that of India, China and the Islamic world. Burmese forces were, for example, said to be unable to overcome large wooden stockades in the early twelfth century.

Glossary

archon: (plural: archontes) commander of a Byzantine foideraton unit.

arrada: simple form of beamsling stone-throwing engine, Arabic.

arrière-ban: general levy in French-language states.

arsenal, arsenale: originally a shipbuilding yard, subsequently meaning a military storage depot (from the Arabic term *dar al-sina*).

bailli: ruler's representative or commander in a castle or fortified place, French.

ballista: large crossbow probably spanned by a windlass.

ban: provincial lord or governor, late medieval Hungary.

bard: horse armour.

batailles: army divisions, France.

benefice: land given in return for military service, Europe.

biffa: trebuchet with an adjustable counterweight, late thirteenth and fourteenth centuries.

bombard: most common early form of short-barrelled cannon, fourteenth century.

boves: form of beam-sling mangonel, France and Italy (see also *biffa*).

boyar: tribal nobleman, military commander or senior aristocrat, Russia, Bulgaria and the Romanian principalities.

buchsenmeister: master gunner, fourteenth-century Germany.

burj: wooden mobile siege-tower, Arabic.

caparison: medieval European horse covering, often including a protective layer.

captain: middle-ranking military commander, usually appointed by a government authority.

carroccio: banner-wagon and rallying point, medieval Italy.

chats châteaux: 'cat-castle', movable shed-like structure to protect the entrance of a siege-mine, with an additional wooden fortification attached.

chelandre, chelandrion: transport ships, tenth to thirteenth century.

chevauchée: military raid, French.

cog: square-rigged late medieval northern Europe sailing ship with a stern rudder.

condottieri: mercenary troops under contract to a specific employer, later medieval Italy.

conroi: cavalry squadron, France.

constable: a senior officer in a royal or noble household, normally responsible for military discipline and organisation.

couched lance: technique whereby the weapon was held tightly beneath a horseman's upper right arm.

cuir bouilli: hardened leather, soaked in wax then heated and moulded.

cuman: German name for light cavalry auxiliaries of Kipchaq Turkish origin.

damascene: form of metal-working in which an ingot of high or mixed high and low carbon steel produced a weapon, usually a sword-blade, with a distinctive surface pattern commonly called 'watering'.

dienstleute: non-noble 'serf cavalry' in Germany.

dihqan: Persian gentry.

diwan al-jaysh: Islamic-Arabic 'Ministry of War'.

domestic: senior Byzantine military commander.

donjon: stone keep, or central or primary tower of a medieval castle.

dorobanti: local defence formations, probably to guard mountain passes, Wallachia, from Turkish derbend.

droungos (plural: droungoi):   depending on the exact period, either a mobile reserve in a Byzantine field army, or a Byzantine cavalry unit.

druzyna: élite troops of a Polish ruler.

espringal: medieval European frame-mounted large arrow-shooting machine with two separate arms (see also *spingarda, spingala* and *springolf*).

fief: territorial estate to support a knight and his equipment.

fighting castle: wooden structures on the prow and stern of larger sailing ships, where the vessel's defenders were concentrated.

gasmouli: Byzantine marines of mixed Greek and western European descent.

ghulam: slave-recruited professional soldier in Islamic armies (see also *mamluk*).

gleven: cavalry unit usually consisting of a man-at-arms and his followers, Germany.

gonfanon: middle-sized military banner.

great crossbow: large form of crossbow, sometimes on a pedestal or frame.

Greek fire: petroleum-based liquid incendiary weapon.

hoardings: wooden defensive structures on top of a fortified wall.

iqta':   revertable fief, usually military, Islamic world.

irafa: pay unit in many Islamic armies.

jihad: Muslim concept of spiritual struggle, the secondary or inferior form consisting of military struggle in defence of Islam.

jinete: small horse; also light cavalry tactics of later medieval Iberian peninsula.

jund: territorial military organisation, Arab-Islamic areas.

karias, karya: tribal army among Baltic peoples.

karr wa farr: tactics of repeated attack and withdrawal, Arabic.

khamis: five-fold division of an Arab-Islamic army.

latrunculi: banditry or raiding, Baltic states.

lavra: Romano-Byzantine monastic retreat, often fortified.

machicolation: overhanging structure on a fortified wall to enable defenders to shoot down upon the enemy.

mamluk: slave-recruited professional soldier in Islamic armies.

manganikon: Byzantine mangonel stone-throwing siege engine.

mangonel: beamsling stone-throwing siege engine.

manjaniq: Islamic mangonel stone-throwing siege engine.

mantlet: large shield, or a piece of defensive hoarding used in field fortification.

marshal: senior officer in a household responsible for various aspects of military organisation.

masnada, masnata: military retinue in early and high medieval Europe.

melée: individual combat following the break-up of a cavalry formation; also a form of mock-combat cavalry training involving teams of horsemen.

milites, miles: professional soldiers in early medieval western Europe, usually cavalry, forerunners of the knight.

ministeriales: non-noble 'serf cavalry' in Germany; knights, often of non- noble origin, serving in a French lord's court.

mizalla: parasol, mark of rulership in the Islamic world.

motte and bailey: type of castle consisting of a tower on a raised earth mound with a wooden stockaded area around the outside.

mourtatoi: ex-Byzantine crossbow troops in Venetian Crete.

murabitin: religiously motivated volunteers, Arabic.

nacharark: a member of the medieval Armenian military aristocracy.

naft: 'Greek fire' incendiary material, Arabic.

naqb: mining techniques in siege warfare, Arabic.

naqqarah: Arabic term for a small drum, often used in warfare.

ordu: Centra Asian Turkish fortified royal residence.

pattern welding: technique of producing a sword-blade or other weapon from strips of hard and soft iron, twisted together then repeatedly heated and beaten.

pavise: large form of shield or mantlet, normally used by infantry.

pennon: small, usually triangular, flag nailed to the shaft of a lance.

portcullis: iron grid lowered behind the normally wooden gates of fortified town or castle.

protostrator: 'commander of troops', Byzantine military rank, also used in fourteenth-century Italo-Angevin Albania and Epirus.

qa'id: officer in medieval Arab-Islamic armies.

qaws al-ziyar: medieval Islamic frame-mounted large arrow-shooting machine.

razzia: Arabian raiding warfare.

renner: men-at-arms, armoured cavalry 14th century Germany.

reysa: high-speed raiding tactics, 13th and 14th century Northern Crusades in the Baltic States.

ribat: garrison duty or frontier fortification for volunteer troops in Islamic countries.

round ship: medieval merchant ship, so called because it was much broader in the beam than a galley, usually referring to Mediterranean types.

seneschal: governor or ruler's representative in a town or city.

sergeant à cheval: mounted sergeant, non-noble cavalryman.

sergeant: professional soldier of non-noble origin, usually infantry.

sestieri: section or quarter of Italian city or colony, basis for raising militia forces.

shalandi: Arab-Islamic galley, warship.

shaykh: Arabic title of respect, usually given to a tribal chief.

shini: Arab-Islamic galley, warship.

shurta: security troops or police in Arab-Islamic states.

solenarion: arrow-guide to shoot short darts, Byzantine Greek.

spingarda, spingala, springolf: alternative Italian and German names for *espringal*.

squire: member of the military class either aspiring to the status of a knight, or merely having less equipment and thus lower status.

stipendiary knight: knight receiving money payment rather than land in return for feudal military obligations.

stradiotti: light cavalry of the late Byzantine Empire, Balkan states and of Balkan origins in late medieval Italy.

strutere: destruction or raiding, Baltic states.

tagma: small Byzantine unit or company, later a division of the Byzantine army.

tarida: large Mediterranean transport galley, usually for horses, of Arab origin.

tarkhan: Turkish military commander.

theme: Byzantine provincial army, later also referring to a military province.

thughur: military frontier-provinces in Arab-Islamic countries.

tournament: gathering of knights to take part in competitive cavalry exercises of various kinds.

trebuchet: counter-weight beam-sling stone-throwing engine.

uissier, or huissier: large Mediterranean transport ship, believed to have loading doors in the sides of its hull, twelfth and thirteenth centuries.

Varangian guard: palace unit of the later Byzantine Empire, recruited from Scandinavian mercenaries and subsequently from Anglo-Saxon exiles or adventurers.

vicarius: senior officer in an Italian overseas colony, 14th century.

viertelmeister: commander of urban militias, 14th century Germany.

voivode: provincial governor or local ruler, 14th century Hungary, Serbia and Romania.

wagenburg: field fortifications made of wagons or carts.

wali: governor of a province and sometimes commander of the provincial army in Arab-Islamic states.

Further Reading

Abulafia, D S H, *Commerce and Conquest in the Mediterranean* (Aldershot, 1993).

Abu'l-Fida' (P M Holt tr.), *The Memoires of a Syrian Prince: Abu'l-Fida', Sultan of Hamah (672-737/1273-1331)* (Wiesbaden, 1983).

Abun-Nasr, J M, *A History of the Maghrib in the Islamic Period* (Cambridge, 1987).

Ahmad, A, *A History of Islamic Sicily* (Edinburgh, 1975).

Ahrweiler, H, 'Les forteresses construites en Asie Mineure face à l'invasion seldjoucide', in *Akten des XI. Internationaler Byzantinistkongresses, München 1958* (Munich, 1960), 182-189.

Ahrweiler, H, *Byzance et la Mer: La Marine de Guerre, la Politique et les Institutions Maritimes de Byzance aux VIIe-XVe siècles* (Paris, 1966).

Alcocer Martínez, M, *Castillos y fortalezas del antique reino de Granada* (Tangier, 1941).

Alexandrescu-Dersca, M M, *La Campagne de Timur en Anatolie (1402)* (London, 1977).

Allan, J W, *Persian Metal Technology, 700-1300 AD* (Oxford, 1979).

Allouche, I S, 'Un texte relatif aux premiers canons', *Hespéris 32* (1945), 81-84.

Allsen, T T, 'Mongol Census-Taking in Rus, 1245-1275', *Harvard Ukrainian Studies 5/I* (Cambridge, Mass., 1981), 32-53.

Allsen, T T, *Culture and Conquest in Mongol Eurasia* (London, 2001).

Allsen, T T, *Mongol Imperialism: The Policies of the Grand Qan Mönke in China, Russia and the Islamic Lands* (Berkeley, 1987).

Amador de los Rios y Villalta, R, 'Notas acerca de la batalla de Lucera de la prision de Boabdil in 1483', *Revista des archives, bibliotecas y museos*, 16 (1906), 37-66.

Amari, M, 'Su i fuochi da guerra usati nel Mediterraneo nel'Xl e XII secoli', *Atti della Reale Academia dei Lincei* (1876), 3-16.

Amouroux-Mourad, M, *Le Comté d'Edesse* (Beirut, 1988).

Anastasijevic, D, & G Ostrogorsky, 'Les Coumanes pronoïaires', *Annuaire de l'Institut de philologie et d'histoire Orientales et Slaves*, 11 (1951), 19-29.

Andrews, K, *Castles of the Morea* (Princeton, 1953).

Anghel, G, 'Les fortéresses moldaves de l'époque d'Etienne le Grand', *Château Gaillard*, 7 (1975), 21-34.

Anghel, G, 'Les premiers donjons de pierres de Transylvanie', *Château Gaillard*, 8 (1977), 7-20.

Angold, M, *A Byzantine Government in Exile: Government and Society under the Laskarids of Nicea 1204-1261* (Oxford, 1975).

Ansari, 'Umar Ibn Ibrahim al-Awsi al-, (G T Scanlon ed. & tr.), *A Muslim Manual of War: being Tafrij al Kurub fi Tadbir al Hurub* (Cairo, 1961).

Antaki, P, 'Le château Croisé de Beyrouth; étude preliminaire', *ARAM Periodical 13/14* (2001/2), 323-353.

Arbel, B, B Hamilton & D Jacoby (eds.), *Latins and Greeks in the Eastern Mediterranean after 1204* (London, 1989).

Arié, R, *L'Espagne Musulmane au temps des Nasrides (1232-1492)* (Paris, 1973).

Arié, R, *L'Occident Musulman au Bas Moyen Age* (Paris, 1992).

Ashcroft, J, 'Konrad's "Rolandslied", Henry the Lion, and the Northern Crusade', *Forum for Modern Language Studies*, 20 (1986), 184-208.

Ashtor, E, *Histoire des Prix et des salaires dans l'orient médiéval* (Paris, 1969).

Atiya, A S, *The Crusade in the Later Middle Ages* (London, 1938).

Atiya, A S, *The Crusade of Nicopolis* (London, 1934).

Avissar, M, & E Stern, 'Akko, the Citadel', *Excavations and Surveys in Israel*, 14 (1994), 22-25.

Ayalon, D, 'Studies in the Structure of the Mamluk Army – I, The Army Stationed in Egypt', *Bulletin of the School of Oriental and African Studies*, 25 (1953), 203-228.

Ayalon, D, 'Studies in the Structure of the Mamluk Army – II: The Halqa', *Bulletin of the School of Oriental and African Studies*, 25 (1953), 448-476.

Ayalon, D, 'Studies in the Structure of the Mamluk Army – III: Holders of Offices Connected with the Army', *Bulletin of the School of Oriental and African Studies*, 26 (1954), 57-90.

Ayalon, D, 'The Mamluks and Naval Power: A Phase of the Struggle between Islam and Christian Europe', *Proceedings of the Israel Academy of Sciences and Humanities*, 1 (1965), 1-12.

Ayalon, D, *Gunpowder and Firearms in the Mamluk Kingdom* (London, 1956).

Ayalon, D, *The Mamluk Military Society* (London, 1979).

Babingen, F, *Mehmet the Conqueror and his Time* (Princeton, 1978).

Bahnassi, A, 'Fabrication des épées de Damas', *Syria*, 53 (1976), 281-294.

Bak, J M, 'The Price of War and Peace in Late Medieval Hungary', in R P McGuire (ed.), *War and Peace in the Middle Ages* (Copenhagen, 1987), 161-178.

Balard, M, 'Les formes militaires de la colonisation génoise', in *Castrum, III* (1988), 67-78.

Balard, M, *La Mer Noire et la Romanie Génoise (XIIIe-XVe siècles)* (London, 1989).

Baldwin, M W, *Raymond III of Tripoli and the Fall of Jerusalem (1140-1187)* (Princeton, 1936).

Barbaro, Nicolo (J R Melville Jones, tr.), *Diary of the Siege of Constantinople* (New York, 1969).

Barber, M (ed.), *The Military Orders: Fighting for the Faith and Caring for the Sick* (Aldershot, 1994).

Barber, M, 'Supplying the Crusader States: The Role of the Templars', in B Z Kedar (ed.), *The Horns of Hattin* (London & Jerusalem, 1992), 314-26.

Barker, J W, *Manuel II Palaeologus (1391-1425): A Study in Late Byzantine Statesmanship* (New Brunswich, 1969).

Barthold, V V, *Histoire des Turcs d'Asie Centrale* (Paris, 1946; reprint Philadelphia, 1977).

Bartusis, M C, *The Late Byzantine Army: Arms and Society 1204-1453* (Philadelphia, 1992).

Basset, H, & H Terrase, 'Sanctuaires et Forteresses Almohades', *Hésperis*, 7 (1927), 117-156.

Bazzana, A, 'Forteresses du Royaume Nasride de Grenade (XIIIe-XVe siècles: la defense des frontières', *Château Gaillard*, 11 (Caen, 1983), 29-43.

Beldiceanu, N, *Le Monde Ottoman des Balkans (1402-1566)*, (reprint London, 1976).

Ben-Ami, A, *Social Change in a Hostile Environment: The Crusaders' Kingdom of Jerusalem* (Princeton, 1969).

Bennett, M, 'La Règle du Temple as a military manual, or how to deliver a cavalry charge', in C Harper-Bill et al (eds.), *Studies in Medieval History presented to R. Allen Brown* (Woodbridge, 1989), 7-19.

Bennett, M, 'Norman Naval Activity in the Mediterranean c.1060-1108', *Anglo-Norman Studies*, 15 (1993), 41-58.

Benvenisti, M, *The Crusaders in the Holy Land* (Jerusalem, 1970).

Beshir, B J, 'Fatimid Military Organization', *Der Islam*, 55 (1978), 37-57.

Biller, T, 'Der Crac des Chevaliers – neue Forschungen', *Château Gaillard*, 20 (2002), 51-55.

Birge, J K, *The Bektashi Order of Dervishes* (London, 1965).

Bishko, C J, 'The Castilian as Plainsman: The Medieval Ranching Frontier in La Mancha and Extramadura', in A Lewis & T McGunn (eds.), *The New World Looks at its History* (Austin, 1963), 46-69.

Blin, R., 'Châteaux croisés de Grèce: Fortifications franques de Morée', *Histoire Médiévale*, 56 (August 2004), 58-67.

Blondal, S, & B S Beneditz, *The Varangians of Byzantium* (Cambridge, 1978).

Boaz, A, 'Bet Shean, Crusader Fortress – Area Z', *Excavations and Surveys in Israel*, 9 (1989-90), 129.

Bodur, F, *Türk Maden Sanati: The Art of Turkish Metalworking* (Istanbul, 1987).

Bombaci, A, 'The Army of the Saljuqs of Rum', *Istituto orientale di Napoli, Annali*, ns. 38 (1978), 343-369.

Bon, A, 'Fortéresses médiévales de la Grèce centrale', *Bulletin de Correspondence Hellénique*, 61 (1937), 136-209.

Bon, A, *La Morée Franque* (Paris, 1969).

Bosworth, C E, 'Abu 'Amr 'Uthman al-Tarsusi's Siyar al-Thughur and the Last Years of Arab Rule in Tarsus (Fourth/Tenth Century)', *Graeco-Arabica*, 5 (1993), 183-195.

Bosworth, C E, 'Military Organization under the Buyids of Persia and Iraq', *Oriens*, 18-19 (1965-6), 143-167.

Bosworth, C E, *The Ghaznavids* (Edinburgh, 1963).

Bosworth, C E, *The Later Ghaznavids: Splendour and Decay* (Edinburgh, 1977).

Boyle, J A, 'The Capture of Isfahan by the Mongols', in *Atti del Convegno Internazionale sul Tema: la Persia nel Medioevo* (Rome, 1971), 331-336.

Boyle, J A, 'Turkish and Mongol Shamanism in the Middle Ages', *Folklore*, 83 (1972), 177-193.

Brand, C M, *Byzantium Confronts the West* (Cambridge, Mass., 1968).

Brett, M, 'The Military Interest of the Battle of Haydaran', in V J Parry & M E Yapp (eds.), *War, Technology and Society in the Middle East* (London, 1975) 78-88.

Brion, M, *Le Mémorial des Siècles: XIV siècle, les hommes, Tamerlan* (Paris, 1963).

Brodman, J W, *Ransoming Captives in Crusader Spain* (Philadelphia, 1986).

Brown, R M, 'A twelfth century A.D. sequence from Southern Transjordan; Crusader and Ayyubid Occupation at El-Wueira', *Annual of the Department of Antiquities of Jordan*, 31 (1987), 267-287.

Browning, R, 'A Note on the Capture of Constantinople in 1453', *Byzantion*, 22 (1952), 379-387.

Brundage, J A, *The Crusades, Holy War and Canon Law* (London, 1991).

Brunschwig, R, *La Berberie Orientale sous les Hafsides des origines à la fin du XVe siécle* (Paris, 1940-7).

Burns, R I, 'The Muslim in the Christian Feudal Order: The Kingdom of Valencia, 1240-1280', *Studies in Medieval Culture*, 5 (1976), 105-126.

Burns, R I, *Moors and Crusaders in Medieval Spain* (London 1978).

Burridge, P, 'The Castle of Vardounia and defence in the southern Mani', in P Lock & G D R Sanders (eds.), *The Archaeology of Medieval Greece* (Oxford 1996), 19-28.

Burton-Page, J, 'A Study of Fortification in the Indian Subcontinent from the Thirteenth to the Eighteenth Century AD', *Bulletin of the School of Oriental and African Studies*, 23 (1960), 508-522.

Byrne, E H, *Genoese Shipping in the Twelfth and Thirteenth Centuries* (Cambridge Mass., 1930).

Cahen, C, 'L'Administration Financière de l'armée Fatimide d'aprés al-Makhzumi', *Journal of the Economic and Social History of the Orient*, 15 (1972), 163-182.

Cahen, C, 'Note sur l'esclavage musulman et le devshirme Ottoman: à propos des travaux récents', *Journal of the Economic and Social History of the Orient*, 13 (1970), 211-218.

Cahen, C, *Le Régime Féodal de l'Italie Normande* (Paris, 1940).

Cahen, S, *La Syrie du Nord au Temps des Croisades* (Paris, 1940).

Castro y Calvo, J M, *El arte de gobernar en las obras de Don Juan Manuel* (Barcelona, 1945).

Cathcart-King, D J, 'The Trebuchet and other siege engines', in *Château Gaillard*, 9-10 (1982), 457-469.

Chalandon, F, *Les Comnènes – Etudes sur l'Empire Byzantin, vol. I* (Paris, 1900); vol. II (Paris, 1912).

Charanis, P, 'Piracy in the Aegean during the reign of Michael VIII Palaeologus', *Annuaire de l'Institut de Philologie et d'Histoire Orientates et Slaves*, 10 (1950), 27-136.

Charmoy, F-B, *Expédition de Timoûr-i-Lenk (Tamerlan) Contre Toqtamiche* (St. Petersburg, 1835; reprint Amsterdam, 1975).

Chehab, M H, 'Tyr à l'époque des Croisades', *Bulletin du Musée de Beyrouth*, 31 (1979), whole volume.

Cherniavsky, M, 'Khan or Basileus: An Aspect of Russian Medieval Political Theory', *Journal of the History of Ideas*, 20 (1959), 459-476.

Chevedden, P E, 'Fortification and the Development of Defensive Planning in the Latin East', in D Kagay & L J A Villalon (eds.), *The Circle of War in the Middle Ages* (Woodbridge, 1999), 33-43.

Christiansen, E, *The Northern Crusades: The Baltic and Catholic Frontier 1100-1525* (London, 1980).

Christides, V, 'Some Remarks on the Mediterranean and Red Sea Ships in Ancient and Medieval Times II: Merchant-Passenger vs. Combat Ships', *Tropsis*, 2 (1987), 87-99.

Clavijo (G Le Strange, tr.), *Embassy to Tamerlane 1403-1406* (London, 1928).

Cohen, A, 'The Walls of Jerusalem', in C E Bosworth (ed.), *Essays in Honor of Bernard Lewis; The Islamic World from Classical to Modern Times* (Princeton, 1989), 467-477.

Combe, E, & A de Cosson, 'Le Fort de Qait Bay à Rosetta', *Bulletin de la Societé Royale d'Archéologie d'Alexandrie*, ns. 10 (1938-9), 320-324.

Constable, G, 'The Financing of the Crusades in the Twelfth Century', in B Z Kedar et al (eds.), *Outremer: Studies in the History of the Crusading Kingdom of Jerusalem* (Jerusalem, 1982), 64-88.

Cook, R F, 'Crusade Propaganda in the Epic Cycles of the Crusade', in B N Sargent-Baur (ed.), *Journeys toward God: Pilgrimage and Crusade* (Kalamazoo, 1992), 157-175.

Creswell, K A C, 'Fortification in Islam before AD 1250', *Proceedings of the British Academy*, 38 (1952), 89-125.

Crow, J, & S Hill, 'Amasra, a Byzantine and Genoese Fortress', *Fortress*, 15 (1990), 3-13.

Crummey, R O, *The Formation of Muscovy 1304-1613* (London, 1987).

Cuoq, J, *Islamisation de la Nubie Chrétienne VIIe-XVIe Siècles* (Paris, 1986).

Darko, E, 'La Tactique Touranienne', *Byzantion*, 10 (1935), 443-469; 12 (1937), 119-147.

De Foucault, J-A, 'Douze Chapitres inédits de la Tactique de Nicéphore Ouranos', *Travaux et Mémoires*, 5 (1973), 281-311.

De Hoffmeyer, A B, *Arms and Armour in Spain, a short survey, vol. I* (Madrid 1972); vol. II (Madrid 1982).

De Mata Carriazo, J, 'Cartas de la frontera de Granada', *Andalus*, 11 (1946), 69-130.

De Mata Carriazo, J, 'Un alcalde entre los cristianos y los moros, en la frontera de Granada', *Andalus*, 13 (1948), 35-96.

De Mombynes, G, *Syrie à l'Epoque Mameloukes d'après les Auteurs Arabes* (Paris, 1923).

De Moraes Farias, P F, 'The Almoradids: Some Questions Concerning the Character of the Movement during its periods of Closest Contact with the Western Sudan', *Bulletin de l'Institut Fondamental d'Afrique Noir*, ser. B. 29 (1967), 794-878.

De Vries, K, 'Gunpowder Weapons at the Siege of Constantinople,1453', in Y Lev (ed.), *War and Society in the Eastern Mediterranean, 7th-15th Centuries* (Leiden, 1996), 343-362.

Dean, B, 'A Crusader Fortress in Palestine (Montfort)', *Bulletin of the Metropolitan Museum of Art*, 22 (1927), 91-97.

Delaville le Roulx, J, *La France en Orient au XIVe siècle: Expeditions du Maréchal Boucicault* (Paris, 1886).

Dennis, G T, *Three Byzantine Military Treatises* (Washington, 1985).

Deschamps, P, *Les Châteaux des Croisés en Terre Sainte: le Crac des Chevaliers* (Paris, 1934).

Deschamps, P, 'Deux Positions Strategiques des croisés à l'Est du Jourdain: Ahamant et el Habis', *Revues Historiques*, 175 (1933), 42-57.

Diaconu, P, *Les Coumans au Bas-Danube aux XIe au XIIe siècles* (Bucharest, 1978).

Digby, S, *War-Horse and Elephant in the Delhi Sultanate, a study of military supplies* (Oxford, 1971).

Dimnik, M, *Mikhail, Prince of Chernigov and Grand Prince of Kiev 1224-1246* (Toronto, 1981).

Dinic, M J, 'Spanski najamnici u srpskoj sluzbi (Spanish mercenaries in Serbian Service)', *Zbornik Radova Visanloloskog Instituta*, 6 (1960), 15-28.

Dodu, G, *Histoire des Institutions Monarchiques dans le Royaume Latin de Jerusalem 1099-1291* (reprint New York, 1978).

Dotson, J E, 'Merchant and naval influences on galley design at Venice and Genoa in the fourteenth century', in C L Symonds (ed.), *New aspects of naval history: selected papers presented at the fourth naval history symposium* (Annapolis, 1979), 20-32.

Doukas (H J Magoulias tr.), *Decline and Fall of Byzantium to the Ottoman Turks* (Detroit, 1975).

Ducellier, A, *L'Albanie entre Byzance et Venise (Xe-XVe siècles)* (London, 1987).

Dujcev, I, 'La conquête turque et la prise de Constantinople dans la literature slave contemporaine', *Byzantinoslavica*, 17 (1956), 278-340.

Dzis, I, & A Sherbakov, 'Novgododtsi Vremen Kulikovskoy Bitivi 1380 (Novgorod Warriors of the time of the Battle of Kulikovo 1380)', *Zeughaus*, 12 (2002), 5-7.

Edbury, P W, 'Castles, towns and rural settlements in the Crusader kingdom', *Medieval Archaeology*, 42 (1998), 191-193.

Edbury, P W, *The Kingdom of Cyprus and the Crusades 1191-1374* (Cambridge, 1991).

Edwards, R W, *The Fortifications of Armenian Cilicia* (Washington, 1987).

Ehrenkreutz, A S, 'The Place of Saladin in the Naval History of the Mediterranean Sea in the Middle Ages', *Journal of the American Oriental Society*, 75 (1955), 100-116.

Elbeheiry, S, *Les Institutions de l'Egypte au Temps des Ayyubides* (Lille 1972).

Elisseeff, N, *Nur al-Din: un Grand Prince Musulman de Syrie au Temps des Croisades* (Damascus, 1967).

Ellenblum, R, 'Frankish and Muslim Siege Warfare and the construction of Frankish concentric castles', in M Balard (ed.), *Die Gesta per Francos* (Aldershot, 2001) 187-198.

Ellenblum, R, 'Three generations of Frankish castle-building in the Latin Kingdom of Jerusalem', in M Balard (ed.), *Autour de la Première Croisade* (Paris, 1996) 517-551.

Enveri (I Melikoff-Sayar ed. & tr.), *Le Destan d'Umur Pasha* (Paris, 1954).

Erdmann, C, *The Origin of the Idea of Crusade* (Princeton, 1977).

Esin, E, *A History of Pre-Islamic and Early Islamic Turkish Culture* (Istanbul, 1980).

Eydoux, H-P, 'L'architecture militaire des Francs en Orient', in J P Babelon (ed.), *Le Château en France* (Paris, 1986), 61-77.

Faris, N A, & R P Elmer (trs.), *Arab Archery*, (Princeton, 1945) – translated as a late fifteenth-century Mamluk treatise on archery, but in reality the thirteenth century Moroccan *Kifayat* treatise by Ibn Maymun).

Farmer, H.G., 'Turkish Artillery at the Fall of Constantinople', *Transactions of the Glasgow University Oriental Society*, 6 (1929-33), 9-14.

Faucherre, N et al (eds.), *La Fortification au Temps des Croisades* (Rennes, 2004).

Favreau-Lilie, M L, 'The Military Orders and the Escape of the Christian Population from the Holy Land in 1291', *Journal of Medieval History*, 19 (1993), 201-227.

Fedden, J, & J Thomson, *Crusader Castles, a brief study in the military architecture of The Crusades* (London, 1977).

Ferrandis Torres, J, 'Espadas Granadinas de la Jineta', *Archivo Española Arte*, 16 (1943), 142-166.

Fiene, E, *Die Burg von Kyrenia* (Hannover, 1993).

Fiene, E, *St. Hilarion, Buffavento, Kantara: Bergburgen in Nordzypern* (Hannover, 1992).

Fino, J F, *Origine et puissance des machines à balancier médiévales; Société des antiquites nationales, n.s. 11* (1972).

Flori, J, 'Encore l'usage de la lance. La Technique du combat chevaleresque vers l'an 1100', *Cahiers de Civilisations Médiévale*, 31 (1988), 213-240.

Foley, V, & K Perry, 'In Defence of LIBER IGNEUM: Arab Alchemy, Roger Bacon and the Introduction of Gunpowder into the West', *Journal for the History of Arabic Science*, 3 (1979), 200-218.

Forey A J, *The Military Orders from the Twelfth to the Early Fourteenth Century* (London, 1991).

Forey, A J, *Military Orders and Crusades* (London, 1994).

Foss, C, & D Winfield, *Byzantine Fortifications; an Introduction* (Pretoria, 1986).

Fournet, T, 'Le Château de Aakar al-Atiqa (Nord-Liban)', *Bulletin d'Archéologie et d'Architecture Libanaises*, 4 (2000), 149-163.

France, J, *Victory in the East: A Military History of the First Crusade* (Cambridge, 1994).

Frye, R N, *The Golden Age of Persia: The Arabs in the East* (London, 1975).

Fügedi, E, *Castles and Society in Medieval Hungary, 1000-1437* (Budapest, 1986).

Gaier, C, 'La cavalerie lourde en Europe occidentale du XIIe au XIVe siècle: un problème de mentalité', *Revue Internationale d'Histoire Militaire* (1971), 385-396.

García Fuentes, J M, 'Las armas hispano-musulmanas al final de la Reconquista', *Crónica Nova*, 3 (1969), 38-55.

García Gomez, E, 'Armas, banderas, tiendas de campaña, monturas y correos en los "Anales de al Hakam II" por 'Isà Razi', *Andalus*, 32 (1967), 163–179.

Geanakoplos, D J, 'Greco-Latin Relations on the Eve of the Byzantine Restoration: The Battle of Pelagonia – 1259', *Dumbarton Oaks Papers, 7* (1953), 99-141.

Gerö, L, *Castles in Hungary* (Budapest, 1969).

Gertwagen, R, 'The Crusader Port of Acre: Layout and Problems of Maintenance', in M Balard (ed), *Autour de la Premiere Croisade* (Paris, 1996), 553-582.

Gertwagen, R, 'The Venetian Colonies in the Ionian Sea and the Aegean in Venetian Defence Policy in the Fifteenth Century', *Journal of Mediterranean Studies*, 12 (2002), 351-384.

Gillingham, J, 'Richard I and the Science of War in the Middle Ages', in J Gillingham & H C Holt (eds.), *War and Government in the Middle Ages: Essays in Honour of J O Prestwich* (Cambridge, 1984), 78-91.

Gillingham, J, *Richard Coeur de Lion: Kingship, Chivalry and War in the Twelfth Century* (London, 1994).

Glick, T F, *From Muslim Fortress to Christian Castle: Social and Cultural Change in Medieval Spain* (Manchester,1995).

Gode, P K, *Studies in Indian Cultural History* (Poona, 1960).

Godfrey, J, 'The Defeated Anglo-Saxons Take Service with the Eastern Emperor', in *Proceedings of the Battle Conference on Anglo-Norman Studies, I* (1978), 63-74.

Goiten, S D, 'Contemporary Letters on the Capture of Jerusalem by the Crusaders', *Journal of Jewish Studies*, 3-4 (1952), 162-177.

Gomez-Moreno, M, 'Pinturas de Moros en el Partal (Alhambra)', *Cuadernos de la Alhambra*, 6 (1970), 141-182.

Gorelik, M V, *Armii Mongolo-Tatar X-XIV vekov* [Mongol-Tatar Arms 10th-14th centuries] (Moscow 2002).

Gorelik, M.V., 'Kulikovskaya Bitva 1380. Russki i Zolotoordinski Voini' [The Battle of Kulikovskaya 1380. Russian and Golden Horde Warriors], *Zeughaus*, 1 (1992), 2-7.

Gorelik, M V, 'Oruzhye Vorsklinskoy Bitvi' [Weapons of the Battle of Vorskla], *Zeughaus*, 3 (1994), 21-25.

Gross, M L, 'The origins and role of the Janissaries in early Ottoman history', *Middle East Research Association* (1969-70), 1-6.

Gultzgoff, V, 'La Russie kiévienne entre la Scandinavie, Constantinople et le royaume france de Jérusalem', *Revue des Etudes Slaves*, 55 (1983), 151-161.

Gumilev, L N, 'Les Mongoles de XIIIe siècle et la Slovo o polku Igoreve', *Cahiers du monde russe et sovietique*, 7 (1966), 37-57.

Haidar, S Z, *Islamic Arms and Armour of Muslim India* (Lahore, 1991).

Haldane, D, 'The Fire-Ship of Al-Salih Ayyub and Muslim use of Greek Fire', in D J Kagay & L J A Villalon (eds.), *The Circle of War in the Middle Ages* (Woodbridge, 1999), 137-144.

Haldon, J, & M Byrne, 'A Possible Solution to the Problem of Greek Fire', *Byzantinische Zeitschrift*, 70 (1977), 91-99.

Halperin, C J, 'Know Thy Enemy: Medieval Russian Familiarity with the Mongols of the Golden Horde', *Jahbücher für Geschichte Osteuropas*, 30 (1982), 161-173

Halperin, C J, 'Tsarev ulus: Russia in the Golden Horde', *Cahiers du monde russe et soviétique*, 23 (1982), 257-263.

Halperin, C J, *Russia and the Golden Horde* (London, 1985).

Halphen, I, 'La conquête de la Mediterranée par les Européens au XIe et au XII siècles', in *Melanges d'histoire offerts à Henri Pirenne, vol. I* (Bruxelles, 1926), 175-180.

Hamdun, S, & N King, *Ibn Battuta in Black Africa* (London, 1975).

Hartal, M, 'Excavations of the Courthouse Site at "Akko"', *Atiqot*, 31 (1997), 1-2, 3-30 & 109-114.

Harvey, L R, *Islamic Spain, 1250 to 1550* (London, 1990).

Hassan, A Y al-, & D R Hill, *Islamic Technology: An Illustrated History* (Cambridge, 1986).

Hatto, A T, 'Archery and Chivalry: A Noble Prejudice', *The Modern Language Review*, 35 (1940), 40-54.

Hendrickx, B, 'Les Armeniens d'Asie Mineure et de Thrace au début de l'Empire Latin de Constantinople', *Revue des Etudes Armeniennes*, 22 (1991), 217-223.

Herde, P, 'Taktiken muslimische Heere vom ersten Kreuzzug bis Ain Djalut (1260) und ihre Einwirkung auf die Schlacht bei Tagliacozzo (1268)', in W Fischer & J Schneider (eds.), *Das Heilige Land im Mittelalter: Begegnungsraum zwischen Orient und Okzident* (Neustadt, 1982), 83-94.

Hess, A C, 'The Evolution of the Ottoman Seaborne Empire in the Age of Oceanic Discoveries, 1453-1525', *American Historical Review*, 75 (1969-70), 1892-1919.

Hill, D R, 'Trebuchets', *Viator*, 4 (1973), 99-114.

Hillgarth, J N, *The Spanish Kingdoms 1250-1516* (Oxford, 1976-78).

Holstein, P, *Contribution à l'étude des Armes Orientales. Inde et Archipel Malais* (Paris, not dated).

Holt, P M (ed.), *The Eastern Mediterranean Lands in the Period of the Crusades* (Warminster, 1977).

Hopkins, J F P, & N Levtzion, *Corpus of Early Arabic Sources for West African History* (Cambridge, 1981).

Hopkins, J F P, *Medieval Muslim Goverment in Barbary, until the sixth century of the Hijra* (London, 1958).

Housley, N, 'The mercenary companies, the papacy and the Crusades, 1356-1378', *Traditio*, 38 (1982), 253-280.

Housley, N, *The Later Crusades, 1274-1580: From Lyons to Alcazar* (Oxford, 1992).

Huici Miranda, A, *Las grandes batallas de la Reconquista durante los invasiones africanas* (Madrid, 1956).

Humphreys, R S, 'The Emergence of the Mamluk Army', *Studia Islamica*, 40 (1977), 67-99 & 147-182.

Huuri, K, *Zur Geschichte des mittelalterlichen Geschützwens aus Orientalischen Quellen. Studia Orientalia* (Helsinki, 1941).

Ibn Hudayl (Ibn Hudayl al Andalusi) (M. J. Viguera tr.), *Gala de Caballeros, Blason de Paladines* (Madrid, 1977).

Ibn Hudayl al Andalusi (L Mercier tr.), *La Parure des Cavaliers et l'Insigne des Preux* (Paris, 1922).

Inalcik, H, 'Mehmed the Conqueror (1432-1481) and his Time', *Speculum*, 35 (1960), 408-427.

Inalcik, H, 'Ottoman Methods of Conquest', *Studia Islamica*, 2 (1954), 103-129.

Irwin, R, *The Middle East in the Middle Ages: The Early Mamluk Sultanate 1250-1382* (London, 1986).

Jackson, P, 'The Crusades of 1239-41 and their aftermath', *Bulletin of the School of Oriental and African Studies*, 50 (1987), 32-60.

Jacoby, D, 'Crusader Acre in the Thirteenth Century; urban layout and topography', *Studi Medievali*, 3 ser. 20 (1979), 1-45.

Jacoby, D, 'Knightly Values and Class Consciousness in the Crusader States of the Eastern Mediterranean', *Mediterranean Historical Review*, 1 (1986), 158-186.

Jawish, H, *Krak des Chevaliers und die Kreuzfahrer* (Damascus, 1999).

Johns, C N, 'Excavations of Pilgrim's Castle, 'Atlit (1932-3): Stables at the south-west of the suburbs', *Quarterly of the Department of Antiquities of Palestine*, 5 (1935), 31-60.

Jurji, E J, 'The Islamic Theory of War', *The Moslem World*, 30 (1940), 332-342.

Kaegi, W E, 'The Contribution of Archery to the Turkish Conquest of Anatolia', *Speculum*, 39 (1964), 96-108.

Kaldy-Nagy, G, 'The First Centuries of the Ottoman Military Organisation', *Acta Orientalia Academiae Scientiarum Hungarica*, 31 (1977), 147-183.

Katele, I B, 'Piracy and the Venetian State: The Dilemma of Maritime Defence in the Fourteenth Century', *Speculum*, 63 (1988), 865-889.

Kazhdan, A, 'Armenians in the Byzantine Ruling Class; predominantly in the ninth through twelfth centuries', in T J Samuelian & M E Stone (eds.), *Medieval Armenian Culture, University of Pennsylvania Armenian Texts and Studies 6* (Chico, California, 1984) 439-451.

Kedar, B Z, 'The Outer Walls of Frankish Acre', *Atiqot*, 31 (1997), 157-180.

Kedar, B Z, 'The Passenger List of a Crusader Ship, 1250: Towards the History of the Popular Element on the Seventh Crusade', *Studi Medievali*, 13 (1972), 267-279.

Kedar, B Z, *The Franks in the Levant, eleventh to fourteenth Centuries* (London, 1993).

Kelsay, J, & J T Johnson (eds.), *Just War and Jihad* (New York, 1991).

Kennedy, H, *Crusader Castles* (Cambridge, 1994).

Khan, G M, 'The Islamic and Ghaznawide Banners', *Nagpur University Journal*, 9 (1943), 106-117.

Kirpichnikov (Kirpitchnikoff), A N, *Drevnerusskoye Oruzhye (Les Armes de la Russia Medievale)* (Leningrad, 1971).

Kirpichnikov (Kirpitchnikoff), A N, *Voennoye Delo na Rusi v XII-XV vv. (Russian Arms of the thirteenth-fifteenth Centuries)* (Leningrad, 1976).

Kirpitchnikoff, A N, 'Russische Waffen des 9.-15. Jahrhunderts', *Zeitschrift für Historische Waffen- und Kostümkunde*, 38 (1986), 1-22.

Kirpitchnikov (Kirpitchnikoff), A N, *Snaryazhenie Vsadnika i Verkhovogo Konya na Rusi IX-XIII vv (Harnachement du Cavalier et de la Monture en Russie aux IX-XIII Siècles)* (Leningrad, 1973).

Kolias, T G, *Byzantinischen Waffen* (Vienna, 1988).

Kosiary, E, *Woyny na Baltyku X-XIX* [Warfare in the Baltic] (Gdansk, 1978).

Kostochkin, V (ed.), *Krepostnoye Zodchestvo Drevniye Rusi (Fortress Architecture in Early Russia)* (Moscow, 1970).

Kradin, N R, *Russkoe Derevjannoe Zodchestvo* [Russian Wooden Defensive Architecture] (Moscow, 1988).

La Monte, J L, *Feudal Monarchy in the Latin Kingdom of Jerusalem* (Cambridge, Massachusetts, 1932).

Ladero Quesada, M A, *Castilla y la Conquista del Reino de Granada* (Valladolid, 1967).

Lambton, A K S, 'Reflections on the Iqta', in G Makdisi (ed.), *Arabic and Islamic Studies in Honour of Hamilton A.R. Gibb* (Leiden, 1965), 358-376.

Lane, F C, 'The Crossbow in the Nautical Revolution of the Middle Ages', in D Herlihy, R S Lopez & V Slessarev (eds.), *Economy, Society and Government, in Medieval Italy: Essays in Memory of Robert L Reynolds* (Kent, Ohio, 1969), 161-171.

Langer, L N, 'The Medieval Russian Town', in M Hamm (ed.), *The City in Russian History* (Lexington, 1976), 11-33.

Lanuza Cano, E, *El Ejército en tiempos de los Reyes Católicos* (Madrid, 1953).

Latham, J D, 'Notes on Mamluk Horse-Archers', *Bulletin of the School of Oriental and African Studies*, 32 (1969), 257-267.

Latham, J D, 'The Strategic Position and Defence of Ceuta in the Later Muslim Period', *Islamic Quarterly*, 15 (1971), 189-204.

Latham, J D, *From Muslim Spain to Barbary* (London, 1986).

Lathan, J D, & W F Paterson, *Saracen Archery: An English Version and Exposition of a Mameluke Work on Archery (ca. A.D. 1368)* (London, 1970).

Lattimore, O, 'The Nomads and South Russia', in *Byzantine Black Sea (symposium, Birmingham University 18-20 March 1978)* (Athens, 1978), 193-200.

Leaf, W, & S Purcell, *Heraldic Symbols: Islamic Insignia and Western Heraldry* (London, 1986).

Leclerq, J, 'St. Bernard's Attitude towards War', in J R Sommerfeldt (ed.), *Studies in Medieval Cistercian History, vol. II* (Kalarnazoo, 1976).

Lev, Y, 'The Fatimid Army, A.H. 358-427/968-1036 C.E.: Military and Social Aspects', *Asian and African Studies*, 14 (1980), 165-192.

Lev, Y, 'The Fatimid Navy, Byzantium and the Mediterranean Sea 909-1036 C.E./2977-427 A.H.', *Byzantion*, 54 (1984), 220-252.

Levi Provençal, E, *L'Espagne Musulmane au Xeme Siècle* (Paris, 1932).

Lewis, A R, *Medieval naval and maritime history, AD 300-1500* (Bloomington, 1983).

Lewis, A R, *The Sea and Medieval Civilisations, Collected Studies* (London, 1978).

Leyser, K, *Medieval Germany and its Neighbours, 900-1250* (London, 1982).

Liebel, J, *Springalds and Great Crossbows* (Leeds, 1998).

Lilie, R-J, 'Die Schlacht von Myriokephalon, 1176', *Revue des Etudes Byzantines*, 35 (1977), 257-277.

Lind, J, 'The Russian Sources of King Magnus Eriksson's campaign against Novgorod 1348-1351 – reconsidered', *Mediaeval Scandinavia*, 12 (1988), 248-272.

Lindner, M, 'Search for Medieval Hormuz: The Lost Crusader Fortress of Petra', *Occident & Orient* (Amman, December 1999), 59-61.

Little, D P, 'The Fall of 'Akka in 690/1291', in M Sharon (ed.), *Studies in Islamic History and Civilization in Honour of Professor David Ayalon* (Jerusalem & Leiden, 1986), 159-181.

Lock, P, 'Castles and Seigneurial Influence in Latin Greece', in A V Murray (ed.), *From Clermont to Jerusalem: The Crusades and Crusader Societies 1095-1500* (Turnhout, 1998), 173-186.

Lock, P, 'The Medieval Towers of Greece: A Problem of Chronology and Function', in B Arbel, B Hamilton & D Jacoby (eds.), *Latins and Greece in the Eastern Mediterranean after 1204* (London, 1989), 129-145.

Lock, P W, 'Castles of Frankish Greece', in A Murray (ed.), *From Clermont to Jerusalem: The Crusades and Crusader Societies* (Brepols, 1997).

Lock, P W, *The Franks in the Aegean* (London, 1995).

Lombard, M, *Les Métaux dans l'Ancien Monde du Ve au XIe siècle* (Paris, 1974).

López de Coca Castañer, J E, 'Institutions on the Castilian-Granadan Frontier,1369-1482', in R Bartlett & A MacKay (eds.), *Medieval Frontier Societies* (Oxford, 1989) 127-150.

Lot, F, *L'Art Militaire et les armées au Moyen Age* (Paris, 1946).

Loud, G A, 'How "Norman" was the Norman Conquest of Southern Italy?', *Nottingham Medieval Studies*, 25 (1981), 13-34.

Lurier, H E (tr.), *Crusaders as Conquerors: The Chronicle of the Morea* (New York, 1964).

Luttrell, A, 'Lindos and the Defence of Rhodes; 1306-1522', *Rivista di Studi Byzantini e Neoellenici*, 22-23 (1985-6), 317-332.

Luttrell, A, 'The Crusade in the Fourteenth Century', in J R Hale et al (eds.), *Europe in the Late Middle Ages* (London, 1965), 122-154.

Lyons, M C, & D L P Jackson, *Saladin, the Politics of the Holy War* (Cambridge, 1982).

Mackay, A, *Society, Economy and Religion in Late Medieval Castile* (London 1987).

Makhdoomee, M A, 'The Art of War in Medieval India', *Islamic Culture*, 11 (1937), 460-487.

Mann, J, 'Notes on the Armour worn in Spain from the Tenth to the Fifteenth Century', *Archaeologia*, 83 (1933), 285-305.

Marino, L (ed.), *La fabbrica dei Castelli Crociati in Terra Santa* (Florence, 1997).

Marshall, C J, 'The French Regiment in the Latin East, 1254-91', *Journal of Medieval History*, 15 (1989), 301-307.

Marshall, C J, *Warfare in the Latin East, 1192-1291* (Cambridge, 1991).

Martin, J, 'Russian Expansion in the Far North, X to mid-XVI Century', in M Rywkin (ed.), *Russian Colonial Expansion to 1917* (London, 1988), 23-43.

Masani, R P, 'Caste and the Structure of Society', in G T Garratt (ed.), *The Legacy of India* (Oxford, 1937), 124-161.

Mayer, H E, *Kings and Lords in the Latin Kingdom of Jerusalem* (London, 1994).

Mayer, L A, *Mamluk Costume* (Geneva, 1956).

Mayer, L A, *Saracenic Heraldry* (Oxford, 1933).

McEwen, E, 'Persian Archery Texts: Chapter Eleven of Fakhr-i Mudabbir's Adab al Harb', *The Islamic Quarterly*, 18 (1974), 76-99.

McGeer, E, 'Byzantine Siege Warfare in Theory and Practice', in I A Corfis & M Wolfe (eds.), *The Medieval City under Siege* (Woodbridge, 1995) 123-129.

Megaw, P, 'A Castle in Cyprus attributable to the Hospital?' in M Barber (ed.), *The Military Orders: Fighting for the Faith and Caring for the Sick* (Aldershot, 1994), 42-51.

Melikan-Chirvani, A S, 'Notes sur la terminologie de la metallurgie et des armes dans l'Iran Musulman', *Journal of the Economic and Social History of the Orient*, 24 (1981), 310-316.

Melville Jones, J R (tr.), *The Siege of Constantinople 1453: Seven Contemporary Accounts* (Amsterdam, 1972).

Menager, L-R, *Hommes et Institutions de l'Italie Normande* (London, 1981).

Menendez Pidal, R, *The Cid and his Spain* (London, 1971).

Mesqui, J, *Châteaux d'Orient, Liban, Syrie* (Paris, 2001).

Mihailovic, K (B Stolz & S Soucek ed. & tr.), *Memoires of a Janissary* (Ann Arbor, 1975).

Mijatovich, C, *Constantine Palaeologus, The Last Emperor of the Greeks: 1448-1453: The Conquest of Constantinople by the Turks* (London, 1892).

Miller, B, *The Palace School of Mohammed the Conqueror* (Cambridge, Massachusetts, 1941).

Miller, Y (ed.), *Russian Arms and Armour* (Leningrad, 1982).

Minorsky, V, 'A Civil and Military Review in Fars in 881/1476', *Bulletin the School of Oriental Studies*, 10 (1939), 141-178.

Mitchell, P D, *Medicine in the Crusades: Warfare, Wounds and the Medieval Surgeon* (Cambridge, 2004).

Molin, K, 'Fortifications and Internal Security in the Kingdom of Cyprus, 1191-1426', in A V Morray (ed.), *From Clermont to Jerusalem: The Crusades and Crusader Societies 1095-1500* (Turnhout, 1998), 187-199.

Molin, K, *Unknown Crusader Castles* (London, 2001).

Mollat, M, 'Essai d'orientation pour l'étude de la guerre de course et la piraterie (XIIIe-XVe siècles)', *Anuario de estudios medievales*, 10 (1980), 743-749.

Morgan, D O, 'The Mongol Armies in Persia', *Der Islam*, 56 (1979), 81-96.

Morgan, D O, *The Mongols* (Oxford, 1968).

Morray, D, 'Then and Now: A Medieval Visit to the Castle of al-Rawandan Recalled', *Anatolian Studies*, 43 (1993), 137-142.

Morris, H T, *Saharan Myth and Saga* (Oxford, 1972).

Mottahedeh, R P, *Loyalty and Leadership in an Early Islamic Society* (Princeton, 1980).

Müller-Wiener, W, *Castles of the Crusaders* (London, 1966).

Munro, D C, 'The Western Attitude Towards Islam during the Crusades', *Speculum*, 6 (1931), 329-343.

Murray, A V, 'The Origins of the Frankish Nobility of the Kingdom of Jerusalem, 1100-1118', *Mediterranean Historical Review*, 4 (1989), 281-300.

Musset, I, 'Problèmes militaires du monde scandinave (VIIe-XIIe siècles)', in *Ordinamenti Militari in Occidente nell'alto medioevo: Settimane di Studio del Centro Italiano di Studi sull'alto medioevo, XV* (Spoleto, 1968), 229-291.

Nesbitt, J W, 'The Rate of March of Crusading Armies in Europe: A Study and Computation', *Traditio*, 19 (1963), 167-181.

Nève, F, *Exposé des Guerres de Tamerlan et de Shah-Rokh* (Brussels, 1860).

Nicol, D M, *The Despotate of Epirus 1267-1479* (Cambridge, 1984).

Nicol, D M, *The End of the Byzantine Empire* (London, 1979).

Nicolle, D C, 'The Reality of Mamluk Warfare: Weapons, Armour and Tactics', *Al-Masaq*, 7 (1994), 77-110.

Nicolle, D C, 'Ain Habis – The Cave de Sueth', *Archeologie Medievale*, 18 (1988), 113-140.

Nicolle, D C, 'Armes et Armures dans les épopées des croisades', in *Les épopées de la croisade (Premier colloque international, Trier University 6-11 August 1984): Zeitschrift für franzosische Sprache und Literatur, 11* (Wiesbaden 1986), 17-34.

Nicolle, D C, 'Arms and Armour illustrated in the Art of the Latin East', in B Z Kedar (ed.), *The Horns of Hattin* (Jerusalem & London, 1992), 327-340.

Nicolle, D C, 'Medieval Islamic Navigation in the Atlantic', *Journal of Medieval and Islamic History* (Cairo), 2 (2002), 3-14.

Nicolle, D C, 'Saljuq Arms and Armour in Art and Literature', in R Hillenbrand (ed.), *The Art of the Saljuqs in Iran and Anatolia, Proceedings of a Symposium held in Edinburgh in 1982* (Costa Mesa, 1994), 247-256.

Nicolle, D C, 'The Cappella Palatina Ceiling and the Muslim Military Heritage of Norman Sicily', *Gladius*, 16 (1983), 45-145.

Nicolle, D C, 'The Monreale Capitals and the Military Equipment of Later Norman Sicily', *Gladius*, 15 (1980), 87-103.

Nicolle, D C, 'Wounds, Military Surgery and the Reality of Crusading Warfare; the Evidence of Usamah's Memoirs', *Journal of Oriental and African Studies* (Athens), 5 (1993), 3-46.

Nicolle, D C, *Arms and Armour of the Crusading Era 1050-1350* (London, 1999).

Nicolle, D C, *Warriors and their Weapons around the Time of the Crusades* (Aldershot, 2002).

Nishamura, D, 'Crossbows, Arrow-Guides and the Solenarion', *Byzantion*, 58 (1988), 422-435.

Noonan, T S, 'Medieval Russia, the Mongols, and the West: Novgorod's relations with the Baltic, 1100-1350', *Medieval Studies*, 37 (1975), 316-339.

Nordiguian, L, & J-C Voisin, *Chateaux et églises du moyen âge au Liban* (Beirut, 1999).

Norris, H T, 'Caves and Strongholds from the Moorish Period around the Rock of Gibraltar', *The Maghreb Review*, 9 (1984), 39-45.

Norris, H T, *The Berbers in Arabic Literature* (London, 1982).

Oikonomides, N, 'L'organisation de la frontière orientale de Byzance aux Xe-XIe siècles et le Taktikon de l'Escorial', *Actes du XIVe Congres Internationale des Etudes Byzantines, Bucarest 6-12 Septembre, 1971, vol. I* (Bucharest, 1974), 285-302.

Olteanu, C, 'L'Organisation de l'armée dans les Pays Roumains', in A Savu (ed.), *Pages de l'histoire de l'armée Roumaine* (Bucharest, 1976) 53-59.

Palmer, J A B, 'The Origins of the Janissaries', *Bulletin of the John Rylands Library*, 35 (1952-3), 448-481.

Paloczi Horvath, A, *Pechenegs, Cumans, Iasians: Steppe Peoples in Medieval Hungary* (Budapest, 1989).

Pant, G, *Studies in Indian Weapons and Warfare* (New Delhi, 1970).

Papacostea, S, 'Byzance et la Croisade au Bas-Danube à la Fin du XIVe siècle', *Revue Roumaine d'Histoire*, 30 (1991), 3-21.

Paradissis, A, *Fortresses and Castles of Greece* (Athens & Thessaloniki, 1972-82).

Partington, J R, *A History of Greek Fire and Gunpowder* (Cambridge, 1960).

Pascu, S (ed.), *Colloquio Romeno-Italiano 'I Genovesi nel Mar Nero durante i secoli XIII e XIV' (Bucharest 27-28 Marzo 1975)* (Bucharest, 1977).

Paviot, J, *'Croisade' bourguignonne et intérês génois en mer Noire au XVe siècle* (Genoa, 1988).

Peirce, I, 'The Knight, his Arms and Armour in the Eleventh and Twelfth Centuries', in C Harper-Bill & R Harvey (eds.), *The Ideals and Practice of Medieval Knighthood (Papers from the first and second Strawberry Hill Conferences)* (Bury St Edmunds, 1986), 152-164.

Pelenski, J, *Russia and Kazan. Conquest and Imperial Ideology 1438-1560* (The Hague, 1973).

Peters, R, *Jihad in Medieval and Modern Islam* (Leiden, 1977).

Petrovic, D, 'Fire-arms in the Balkans on the eve of and after the Ottoman Conquests of the fourteenth and fifteenth centuries', in V J Parry & M E Yapp (eds.), *War, Technology and Society in the Middle East* (London, 1975), 164-194,

Petrovic, D, *Dubrovacko Oruzje u XIV veku (Weapons of Dubrovnik in the fourteenth century)* (Belgrade, 1976).

Pieri, P, 'I Saraceni di Lucera nella Storia militare medievale', *Archivio Storico Pugliese*, 6 (1954), 94-101.

Poliak, A N, 'The Influence of Chingiz Khan's Yasa upon the general organization of the Mamluk State', *Bulletin of the School of Oriental and African Studies*, 10 (1942), 862-876.

Powell, J M (ed.), *Muslims under Latin Rule, 1100-1300* (Princeton, 1990).

Powers, J, 'The Origins and Development of Municipal Military Service in the Leonese and Castilian Reconquest, 800-1250', *Traditio*, 26 (1970), 91-111.

Powers, J, 'Townsmen and Soldiers: The Interaction of Urban and Military Organization in the Militias of Medieval Castile', *Speculum*, 46 (1971), 641-655.

Praga, G, 'L'organizzazione militare della Dalmazia nel Quattrocento', *Archivio Storico per la Dalmazia*, 119 (1936), 463-477.

Prawer, J, 'The Nobility and the Feudal Regime in the Latin Kingdom of Jerusalem', in F L Cheyette (ed.), *Lordship and Community in Medieval Europe: Selected Readings* (New York, 1968), 156-179.

Prawer, J, *Crusader Institutions* (Oxford, 1980).

Prescott, W H, (A.D. McJoynt ed. & intro.), *The Art of War in Spain. The Conquest of Granada 1481-1492* (London, 1995).

Pringle, D & R Harper, *Belmont Castle, the Excavation of a Crusader Stronghold in the Kingdom of Jerusalem: British Academy Monographs in Archaeology 10* (Oxford, 2000).

Pringle, D, & J De Meulemeester, *The Castle of al-Karak, Jordan* (Namur, 2000).

Pringle, D, 'Reconstructing the Castle of Safad', *Palestine Exploration Quarterly*, 117 (1985), 139-149.

Pringle, D, 'Towers in Crusader Palestine', *Château Gaillard*, 16 (1994), 335-370.

Pringle, D, 'Town Defences in the Crusader Kingdom of Jerusalem', in I A Corns & M Wolfe (eds.), *The Medieval City under Siege* (Woodbridge, 1995), 69-121.

Pringle, D, *Secular Buildings in the Crusader Kingdom of Jerusalem; An Archaeological Gazetteer* (Cambridge, 1997).

Pritsak, O, 'The Polovcians and Rus', *Archivum Eurasiae Medii Aevi*, 2 (1982), 321-380.

Pritsak, O, *The Pechenegs: A Case of Social and Economic Transformation* (Lisse, 1976).

Pryor, J H, 'In Subsidium Terrae Sanctae: Exports of foodstuffs and war material from the Kingdom of Sicily to the Kingdom of Jerusalem, 1265-1284', *Asian and African Studies*, 22 (1988), 127-146.

Pryor, J H, 'The Crusade of Emperor Frederick II: 1220-29; The Implications of the Maritime Evidence', *American Neptune*, 52 (1992), 113-131.

Pryor, J H, 'The Naval Architecture of Crusader Transport Ships: a reconstruction of some archetypes for round-hulled sailing ships', *The Mariner's Mirror*, 69 (1983), 171-219, 275-292 & 363-386;

Pryor, J H, 'The Naval Architecture of Crusader Transport Ships and Horse-Transports Revisited', *The Mariner's Mirror*, 76 (1990), 255-272.

Pryor, J H, 'Transportation of Horses by Sea during the era of the Crusades: Eighth Century to AD 1285 (part 1. to c.1225)', *The Mariner's Mirror*, 68 (1982), 9-27.

Pryor, J H, *Geography, technology and war: studies in the maritime history of the Mediterranean 649-1571* (Cambridge, 1988).

Rabie, H, 'The Training of the Mamluk Faris', in V J Parry & M E Yapp (eds.), *War, Technology and Society in the Middle East* (London, 1975), 153-163.

Rappoport, P, 'Russian Medieval Military Architecture', *Gladius*, 8 (1969), 39-62.

Rex Smith, G, *Medieval Muslim Horsemanship* (London, 1979).

Ricard, R, & L Torres Balbas, 'Cácares y su cerca Almohade', *Andalus*, 13 (1948), 446-475.

Rice, D S, 'Medieval Harran: Studies in its Topography and Monuments, I', *Anatolian Studies*, 2 (1952), 36-84.

Richard, J, 'An Account of the Battle of Hattin referring to the Frankish Mercenaries in Oriental Muslim States', *Speculum*, 27 (1952), 168-177.

Richard, J, 'Les causes des victoires Mongoles d'après les historiens occidentaux du XIIIe siècle', *Central Asiatic Journal*, 23 (1979), 104-117.

Richard, J, *Croisades et Etats Latins d'Orient* (London, 1992).

Richard, J, *Croisés, missionaires et voyageurs* (London, 1983).

Richard, J, *Le Comté de Tripoli sous la Dynastie Toulousaine* (Paris, 1945).

Richard, J, *Orient et Occident au Moyen Age* (London, 1976).

Richard, J, *The Latin Kingdom of Jerusalem* (Oxford, 1979).

Riley-Smith, J, *The First Crusade and the Idea of Crusading* (London, 1986).

Riley-Smith, J, *The Knights of St. John in Jerusalem and Cyprus, c.1050-1310* (London, 1967).

Robinson, H R, *Oriental Armour* (London, 1967).

Robson, J A, 'The Catalan Fleet and Moorish Sea-Power, (1337-1344)', *English Historical Review*, 74 (1959), 386-408.

Rogers, R, *Latin Siege Warfare in the Twelfth Century* (Oxford, 1992).

Roll, I, 'Medieval Apollonia – Arsuf; A Fortified Coastal Town in the Levant of the Early Muslim and Crusader Periods', in M Balard (ed.), *Autour de la Premiere Croisade* (Paris, 1996), 595-606.

Rose, W, 'Die deutschen und italianisschen schwarzen (grossen) Garden im 15. und 16. Jahrhunderts', *Zeitschrift für Historische Waffen- und Kostümkunde*, 6 (1912-14), 73-97.

Rosetti, R, 'Notes on the Battle of Nicopolis', *Slavonic Review*, 15 (1936-37), 629-638.

Ross, D J A, 'L'Originalité de Turoldus: le maniement de la lance', *Cahiers de Civilizations Médiévales*, 6 (1963), 127-138.

Ross, D J A, 'The Prince Answers Back: "Les Enseignements de Théodore Paliologue"', in C Harper-Bill & R Harvey (eds.), *The Ideals and Practice of Medieval Knighthood (Papers from the first and second Strawberry Hill Conferences)* (Bury St. Edmunds, 1986), 165-177.

Rosser, J, 'Crusader Castles of Cyprus', *Archaeology*, 39 (1986), 40-47.

Rubio y Lluch, A, 'Els castells catalans de la Grècia continentale', *Annuari de l'Institut d'estudis catalans*, 2 (1908), 364-425.

Runciman, S, *The Fall of Constantinople 1453* (Cambridge, 1965).

Russell, F H, *The Just War in the Middle Ages* (Cambridge, 1975).

Russell, P E, *Portugal, Spain and the African Atlantic 1343-1490* (London, 1995).

Saade, G, 'Le Chateau de Bourzey: Fortresses Oubliées', *Annales Archeologiques de Syria*, 6 (1956), 139-162.

Sadeque, S F, *Baybars I of Egypt* (Oxford, 1956).

Salih, A H, 'Le Role des bedouins d'égypte à l'époque Fatimide', *Rivista degli Studi Orientate*, 54 (1980), 51-65.

Salinger, G, 'Was the Futuwa an Oriental form of Chivalry?', *Proceedings of the American Philosophical Society*, 94 (1950), 481-493.

Sánchez-Albornoz, C, 'El Ejército y la Guerra en al Reino Asturleonés, 718-1037', in *Ordinamenti Militari in Occidente nell'Alto Medioevo. Settimane di Studio del Centro Italiano di Studi sull'Alto Medioevo, vol. XV* (Spoleto, 1968), 299-335.

Santaella, R G P, & J E L De Coco Castañer, *Historia de Granada, vol. II: La Epoca Medieval, Siglos VIII-XV* (Granada, 1987).

Sarraf, S al-, 'Furusiyya Literature of the Mamluk Period', in D Alexander (ed.), *Furuysiyya, volume 1: The Horse in the Art of the Near East* (Riyadh, 1996), 118-135.

Sarraf, S al-, 'L'impact des techniques militaires sur l'evolution politique et sociale dans le Moyen-Orient médiévale: Le cas de l'archerie', *Etudes Orientales/Dirasat Sharqiyah*, 7 (1990), 6-28.

Sauvaget, J, 'Notes sur les defences de Marine de Tripoli', *Bulletin de Musée de Beyrouth*, 2 (1938), 1-25.

Sauvaget, J, *La poste aux Chevaux dans l'Empire des Mamluks* (Paris, 1941).

Schiltberger, J, (J Buchan Teller tr.), *The Bondage and Travels of Johann Schiltberger* (London, 1879).

Schneidman, J L, *The Rise of the Aragonese-Catalan Empire 1200-1350* (London, 1970).

Shepard, J, 'The English and Byzantium: A Study of their Role in the Byzantine Army in the Later Eleventh Century', *Traditio*, 29 (1973), 53-92.

Shepard, J, 'The Russian-steppe frontier', in (anon. ed.), *Byzantine Black Sea (symposium, Birmingham University 18-20 March 1978)* (Athens, 1978), 123-133.

Shepard, J, 'The Uses of the Franks in Eleventh-century Byzantium', *Anglo-Norman Studies*, 15 (1993), 275-305.

Sinor, D, 'The Inner Asian Warriors', *Journal of the American Oriental Society*, 101 (1981), 133-144.

Skrivanic, G A, 'Armour and Weapons in Medieval Serbia, Bosnia and Dubrovnik', *Posedna Izdanja*, 293 (1957), 201-205.

Smail, R C, 'Crusaders' Castles in the Twelfth Century', *Cambridge Historical Journal*, 10 (1950-2), 133-149.

Smail, R C, *Crusading Warfare, 1097-1193* (Cambridge, 1956).

Smith, J M, 'Ayn Jalut: Mamluk Success or Mongol Failure?', *Harvard Journal of Asiatic Studies*, 44 (1984), 307-345.

Smith, J M, *A History of the Sarbadar Dynasty, 1336-1381 AD* (The Hague & Paris, 1970).

Soler del Campo, A, 'Sistemas de Combate en la Iconografia Mozarabe y Andalusi Altomedieval', *Boletin de la Asociación Española de Orientalistastas*, 22 (1986), 61-87.

Soler del Campo, A, *La evolucion del armamento medieval en el reino castellano-leonés y al-Andalus (siglos XII-XIV)* (Madrid, 1993).

Soulis, G C, *The Serbs and Byzantium during the reign of Tsar Stephen Dusan* (Washington, 1984).

Sourdel-Thomine, J (tr.), 'Les Conseils du Sayh al Harawi à un Prince Ayyubide', *Bulletin d'Etudes Orientales*, 17 (1961-62), 205-266.

Spinei, V, *Moldavia in the eleventh-fourteenth Centuries* (Bucharest, 1986).

Spuler, B, *Die Goldene Horde. Die Mongolen in Russland 1223-1502* (Wiesbaden, 1965).

Stoicescu, N, 'La levée en masse en Valachie et Moldavie (XIVe-XVIe siècles)', in A Savu (ed.), *Pages de l'histoire de l'armée Roumaine* (Bucharest, 1976), 60-72.

Tanasoca, N-S, 'Les Mixobarbares et les fonctions Paristriennes du XIe siècle', *Revue Roumaine d'Histoire*, 12 (1973), 61-82.

Tarsusi, al- (A Boudot-Lamotte tr.), *Contribution à l'Etude de l'Archérie Musulmane* (Damascus, 1968).

Tarsusi, al- (C Cahen ed. & tr.), 'Un traité d'armurérie composé pour Saladin', *Bulletin d'Etudes Orientales*, 12 (1947/8), 103-126.

Terrasse, H, 'La Vie d'un Royaume Berbère du XIe siècle Espagnol: L'Emirat Ziride de Grenade', *Melanges de la Casa de Velazquez*, 1 (1965), 73-85.

Terrasse, H, 'Les forteresses de l'Espagne musulmane', *Boletin de la Real Academia de la Historia*, 134 (1954), 474-483.

Thiriet, F, *La Romanie Vénetienne au Moyen Age* (Paris, 1955).

Thompson, M W, *Novgorod the Great* (London, 1967).

Tokati, 'Arif 'Ali of Tokat (I Melikoff ed. & tr.), *Danishmandname: La Geste de Melik Danisment* (Paris, 1960).

Torres Delgado, C, 'El Ejercito y las Fortificaciones del Reino Nazari di Granada', *Gladius: Las Armas en la Historia* [special volume] (Madrid, 1988), 197-217.

Toy, S, *The Fortified Cities of India* (London, 1965).

Toy, S, *The Strongholds of India* (London, 1957).

Traquair, R, 'Laconia, I: Medieval Fortresses', *Annual of the British School at Athens*, 12 (1905-6), 259-276 (plates II-VI).

Traquair, R, 'Medieval Fortresses of the North-Western Peloponnesus', *Annual of the British School at Athens*, 13 (1906-7), 268-284 (plates VIII-IX).

Tsangadas, B C P, *The Fortifications and Defence of Constantinople* (New York, 1980).

Turan, O, 'World Domination among the Medieval Turks', *Studia Islamica*, 4 (1955), 77-90.

Turtushi, Muhammad Ibn Walid al-, (M Alarcon tr.), *Lámpara de los Príncipes: Siraj al-Muluk* (Madrid, 1931).

Tyerman, C, 'Who went on Crusade to the Holy Land?', in B Z Kedar (ed.), *The Horns of Hattin* (Jerusalem & London 1992), 13-26.

Udina Martorell, F, *Ingenieria Militar en las Cronicas Catalanas* (Barcelona, 1971).

Unger, R W, 'Warships and cargo ships in medieval Europe', *Technology and Culture*, 22 (1981), 233-252.

Urban, W, 'The Organisation and Defence of the Livonian Frontier in the Thirteenth Century', *Speculum*, 48 (1973), 523-532.

Urban, W, *The Baltic Crusade* (De Kalb, 1975).

Urban, W, *The Prussian Crusade* (New York, 1980).

Urban, W, *The Samogitian Crusade* (Chicago, 1989).

Verbruggen, J F, *The Art of War in Western Europe during the Middle Ages* (Oxford, 1977)

Vigón, J, *El Ejercito de los Reyes Católicos* (Madrid, 1968).

Viguera Molins, M J, *De las taifas al reino de Granada. Al-Andalus, siglos XI-XV* (Madrid, 1995).

Vryonis, S, Jr, *The Decline of Medieval Hellenism in Asia Minor and the Process of Islamization from the Eleventh through the Fifteenth Century* (Berkeley, 1971).

Waley, D P, 'Papal Armies in the Thirteenth Century', *The English Historical Review*, 282 (1957), 1-30.

Wasserstein, D, *The Rise and Fall of the Party Kings* (Princeton, 1985).

Webster, K G T, 'The Twelfth Century Tournament', in *Kittredge Anniversary Papers* (Cambridge, Massachusetts, 1913), 227-234.

Welsby, D A, 'Soba Excavations', *Azania*, 18 (1983), 165-180.

Werner, K F, 'Heeresorganisation und Kriegsführung im deutschen Königreich des 10 und 11 Jahrhunderts', in *Ordinamenti Militari in Occidente nell'Alto Medioevo. Settimane di Studio del Centro Italiano di Studi sull'Alto Medioevo, XV/2* (Spoleto, 1968), 791-843.

Woods, J E, *The Aqquyunlu: Clan, Confederation, Empire* (Minneapolis, 1976).

Zachariadou, E A, 'The Catalans of Athens and the Beginnings of the Turkish Expansion in the Aegean Area', *Studi Medievali*, 21 (1980), 821-838.

Zachariadou, L A, *Romania and the Turks* (London, 1985).

Zaky, A R, 'Gunpowder and Arab Firearms in the Middle Ages', *Gladius*, 6 (1967), 45-58.

Zakythinos, D A, *Le Despotat Grec de Morée: Vie et institutions* (London, 1975).

Ziada, M M, 'The Fall of the Mamluks 1516-1517', *Bulletin, Faculty of Arts, Foad University*, 6 (1941), 19-36.

Ziada, M M, 'The Mamluk Conquest of Cyprus in the Fifteenth Century' [in two parts], *Bulletin of the Faculty of Arts, Cairo University*, 1 (1933), 90-113; 2 (1934) 37-57.

Ziadeh, N A, *Urban Life in Syria under the Early Mamluks* (Westport, 1953).

Zoppoth, G, 'Muhammad Ibn Mängli: Ein ägyptischer Offizier und Schriftsteller des 14. Jahrs.', *Wiener Zeitschrift für die Kunde des Morgenlandes*, 53 (1957), 288-299.

Zozaya, J, 'The Fortifications of al-Andalus', in J D Dodds (ed.), *Al-Andalus: The Art of Islamic Spain* (New York, 1992), 63-73.

Index